Contents

THE CULTURAL ADJUSTMENT OF ASIAN LONE
MOTHERS LIVING IN LONDON

This book is dedicated
to my parents and brother

The Cultural Adjustment of Asian Lone Mothers Living in London

DR RACHANA SINHA MA.PhD

Ashgate

Aldershot • Brookfield USA • Singapore • Sydney

Published by
Ashgate Publishing Limited
Gower House
Croft Road
Aldershot
Hants GU11 3HR
England

Ashgate Publishing Company
Old Post Road
Brookfield
Vermont 05036
USA

British Library Cataloguing in Publication Data
Sinha, Rachana
  The cultural adjustment of Asian lone mothers living in
  London
  1.Single mothers - England - London 2. Culture conflict
  3.Women immigrants - England - London 4.Asians - England -
  London - Social conditions
  I. Title
  306.8'56'089914'0421

Libray of Congress Catalog Card Number: 98-074123

ISBN 1 84014 806 3

Printed in Great Britain by The Book Company, Suffolk

List of Tables

Preface

This book primarily attempts to examine how 90 Asian lone mothers from the Indian and African sub-continent living in London in 1993 resolve their two situational difficulties - firstly that of being lone mothers, and secondly that of being of ethnic origin. A secondary aim of the research is to compare the material and living conditions of the Asian lone mothers with those of their British counterparts, although this can only be tentatively done, given the small size of this sample.

The culture conflict thesis discussed in the first chapter argues that an ethnic population will inevitably encounter adjustment problems as a result of cultural differences and the possible conflict of interests between them and the host society. The literature in Chapter Two shows that the Asian culture is far more traditional than the British culture regarding issues such as marriage, the family, the position of women, marriage breakdown and lone parenthood.

Evidence from this study suggests that although most of the women acknowledged that these cultural differences could cause them difficulties, this did not necessarily mean that all their experiences of lone parenthood were negative. Even though the majority of the mothers no longer saw the father, they did not feel that they were isolated from their family and friends or the local community, with whom they shared amicable relationships, in addition to receiving various types of support.

Most of the respondents also claimed that they had culturally adjusted to their immigrant status, with none of them being totally assimilated into the British way of life. Despite the fact that many of the women were suffering from some mental and emotional complaints, their general outlook was largely positive. Finally it was found that many of the living conditions of this sample were similar to those of the national lone parent population.

Acknowledgements

I would like to convey my special thanks to everyone who has offered me their support following my decision to undertake this research. Firstly, my deepest gratitude must go to my supervisor, Professor Vic George, who has guided me throughout the last few years, whilst successfully helping me to overcome any of the difficulties I faced. I have very much appreciated his unfailing encouragement, advice and valuable suggestions, as well as his patience in reading through my drafts.

My thanks go to all the Asian lone mothers, without whose co-operation this study would not have been possible, and to the various women's centres and other agencies who so enthusiastically helped in providing me with my sample.

Finally, I would like to take this opportunity of thanking my parents and my brother for their unfaltering support in inspiring me to continue and complete the writing of this book.

Introduction

The main purpose of this research is to investigate whether Asian lone mothers living in London face and experience additional problems to British lone mothers because of their different ethnic and cultural background. A subsequent aim of the study is to compare the standards of living between the two groups of women. This kind of research inevitably has policy implications, which shall also be drawn out from the relevant findings.

In Britain today the typical household consisting of a married or co-habiting couple and their children is increasingly being challenged by the growing prevalence of lone parent families, the proportion of which rose from nearly 8 per cent in 1971 to 22 per cent in 1993. The overwhelming majority of lone families are headed by mothers, with only ten per cent of such families headed by fathers (OPCS 1996:54). The recent demographic changes have, therefore, meant that fewer women now have lives which fit the conventional assumptions on which social policy has traditionally been based.

According to Morgan, current "discussion of family affairs is heavily focused on lone parents, and a plethora of reports now dwell upon their disadvantaged position and how this might be addressed" (1995:1). Most studies of lone parenthood in this country, however, tend to be both partial and over-generalised, and based on predominantly white samples, with the result that they have treated the lone parent population as a homogeneous group. Despite the fact that some researchers have included ethnic participants in their recent large scale surveys (Bradshaw and Millar 1991, McKay and Marsh 1994), their numbers have, on the whole, been negligible, so that any problems which may be specific to their group remain largely hidden.

This study proposes to bridge this gap of knowledge by focusing exclusively on Asian lone mothers from the Indian and African sub-continent, who have largely been ignored by investigators to date. Although there may be some similarities in the experiences of British and Asian lone mothers, in that most of them live in a constant state of poverty and are heavily dependent on the state for their incomes, the Asian women may face additional difficulties due to their primarily dissimilar cultural backgrounds.

The first chapter of this book begins with a review of the various models of race relations developed over the years to conceptualise the conflict of relationships between the immigrant and the host nation. Although they differ in their perceptions and resolutions of the problem, all the models show that culture conflict is an inevitability in a society with an ethnic population. Chapter Two, also literature based, concerns itself with a portrayal of Hindu, Muslim and Sikh cultures regarding marriage, the family, the position of women, marriage breakdown and lone parenthood, essentially showing how these values differ from their western equivalents. The methodology procedures used to undertake the fieldwork and a brief profile of the sample are described in Chapter Three.

Chapter Four is the first of five chapters presenting and analysing the results of this study, and records the living conditions of the sample. The areas covered are employment, income, housing and physical health, the main indicators of standards of living, with the findings being compared, wherever possible, to those of the lone parent population at large. Such comparisons, however, must be treated with caution because of the manifold differences between the sample of this study and those of other studies. In Chapter Five the mothers' attitudes towards marriage, the family and the position of women are explored, whilst Chapter Six discusses their attitudes towards marriage breakdown and lone parenthood. The women's experiences of lone motherhood through their relationships with the father, their family and friends and with contacts with social organisations are documented in Chapter Seven. There will additionally be a section on the effects of lone parenthood on the children. Chapter Eight examines the types of adjustments the women have had to make, both culturally as immigrants living in London and psychologically as lone mothers. The final chapter concludes by summarising the major findings of the study whilst analysing the implications of lone parenthood for the 90 women in the sample.

Being one of only a few investigations devoted to Asian lone mothers in Britain, this project will try to shed some light on the cultural problems they may encounter, and will hopefully be a step in the right direction in acknowledging that this specific group is now worthy of serious study in their own right.

1 Models of Race Relations

This chapter is concerned with reflecting the changes over the years in conceptualising the relationship between the ethnic and the native population. As earlier stated, this study proposes to show how Asian lone mothers from the Indian and African sub-continent resolve their two situational difficulties - firstly that of being lone parents, and secondly that of being of ethnic origin and living in London. The changes in the ethnic/native model will show how many of the dilemmas faced by ethnic minorities are essentially the result of differences in cultural background between the two groups. Since the notions of "ethnicity" and "culture" are used many times throughout this book, it will, therefore, be valuable to distinguish between the two. According to Marsh et al (1996:350), ethnicity refers to "a sense of cultural awareness and identity within groups that share a common history or heritage," whilst culture is used to refer to the "values, customs and styles of behaviour of a society or social group and socialisation to the process by which people learn the norms, values and roles approved in their society" (1996:33).

Eidenstadt claimed that all migratory movements are motivated by the migrants' feeling of insecurity or inadequacy in the homeland, although this insecurity may not apply to all spheres of social life (Richmond 1965). The dominant aim is to initially achieve optimum satisfaction by raising their standard of living through secure employment. However, when sizeable groups of people of any ethnicity, religion or colour arrive to settle in a new country, many difficulties which may or may not be foreseen, are bound to arise. As well as the more "material" problems of housing, employment and income, there is initially much misunderstanding between the host nation and the newcomers due to a lack of communication, differences in beliefs and values and real or perceived conflicts of interest (Tajfel 1965). As the migrants begin to adapt to their new environment, new relationships develop between them and the larger society.

Over the years various models have been put forward conceptualising the conflicts of relationship between the ethnic/native groups. The first model was developed by Park and Stonequist in the

1920's and 1930's and emphasises the association of marginal personality traits with the immigrant. The second later model presented by Goldberg, Green and more specifically Dickie-Clark, points at some of the flaws inherent in the Park/Stonequist theory by concentrating on the importance of the marginal situation rather than the marginal personality. The cultural deficit model which emerged during the 1960's similarly assumes that the culture of the host nation is superior to that of the ethnic population, with the immigrant expected to assimilate into the host nation's way life. The remainder of the chapter will show how these three models are now outdated and of historical interest only, by tracing other more contemporary perspectives which have been developed since this period, such as liberal pluralism, Marxist, Black and feminist approaches. However, it is the current model of culture conflict between two equal but different cultures, supported by Anthias and Hiro, amongst others, which is of importance in relating to the situation of the lone mother from the Indian and African sub-continent living in London today.

There have been several writers who have claimed that in the long run, immigrants' descendants would be so incorporated into the majority culture that they would feel as part of it as those whose ancestors were of the host nation. Thus Park claimed that assimilation was the inevitable last stage of the relationship between the host society and any new immigrant group (Banton 1967:75). Some governments, too, have pursued assimilationist policies. A notable example of this is the longstanding policy of Israeli governments to absorb and assimilate various Jewish ethnic immigrant groups. There is today, however, general acknowledgement that assimilation is an impossible process, and some would argue an undesirable policy, from the short and medium points of view.

Since this study is concerned with first generation women, some of whom have only been in this country for a few years, the issue of assimilation appears to be of no relevance. Nevertheless, the mothers' replies will be examined to see whether any of them felt assimilated in the sense of feeling predominantly British and if they were accepted as such by the British population.

The marginal personality

The pioneer of the marginal thesis was Park, a leading figure in the inter-war "Chicago School" of sociologists. Although the term had been used earlier in anthropological studies, it was Park who formally introduced the phrase into the study of society with the publication of his essay "Human Migration and the Marginal Man" in 1928 (Hughes 1968).

Park saw the vast expansion of Europe over four centuries as the starting point for a mixing of populations and cultures (Mann 1973). However, he claimed that "where peoples who come together are of divergent cultures and widely different racial stocks, assimilation and amalgamation do not take place as rapidly as they do in other cases" (1950:353). Instead, when people of dissimilar races and cultures live together, then under the conditions of modern life, culture conflicts arise (Dickie-Clark 1966). When cultures come into conflict, some individuals find themselves on the margin of these two cultures, neither fully nor permanently accommodated into either. Living simultaneously in two worlds, the individual is forced to become both a cosmopolitan and a stranger. On the one hand, he is never quite willing to break with his past and traditions, whilst on the other, he is not quite accepted by the new society.

According to Park, "it is in the mind of the marginal man that the moral turmoil which new contacts occasion, manifests itself in the most obvious forms" (1950:356). Although all immigrants are bound to experience some sort of cultural conflict, it is more likely to be relatively permanent for the marginal man. This results in him becoming a personality type, characterised by instability, restlessness and with there being "inevitably a period of inner turmoil and intense self-consciousness" (1950:355).

Park also went on to associate certain other personality traits with the marginal man. In his publication (1950:386-392), he stated that mulattos, or those of mixed blood are more intelligent, enterprising and aggressive, far tenser and prone to taking themselves more seriously. They are also more egocentric and sensitive, and more obsessed with their ambiguous position in society. Park argued that the mulattos' progress has been more rapid than that of the Negro, in securing recognition for themselves in the fields of leadership, writing and teaching, amongst other professions. He concluded by claiming that the migrant of mixed blood is the one condemned to be the most marginalised.

For Park, the dilemma of the marginal man's mental conflict would be resolved by an inevitable process of assimilation into the dominant society. This would begin with the initial stage of "contact," developing to "competition" over housing, jobs and political power. This is followed by "accommodation" involving peaceful co-existence, and lastly "assimilation" whereby "the conquering peoples impose their culture and their standards upon the conquered" (1950:354). Thus, the newcomer would finally be completely incorporated into the native country's way of life. This progression to full assimilation may not necessarily proceed regularly in all spheres of life and could drag over several generations (Richardson and Lambert 1985).

This first model of thought was taken up and elaborated on in the 1930's by Stonequist who began his work under Park's direct influence. Although he paid much attention to Jews and mixed bloods, Stonequist also widened the scope of those labelled marginalised by including such categories as Europeanised Africans and westernised Orientals (Berry 1965). Stonequist's theory was also more detailed, greatly emphasising the effects of conflicts on the personality of the immigrant. According to Stonequist, the marginal man is:

> one who is poised in psychological uncertainty between two or more worlds, reflecting in his soul the discords and harmonies, repulsions and attractions of these worlds, one of which is dominant over the other (1961:8).

Thus, the marginal man will see himself from two conflicting viewpoints – those of the two groups between which he is poised.

Like Park, Stonequist stressed the negative features of personality, though to a greater extent. He claimed that the marginal man will show an ambivalence in both attitudes and sentiments, and will experience a divided loyalty. It is this ambivalence which is essentially at the root of the traits which characterise the marginal man and helps to explain his dual personality and double consciousness. Because his status is often called into question, he is likely to be moody, temperamental and irrational, and excessively self and race-conscious (Berry 1965).

Made to feel unacceptable, he is likely to be hypocritical and show feelings of inferiority, for which he may compensate by becoming egocentric or pushing, or by rationalising or daydreaming. By self-consciously seeing himself through the eyes of others, he is prone to be hyper-sensitive and liable to withdrawal tendencies. He will show skill in noting contradictions and hypocrisies among people of the dominant culture, and be contemptuous of those living below him (Mann 1973). Stonequist believed that the individual's heightened mental activity may often enable him to be more reflective and creative. However, at other times, he is merely imitative and conformist in outlook. These personality traits may vary in strength from very little to great (Dickie-Clark 1966).

One way of adjusting to the ambiguous situation is assimilation into the dominant group, another way is assimilation into the subordinate group and a third way is accommodation to an intermediate position between the two groups. The degree of adjustment may differ, although there will always be some degree of personal maladjustment inherent in the marginal situation. Stonequist stated that at a minimum it consists of an inner strain and malaise, a feeling of isolation or of not quite belonging. He went on to say that:

> at the other extreme are those conflicts which are severe enough to demoralise the individual, throwing him into continual restlessness, and initiating a process of disorganisation which ends in dissipation, crime, suicide or psychosis (1961:159).

The marginal situation

Contemporary critics of the Park/Stonequist thesis developed the second model of immigrant/native relationships – the culture conflict theory.

Goldberg (1941) forwarded the concept of a "marginal culture" in which marginalised peoples need not necessarily develop psychological marginality. This is because, although they live within a minority culture, it is nonetheless sufficiently complete and satisfying enough to prevent personality traits emerging. Unlike Stonequist, Goldberg saw American Jews as an example of a group with such a minority culture within which the members can function quite normally. Safely enclosed in their own culture they cannot be torn between two cultures (in Mann 1973).

Green (1974) followed up Goldberg's idea by claiming that migrant groups do not necessarily experience a culture conflict since they can keep their initial cultures intact. In his work with second generation Greeks and Poles in America, he found that although both groups were culturally equi-distant from the dominant culture, only one of the groups experienced culture conflict and went on to show the particular associated personality traits. Green believed that this would partly depend on the degree to which he is attracted to the group he is attempting to leave, and repulsed by the group he is trying to become a member of. According to Green, only where there are major cultural differences is it likely that marginal personality traits will appear. He also saw absolute rejection as being easier to bear than uncertain and unpredictable acceptance (in Mann 1973).

Green's theory that only some of those marginalised will be torn by conflicts was supported by Antonovsky's study in 1956 of 58 second generation Jews (in Dickie-Clark 1966). He discovered that no less than eight of his sample held ambivalent views about their identities, with the results that their relationship with both Jewish and non-Jewish life was found to be unsatisfactory and filled with conflict. The remainder of the sample, however, had come to terms with their Jewishness and could identify with their lives in various ways. It remains unclear, though, as to whether or not all those in the study had initially experienced culture conflict, and barring the ambivalent eight, had finally managed to resolve their dilemmas.

It was Dickie-Clark (1966) who concentrated his work more specifically on the marginal situation, by stressing its importance in its own right without any psychological components. Marginal situations, he argued, are hierarchical in character and:

> while many of those situations are either or of no great importance, others are very important and last a long time. The situation of the world's minority groups is of this second kind and this fact indicates the scale on which marginal situations are found (1966:47).

A resistance is offered by members of the host society to the newcomer's entry into the majority group and the enjoyment of its privileges. This resistance has its origins in the attitudes of the majority group towards those who are excluded. Subordinate group members may be permitted into the system of social relations at certain points but are kept out of the rest. What the dominant group would regard as being desirable and worthy of encouragement and what it would look upon as being objectionable or feel indifferent to, would partly be dependent upon factors like the political ideology, the demands of the economy and the colour of the immigrant group. Moreover, the individual's own subjective attitude towards the obstacle to be overcome may vary. One individual may feel totally excluded, whilst another may only feel partially so.

Thus, whilst the obstacle between the groups is effective in preventing the full enjoyment by the marginalised group of the power and privileges of the dominant group in the hierarchy, it does not prevent the absorption by individuals of the former group of the latter's culture. This results in the marginalised individual possessing characteristics which would otherwise give him a higher status but does not. Dickie-Clark went on to use colour as another dimension to the marginality thesis to validate this point. He claimed that although a "coloured" individual may possess all the cultural traits of a dominant white of equal standing, he does not share the status of a white person, nor will he enjoy the same opportunities in life. This, in effect, will lead to a status dilemma, leaving the "coloured" individual with a confused social identity. However, Dickie-Clark believed that there is no evidence to show that being in this situation necessarily produces marginality traits. One of his arguments was to state that the attitudes of these people "can be held without personal maladjustment or undue inner turmoil or emotional imbalance" (1966:190). Thus, a marginal situation does not necessarily lead to a marginal personality.

Sometimes a marginal group may feel itself to be superior concerning particular matters, to the dominant group, and thus erect its own barrier. For example, a cultural group may retain a specific value and the behaviour based on it. Therefore, even in the process of being acculturated, the marginal group may not accept all the elements of the dominant culture so readily.

Dickie-Clark concluded by stating that the marginal situation distinguishes between the learning of cultural elements on the one hand and acceptance into the dominant system of social relations on the other. Complete exclusion and complete inclusion are incompatible with the notion of marginality, so where barriers are complete, marginal situations cannot occur. However, where there are inconsistencies, this provides the most significant and historically important marginal situations, like those of minority groups in general.

Cultural deficit model

The post-war period in Britain saw an acute shortage of labour, and with it, the recession of its major industries (Cashmore and Troyna 1983). In an attempt to boost the economy, the government allowed the unregulated arrival of primary labour migrants from the Caribbean and Indian sub-continent, the heaviest flow of which began in the late 1940's and early 1950's (Saggar 1992).

Banton's "Black and Coloured" (1959) saw the departure from the earlier psychological explanations of individual behaviour by attempting a sociology of race relations which studied the structures and norms governing behaviour. The author argued that although the host nation seemed well-disposed to the "Blacks," they preferred to keep a "social distance" due to the pressure of group norms (in Bourne with Sivanandan 1980).

As immigration continued, a more disciplined and academic body of research began to emerge. These studies, however, were mainly of a descriptive nature and concerned with narrating how the immigrants lived, what their customs were and how they were fitting into British society (Bourne with Sivanandan 1980). Thus, these pieces of literature appeared to condone an assimilationist position.

In her book "Dark Strangers" (1965), Sheila Patterson rejected the relevance of colour to the whole issue by explaining the findings of her field-work in Brixton within a neutral "host-immigrant" framework. She saw the incoming group, through its own organisation, as adapting itself to the permanent membership of the receiving nation in certain major spheres of association, notably in economic and civic life (Patterson 1965).

Stuart Hall's early work within the field of education (1967) gave vivid accounts of what life was like for young Black people in the inner cities. Discrimination was explained in terms of practices which impeded Blacks from gaining access to sources of power, and the teacher's role was to help the whites to understand the needs of vulnerable Black people and to assist them through their difficulties (in Denney 1983). Fitzherbert's study of West Indian children in London (1967) blamed Black people for inappropriate use of welfare services, with the perceptions of whites being inherently superior to that of the Black person due to the white social worker being able to function more adequately in society (in Denney 1995).

During this time, however, no provision was made for the social needs of the immigrants. Rather, they were merely regarded as units of labour who were in competition with the white working classes in the run-down inner-cities for schools, housing and welfare services. In the process the Blacks became defined as the cause of social decay and not its symptoms (Bourne with Sivanandan 1980).

Viewed today, however, the three models outlined above are greatly outdated and of no more than historical interest, serving only to trace the change in thought over the decades in the relationship between immigrants and the native population.

The first model, presented by Park and Stonequist, incorrectly shows the ethnic individual, by virtue of being an immigrant, as developing an inferior personality to the majority population. This assumption is both unrealistically one-sided and derogatory. The second model, concentrating on the marginal situation of the immigrant, although less patronising, is nevertheless biased in assuming that the majority culture is superior to the ethnic culture at all times and in all respects. Likewise, the cultural deficit model takes a similar stance by presuming that the immigrant will readily absorb into the host culture.

The first three models had implications for the understanding of racism. They implied that racism is caused by the "strangeness" of the ethnic population, and that with the acculturation and eventual assimilation of the immigrants and their children, the issue would disappear. This early tendency postulated the need for ethnic groups to abandon their distinct identity in order to acquire full status as equal members of society. Racism was largely defined as a problem of cultural difference, and hostility regarded as mainly the result of ignorance (Anthias 1992:157).

Liberal pluralism

In the early 1970's the liberal pluralists came to dominate welfare discourse. Within this framework society is conceptualised in terms of competing elite groups, each deriving their power from a variety of political, religious and military sources. Thus, power is diffused through society and is not concentrated in the hands of any one group (Denney 1983). Because of discriminatory practices, Black people are excluded from gaining access to the sources of power, which impinges on many aspects of their day-to-day lives (Denney 1995).

Liberal pluralists recognised that this multiple deprivation affected Black people differentially, and in order to correct the balance, corrective action was seen as being needed within existing systems of welfare (Denney 1995). In principle, the liberal standpoint argues that equal opportunity exists when all individuals are enabled freely and equally to compete for social rewards. Policy makers are, therefore, required to ensure that the rules of competition are not discriminatory and that they are fairly enforced on all (Jewson and Mason 1992). Although the prejudice of some whites was acknowledged as a factor, it was believed that as time passed, anti-discrimination legislation, education and a willingness to adapt on the part of the immigrants would remove the ethnic dimension in the stratification system. It was thought that racism as a barrier to social advancement would be overcome and recent immigrants and their children would be represented in proper proportions and at all parts of the stratification hierarchy, depending on their abilities and hard work (Thompson and Priestley 1996).

Policies with the objective of giving people access to equal educational opportunity have always been an important feature of liberal pluralism, with full entitlement to housing and social work services through policies to reduce inequality also being emphasised. The role of welfare is regarded in terms of assisting Black people through the inevitable difficulties which they experience in attempting to utilise state services for their own advancement. Understanding individual problems and developing relationships with Black people also helps to provide an essential bridge between them and the white population. Therefore, for the pluralist, the overall race relations goal is a complex blend of integration and assimilation (Denney 1995).

In Great Britain during the 1970's the official view of ethnic relations was more on integration. As a goal to be achieved, the then Home Secretary, Roy Jenkins, defined integration as "not a flattening process of assimilation but as equal opportunity accompanied by cultural diversity, in an atmosphere of mutual tolerance" (quoted in Denney 1983:154). It was hoped by the Labour government that if intolerance of different racial groupings was eradicated, then equal opportunity could develop, with anti-discrimination legislation also aiding this process (Denney 1983). Although it was not made clear whether minority groups should retain all or only part of their cultures and religions, it was hoped that they would be accepted as permanent members of the majority group in all external aspects of association (Rose et al 1969). Therefore, it was recognised that a certain amount of responsibility lay with the white "host" community to adapt to a situation in which Black people were a permanent part of many communities (Denney 1995). This set the terms of an agenda where citizenship rights involved a commitment to a shared political culture (Anthias 1995).

Yet, what was not sufficiently examined was the potential possibility of conflict between a shared culture of the public domain and the rights to cultural differences which had been cited by Jenkins. The concept of two divided provinces, those of a shared public domain and a differentiated private cultural domain, did not allow for the difficulties in this depiction. Rex challenges the two domains thesis, both on a theoretical and a practical level. There appears no sociological validity to the view that two spheres of social life could exist without influencing each other. Nor can it be alleged that the numerous elements of one could be easily distinguished from the other. For instance, the question of what constitutes the shared public domain could be answered in differing ways from different political or cultural positions (Anthias 1995). Some like Honeyford (1988), for example, have identified the shared public domain as being comparable to an all-inclusive British national culture. But this is problematised both by class and political differences. Feminists have also challenged the opinion that values and organisations around gender and the family are private, by arguing for the breakdown of the dualism inherent in the distinction between the public and the private (in Anthias 1995).

However:

> the most important feature of the pluralist paradigm was that it was dominated by white academics and policy makers who set the agenda without reference to the perceptions of Black people or the need to analyse the nature of racism and other forms of discrimination within welfare institutions (Denney 1995:319).

This perspective supposes that the removal of collective barriers to the expression of individual talent will enable the best person to be the most successful, and in general, allow all individuals to make the best of themselves. Because the principles embodied in equal opportunities policies are procedural ones, the liberal pluralist has ignored or has great difficulty in accommodating the structural sources of social capabilities and skills, and hence the structural sources of social inequality (Jewson and Mason 1992).

The Marxist perspective

The late 1970's saw a new position emerge which was quite distinct from the previous approaches taken, in that it emphasised the racially structured nature of British society. A discourse dominated by white males, Marxist writers stress that racism must be viewed in the context of capitalist relations of production. In this form of analysis, the state, class and race divisions are inextricably linked. Efforts to focus purely on cultural or ethnic differences are seen as diverting attention away from practices which perpetuate and legitimise racism (Denney 1983). This notion of institutionalised racism reflects an attempt to move away from the individual as the focus of attention in understanding how racism works (Marsh et al 1996) .

Racism is regarded as the ideology of inferiority and is part of the superstructure of capitalist society. Racist ideas, practices and institutions enhance the control of the ruling class over the workers. The effects of racism include legitimising slavery, colonialism and continued deprivation in capitalist society; dividing the working class, thereby helping prevent the development of class-consciousness, with the segregation of the labour market allowing further exploitation; and providing scapegoats for the inevitable tensions and frustrations of capitalism, whereby such issues as unemployment, poverty, crime and poor housing can be blamed on a visible and vulnerable group (Richardson and Lambert 1985).

Stuart Hall can be regarded as developing "core" concepts in relation to race, racism and the state through the 1970's, by claiming that sociological theories of race and racism failed to take into account the historical, economic and structural features of societies which allowed racism to be reproduced. He thus moved beyond a simplistic form of Marxist analysis which reduced all social relations to the productive process (Denney 1995). One of the most illuminating of the above mentioned effects of racism can be seen in the study by Hall et al (1978) which offers an interesting and immensely detailed version of the scapegoating argument (in Richardson and Lambert 1985). The research undertaken entitled "Policing the Crisis" was a major intellectual achievement which still has an enduring influence in social science today (Denney 1995).

Hall et al's starting point is the debate about "mugging" in Britain, one which became more prominent in the early 1970's following some heavily publicised cases. Curiously, the mugging scare did not seem justified in terms of an unprecedented increase in the relevant crime figures and so the notion of a "moral panic" was used to draw attention to the exaggerated nature of the fears and rumours surrounding the issue. Moreover, a central feature of the debate was the close identification of mugging with Blacks, an identification which seemed "natural" and "reasonable" in light of some familiarity with the crime debates in America. Hall et al skilfully demonstrate how certain groups created, sustained and transformed the moral panic about mugging. Thus, police groups seized the initiative, forming pre-emptive patrol groups even before the media bestowed a great deal of publicity. However, media coverage was certainly important in orchestrating public opinion and shaping public debate (Richardson and Lambert 1985).

The construction of the Black mugger at a particular historical moment therefore challenged the view that the relation between news and crime is a simple one. Hall et al argue that definitions of crime, and in this case, Black crime, are socially constructed officially by agencies responsible for crime control, with the police and the courts being the "primary definers of crime." Such definitions reflect the selective attention of journalists and the routine practices of news gathering and presentation, while official definitions of crime are transformed into the vigorous public language of popular journalistic rhetoric. The public definition of crime is therefore dependent on the official and media definitions of crime (Denney 1995).

Following Gramsci, Hall et al focus on the crisis of "hegemony," which draws attention to the ways in which ruling classes attempt to maintain their domination by ideological and cultural means. As well as exercising economic power and state coercion (the police and military), the ruling class strive to win the hearts and minds of people and thereby gain "consent" rather than mere obedience. However, this bid for hegemony is not always successful, and a crisis in hegemony occurs when there is a loss of faith in the social order, or when opposing groups challenge the legitimacy of the ruling groups (Richardson and Lambert 1985).

However, by focusing on such a potent symbol as "law and order," the state was able to rally support for its campaign against not just Black youth alone, but also against the wider sources of political, social and economic unrest which "threatened" the fabric of post-war consensus. Such sources of conflict included politicised youth protest, women's movements, industrial unrest and an acceleration of violent protest in Northern Ireland. The main argument is that the association of mugging with the Black presence in Britain was not simply accidental, a case of mistaken perceptions or unfortunate speculation (Richardson and Lambert 1985). For Hall et al, the crisis of the Black mugger was directly linked to a broader crisis – a crisis within capitalism itself (Marsh et al 1996).

The state was also able to capitalise on the symbolism of "race," and that is why the identification of mugging with Blacks was so important, with the symbolism of the young Black mugger proving very powerful in its effects – in offending the latent "sense of Englishness;" in connecting up the fears about "youth today;" in offering a credible explanation for the very real difficulties people were experiencing; and in outlining fears about "inside conspiracies" by liberals who were imposing an alien presence and destroying valuable traditions and institutions. Race was undoubtedly not the only symbol, but it brought together many of the preoccupations and fears of people living in a capitalist society experiencing deep crisis. Yet it enabled this crisis to be masked by a series of false resolutions such as cries for law and order, a desire for re-establishment of firm authority and stricter immigration legislation, which deflected attention away from the true source of the troubles. In the process, the moral panic also inflamed racism and made life much harder for the scapegoated Black communities residing in this country (Richardson and Lambert 1985).

Black perspectives

Hall's important contribution during the 1970's enabled the breakthrough of a Black perspective of race relations (Denney 1995). This began to take place in the early 1980's with an interpretation of the Black experience in Britain emerging from those who experienced it rather than from those who observed it. According to Williams (1994), this located the problem as stemming from a white society and its institutions steeped in racism, and it transposed Black people from being problems and victims to a people with a history of struggle against imperialism, colonialism and racism in its various forms.

Rather than targeting individual prejudice as in the past, anti-racist movement at this time stressed the role of racism and provided the idea of Black autonomous organisation, whereby people gained the power to have a voice in formulating policies which were of direct relevance to their needs. The objective was to build an anti-racist society and culture, stressing race differences and awareness rather than the colour blindness approach promoted by liberalism (Anthias 1995).

Political resources were to be marshalled through Black councillors and Black MP's, with a growth of Black political activism inside the Labour Party. The group of Blacks, which also organised itself around the demand for a Black section within the party, issued warnings that the electoral allegiance of Black populations in urban areas could no longer be taken for granted by Labour (Gilroy 1993).

Race awareness workshops were promoted, whilst ideas about Black culture and identity and ethnic monitoring were fought for. Black groups were funded, and there was a greater presence of Blacks in the media (Anthias 1995). Mixed race adoption was challenged in response to Black family pathology, demanding the right and need for Black children in care to be fostered with Black foster parents or remain in children's homes where there were Black residential workers. Small's argument, in brief, is that in a society structured by racial domination, a Black child can only acquire a positive Black identity from a Black parent who has learned to cope with day-to-day racism. Clearly, in this argument "Blackness" is seen as the most fundamental division in both the child and parent's world and in shaping identity (in Williams 1994).

During this time, numerous Black and Black women's organisations defined their constituencies to comprise members from all three communities - Caribbean, African and Asian, for example "Southall Black Sisters." There also continued to be Asian women's organisations excluding African or Caribbean people and Black organisations not including Asians, for instance "Camden Black Sisters" and "Grassroots" (Mama 1992).

Hall, however, has argued that the word "Black" itself was coined as a way of referencing:

> the common experience of racism and marginalisation in Britain and came to provide the organising category of a new politics of resistance amongst groups and communities, with in fact very different histories, traditions and ethnic identities (quoted in Denney 1995:321).

These identities never remain the same but are "historically contingent fields of contestation within the nature of a hierarchical, racialised and gendered society" (quoted in Denney 1995: 321).

This period saw the emphasis on common experience of racial oppression in particular as the rationale for Black unity, which led to a further change in the meaning of the term "Black," as it came to mean "people affected by racism." There were actually debates about whether Irish people and other migrant groups should be defined as "politically Black" on account of their experience of British colonisation (Mama 1992). Therefore, "Black" as a basis for solidarity communal grouping has been a shifting and confusing category, at times denoting both Asians and African Caribbeans and at other times only the latter (Anthias 1995).

According to Anthias (1995), an even more important objection to the use of the term "Black" is that it cannot articulate processes of racialisation in general or in their specificity. It is too limited since it excludes those who do not experience what can be called "colour racism," like the Jews and migrant workers. It is also too broad because it cannot tackle specific forms of racism, such as those against Asian women or African Caribbean youth, in the first case linked to gender and sexuality (such as the practice of virginity tests at immigration control) and in the second case linked to gender, generation and unemployment (whereby young, Black men not in work are often labelled as criminals). It reduces racism to a homogeneous set of experiences and practices organised around the centrality of skin colour as the visible marker of racist intentionality. Racism is therefore defined in inter-subjective terms, being seen as exercised in and against subjects with particular ascriptive characteristics, rather than being a set of outcomes of a large range of legal, policy, institutional and discursive practices.

Mama (1992) has discussed the culturalisation or ethnicisation of race as a state-orchestrated process, by which focusing on the language, food, habits and clothing of Black (African, Caribbean and Asian) people, masks and denies the fact of discrimination. Systematic and institutionalised racism is thereby reduced to cultural misunderstanding and so is depoliticised. Even more mystifying is the manner in which class politics have been superseded by the new identity politics of gender, ethnicity, sexuality and disability.

One aspect of the changing policy climate has been the development and then retraction of ethnic funding. The narrow focus on specific cultural and ethnic needs has produced a fragmented and competitive identity politics which failed to advance the anti-racist campaigns that guided Black struggles into the 1980's. This is not to suggest that diverse positive cultural identifications are incompatible with a politics of "Black unity." However, it is now clear that in the early 1980's "Black unity" was more of an aspiration than an actuality (Mama 1992). Anti-racism has thus been responsible for Black people being conceived as victims and not as an active force (Denney 1995). Furthermore, it is also now clear that the contradictory policy climate of municipal socialism and Thatcherism generated a scramble for the suddenly available but limited funding for ethnic needs, which did not help. The minority communities remain largely separate, although amongst the younger generation there is evidence that new syncretic Black identities are being formed, and at least some of these are inclusive rather than exclusive (Mama 1992).

Feminist perspectives

The feminist critiques of the welfare state which have emerged since the 1960's, diverse and complex as they are, have been responsible for enriching the analysis of social policy by throwing new light on old concepts, by adding new policy concerns to the agenda of welfare strategy and new analytical and methodological considerations which need to be acknowledged in any account of welfare which aims for theoretical adequacy (Williams 1994).

In her book "Social Policy – A Critical Introduction" (1994:81), Williams summarises these various feminist perspectives. Libertarian feminism hardly advances the analysis of women's oppression or of social policy, being both individualist and biologically determinist in method. Liberal and welfare feminism – the two faces of reformist feminism – have brought to attention women's inequalities and special needs, and the potential of the welfare state to ameliorate these, but neither has sufficiently dealt with the division between the private and the public, or the question of women's biology. Liberal feminism mainly emphasises the change in the public domain and fails to recognise any aspect of women's biology. Welfare feminism, being the antithesis, pertains to change for women as wives and mothers in the private sphere, and tends towards a biologically determinist method of analysis. Additionally, both are idealist in outlook, expecting reformation through changing ideas and attitudes, whilst appealing to a neutral state.

Radical feminism has vehemently highlighted elements of women's personal lives which merit political consideration - sexuality, reproduction, the family and divisions within it - but in its different definitions of male power and its appeals to "women's special nature" leans towards both biological determinism and idealism. Social feminism, however, has more suitably provided a consistent theoretical basis for understanding the issues highlighted by radical feminists, a framework that explores the relationship between the personal and political, between women's biology and its material context, in terms of the social and economic organisation of patriarchal capitalism and its implications for change. This has been done in a materialist way, by attempting to avoid both economic reductionism or biological determinism.

Today, there is a further dimension to the divisions amongst women along racial lines. Many Black feminists, such as Amos and Parmar, argue that the above mentioned feminist perspectives all share racist assumptions and have failed to relate to the specific experiences of Black women (Dale and Foster 1986). Black feminism's contribution and critique of feminism is crucial, in that it rejects the biological explanations for racial inequalities, and has instead highlighted the ways in which, subjectively and objectively, Black women's oppression is different, and how not only the sexual division of labour but the racial and international division of labour, not only patriarchy and capitalism but also imperialism, must be brought into the analysis of social policy to understand the relationship between the state, the family and women (Williams 1994). Thus, Black feminists have stressed that any theoretical models that deal sufficiently with the experience of all women must recognise and explore the interlocking nature of class, race and gender (Marsh et al 1996).

Williams (1994) argues that Black feminists have criticised the use of the concept of patriarchy by many radical feminists in that it emphasises women being oppressed as women, and therefore suggests, firstly, that universal solidarity exists between women as women, and secondly, that stressing men as oppressors implies a collective sense of power used by all men. It is argued that this interpretation has led to a blindness of differences of power between women, particularly the racism of the state as well as its sexism.

A significant amount has been written articulating the experiences of Black women, how their relationship to the family, men, sexuality, reproduction, work and the state, including the welfare state, is structured not only by gender but by race as well, and how this renders their experiences different from those of white women. The simultaneous experiences for Black women of racism and sexism not only compounds those oppressions but reconstitutes them in specific ways (Williams 1994).

This can be illustrated by the argument centring around the abortion campaigns of the 1970's where the "right to choose" an abortion was seen as a demand only appropriate to white women, whose fertility was taken for granted and approved. For Black women, however, the experience was one where their "right to reproduction" was being questioned and often controlled by a health service operating under a concern about "Black numbers," a racist view of Black female sexuality and a tradition of eugenicism (Williams 1994).

For Black women, the oppression of racism may often take precedence over their oppression as women, or they may wish to organise separately as Black women, thus struggling around gender issues within their own communities, rather than as part of an all-embracing women's movement (Dale and Foster 1986). In post-war Britain, for instance, Afro-Caribbean, Afro-American and Asian women have fought over issues affecting them as Black mothers, workers, tenants, patients and claimants; for better pay and conditions (Chix, Grunwick and the health workers strikes of the 1970's); against racist and sexually discriminatory controls and deportations; for the right to organise autonomously against domestic violence (Asian women's refuges); and against the practice of social services departments of blaming the problems Black families face upon their own cultures or traditions - a racialised form of blaming the victim (Williams 1994).

Williams (1994) has claimed, however, that within this movement there is also the need to recognise that "Black" should not imply homogeneity of experience, since the histories and struggles of Afro-

Caribbean, Afro-American and Asian women are mediated by different experiences of racism. For example, the operation of racism and sexism does not apply in a uniform manner to Black women, as the notions of "Black family pathology" shows. The idea that the cultural characteristics of Black families are the cause of poverty, inadequate housing, poor schooling and other social problems has long been part of the common sense practice of doctors, teachers and social workers. However, these are applied in different and contradictory ways to different cultural groups:

> Black children are seen to fail at school because their Asian mothers are too passive and withdrawn and stay at home, or because their Afro-Caribbean mothers are too assertive and go out to work. Black adolescents' problems are supposed to derive from too much or too little discipline, from being kept in the home or not kept off the streets (1994:78).

After at least 30 years of debates within feminist political groups and feminist theory, few contemporary feminist sociologists would now underestimate the significance of ethnicity in structuring women's experiences and oppression, and would recognise the urgency of redefining feminist theories to take into account both diversity and commonality in women's lives and the ways in which ethnicity, gender, class, social class, sexuality and age all help to shape the pattern of women's experience and the making of their identity (Thompson and Priestley 1996). Williams (1994) has claimed that whilst the welfare state plays an important role in defining the boundaries of women's lives, in underpinning female dependency and the sexual division of labour within and outside the home, Black feminist analysis forces us to acknowledge that the state, nevertheless, treats different groups of women in different ways.

Cultural pluralism

An important breakthrough in our understanding of racism was the militant Black American movement in the 1960's with its strong affirmation of "Black" identity, best reflected in the slogan "Black is Beautiful," whereby Black minorities need not become "white" to "merit" equal economic and social opportunities (Tajfel 1982, Sivanandan 1983). The Black Power movement gave people a voice, and by establishing the principle of self-empowerment, the negative embedded value judgements were reversed. It was out of this movement that the current model gradually surfaced. First appearing during the 1970's, cultural pluralism has re-emerged in the 1990's as a counter to the total absorption model suggested by the assimilationists (Denney 1995).

More recently, the term multi-culturalism has evolved, originally in America, and then in Britain, with the realisation that the "melting pot" does not melt, and that ethnic and racial divisions get reproduced from generation to generation. Assimilation is thus "clearly regarded as unrealistic" (Denney 1983:163). Anthias (1992) has argued that a multi-cultural society is made up of a homogeneous majority and smaller "unmeltable" minorities, the latter groups having their own essentially different communities and cultures. These differences, which are compatible with the majority society, need to be understood, accepted and basically be left alone in order to create harmonious relations.

It is no longer feasible for the state to treat the population as unitary and static, and to enforce policies which will lead to acculturation and accommodation for the minorities into the native culture. State nations now contain within them diverse ethnicities, cultures and religions and there is an increasing tendency to recognise racial differences, rejecting the notion that white is superior (Jacobs 1988).

Integrationism and multi-culturalism have been two recent responses to the "different but equal" situation of ethnic populations in modern day societies. Advocates of both terms insist that pluralism provides the most desirable socio-political arrangement for post-imperial Britain (Goulbourne 1991). Pluralism states that groups of people are encouraged to maintain their own communal social structure and identify and preserve certain of their values and behavioural patterns which are not in conflict with broader values, patterns and legal norms common to the entire society (Gordon 1978:160). Any differences in thinking between integrationism and multi-culturalism are, in reality, only a matter of degree. The former encourages the immigrant population to retain some of their cultural values on the one hand, and also to adapt and fit into the whole of society on the other. Multi-culturalism claims to be more tolerant in practice, by insisting that ethnic minorities retain their cultural values eternally.

Welcome though it is, this present model is not problem free. Even in countries where there is a formal policy of multi-culturalism, complications may arise (Anthias 1992). As a method of resolving the conflict between dissimilar groups inhabiting the same territory, pluralism has an appeal to those committed to the ideals of democracy and tolerance (Berry 1965). Separate national majorities, however, are constructed with varying degrees of tolerance to cultural difference, with the state responsible to defend the general will of the people. National cultural unity must not be seen to be jeopardised by an exaggerated development of cultural diversity. According to Anthias:

> first of all, defining the boundaries of difference between the actual different cultures is problematic. Which cultures or elements of cultures would be 'legitimately' included in the multi-culturalist vision and which would not? (1992:37).

Supporters of pluralism recognise the fact that there are limits beyond which cultural freedom cannot go. Depending on how tolerant the hegemonic culture is concerning various social practices, will clearly determine what can or cannot be allowed. Ethnic groups which differ radically in their fundamental value systems could hardly become accommodated on a plane of equality and tolerance (Berry 1965). Those minority cultural practices which contravene the country's legal system will not be acceptable to the majority society. Such examples are polygamy, wife beating and forced childhood marriages. More specifically, the more traditional Muslim leaders have made demands for their Islamic family law to be incorporated into the British legal system. In Hiro's own words:

> any serious consideration of the Muslim demand by the British authorities would imply treating Islam on a par with Christianity in a Christian land, an idea far too antithetical to western values to be entertained (1991:312).

The stock response by the government has been that there is and can only be one family law in Britain. If different family laws were to be permitted, then this would lay down the foundations for social segregation. Immigrants, however, are allowed to preserve other elements of their cultures from their countries of origin. The government in Britain has also recognised that racial equality may not always mean that public institutions and the law itself should treat everyone by the norms and convenience of the majority (Modood 1990). An illustration of this is the exemption of turban-wearing Sikh men from wearing a crash helmet when riding a motor bike. Indirect provision has also been made for Sikh men to wear their religious daggers in public places without being guilty of an offence.

By the early 1980's Britain was routinely described both officially and unofficially as a multi-racial, multi-cultural society (Hiro 1991). The controversy over "The Satanic Verses" in 1988, however, challenged this view. Modood states that:

> the Rushdie scandal has exposed the weaknesses of any benign multi-culturalism premised on the assumption of easy harmony and pluralism (1992:39).

The Muslim minority were incensed that, unlike Christianity, Islam had been denied legal protection against blasphemy. Feeling unprotected and powerless against a majority community overwhelmingly Christian in law and institutions, Muslims in this country and worldwide took to rioting, with mass book burnings as a symbol of their outrage and condemnation. Moderates among the Muslim leaders made demands for the law to be extended to make religious blasphemy a criminal offence.

Britain is happy in offering its Muslims a formal equality, but is not yet willing to acknowledge, in its legal and institutional arrangements, the existence of a Muslim community which, for example, may be deeply hurt and provoked to violence by forms of literature to which the majority of citizens have become accustomed to tolerating.

Another example where governments in this country have not, in practice, supported the notion of multi-culturalism, is in the area of education. The present government appear committed to "rolling back" any little progress made in multi-ethnic education in the 1980's by permitting schools to opt out of local authority control (Hiro 1991). In the name of freedom of choice, parents can now select to which schools to send their children.

With the pressure now on the majority of white head teachers to attract the maximum number of white pupils, this may result in many ethnic students with special needs being neglected and no longer catered for. Some schools still refuse to allow Sikh boys to wear a turban or Muslim girls to cover their legs. Others do not cater for children who only eat halal meat (Modood 1992). Many ethnic parents want non-Christian faiths to be taught to their children, and have consequently withdrawn them from religious education and from assemblies (Tomlinson 1991). As a result of these cultural differences, separated schooling for ethnic minority children has been increasing steadily. Many among the Muslim community now want to start schools where the Muslim religion and Islamic values are taught to their children. However, state aid has been refused and several applications have been turned down. Thus, the very notion of a multi-cultural educational system for all, has in reality, been dampened by a creeping form of segregation.

According to Rex (1986), multi-culturalism is a feasible social and political ideal, but it is only likely to be tolerated if it does not threaten the shared civic culture. One of the main important aspects of living in a plural society is that minority group members are always, to some degree, caught between their identities as members of the larger society and their identities as members of their particular groups (Newman 1976:40). In a society seeking to achieve equal opportunities and the toleration of cultural diversity, institutional arrangements will inevitably evolve to deal with any arising problems.

Conclusion

In conclusion, all the models of race relations have shown that culture conflict is an inevitability in a society with an immigrant population. Their differences lie, however, in their perceptions and resolution of the problem. The current notion of ethnic and cultural pluralism means that migrants and their children face a dilemma of culture conflict between two equal but different cultures, without implying either a presence of a marginal situation or marginality personality traits. Whichever model is examined, however, it is well documented that second generation immigrants, learning the civic culture and sharing the interests of their non-ethnic peers, are more likely to accept the values of the dominant society than their parents (Dickie-Clark 1966, Gordon 1978, Rex 1986, Ballard 1994).

This investigation will attempt to show how such members of an ethnic group deal with the dilemma of being pressed between two cultures whilst examining the plight of lone parent Asian women from the Indian and African sub-continent living in London today.

2 Family Values in Hindu, Muslim and Sikh Cultures

The previous chapter has argued that ethnic minorities experience a form of culture conflict due to cultural differences between themselves and the host society. This chapter will examine those differences with specific reference to Asian women from the Indian and African sub-continent, by tracing the values inherent in their ethnic culture towards marriage, the position of women, relationships with men, divorce, separation and widowhood. Although some values overlap, there are also differences between Hindu, Muslim and Sikh cultures which shall be brought to the fore. These old, established principles are very difficult to change, even when becoming an immigrant, and continue to be upheld in the new country of residence. The traditional ideology regarding Asian women's position in the family may influence the latters' decisions to become lone mothers as well as shaping their self-perceptions following marriage breakdown. The chapter will conclude by drawing together the similarities between the three cultures and will show how these male dominated views on women may have important implications for the outcome of this study.

Hindu culture

According to Ghadially (1988), in a patriarchal culture like India's, the ideals and images of women are not female but male defined. Hindu women's roles in society and their images are very deeply embedded in the myths and legends of the Hindu culture. The ideal model of womanhood in Hindu culture is incorporated by Sita in the epic "Ramayana," who shows her devotion by following her husband, Rama, into fourteen years of forest exile, before placing herself on a lighted pyre to prove her wifely virtue. Unscathed by the flames, Sita is finally accepted by Rama into his household.

Sita is only one of many women in Hindu tradition and legend. The ideal of womanhood incorporated by Sita is one of chastity, purity, gentle tenderness and a single-minded faithfulness which cannot be disturbed or destroyed even by one's own husband's rejections, cruelty

24

or infidelity. For most men and women in Hindu society, Sita is the epitome of the proper woman, representing the ideal towards which all females should strive, regardless of age, caste, region, social class, education or modernisation (Kakar 1988).

Classical Hindu laws have mainly focused on the dominant role of women as wives, with role models for mothers, daughters and sisters being less dominant. The basic rules for a woman's proper behaviour are that she should never be independent, must show a duty to her husband who controls her, and be obliged to faithfully worship her husband or else be disgraced (Wadley 1988).

These ideals are instilled into Hindu girls from the earliest age to prepare them for the inevitability of marriage. Marriage is almost a universal norm in Indian society for a variety of reasons. Firstly, most women are economically dependent and thus could not choose to remain unmarried, except for a tiny minority, and secondly it is believed that a woman's sexuality is dangerous unless it is controlled by a man. Therefore a woman's power must be "tamed" and then channelled into useful purposes, namely childbearing, especially sons (Caplan 1985). Spinsters are rare and viewed with a certain amount of distrust (Gaur 1980).

A Hindu girl spends only a few years of her childhood in mixed company (Parikh and Garg 1989). She is soon separated from boys and the process of her grooming for adulthood begins. A girl is usually married during adolescence between the ages of twelve and eighteen to guard against any future promiscuity. Significantly, she is not expected to have any say in the matter. In big cities and urban areas, or among high castes where girls are likely to be educated or go on to university, the marriage age is higher.

Marrying off one's daughter successfully is considered one of the primary religious duties of Hindu parents. Arranged marriages in India are the norm for the vast majority, where the prospective bride or groom is chosen by respective parents (Gaur 1980, James and Wilson 1986). Love marriages are believed to be highly dangerous, implying that the behaviour had not been circumspect, or the couple could not have got to know one another in the first place (Caplan 1985:42). In cases where girls choose their own partners, considerable parental disapproval is provoked, and marriages may not take place as parents nearly always have different aspirations for their daughters. In many areas of India such as in the south where norms of extended family support exist, if a couple marry in defiance and have their support withdrawn, it is very difficult for them to manage alone.

Arranged marriages are based on finding a suitable match in class, caste, religion, social status and education. The groom must be older and more mature. The Hindu girl tries to derive security from being desirable in both appearance and conduct, and being useful around the house. All these modes of security are linked to her future. Being physically desirable ensures a husband (Parikh and Garg 1989). A plain girl is encouraged to become skilful and accomplished in household chores in order to compensate for her lack of beauty.

If all negotiations prove satisfactory and the "girl viewing" goes well, the betrothal follows shortly afterwards. Even once engaged very few girls are permitted much contact with their fiancees (Caplan 1985). Although the couple may be allowed to write to one another, it is extremely rare for them to go out together. In any case, the marriage usually follows soon after the engagement.

The girl's parents also have the burden of giving an appropriate dowry to the groom's family. Although the giving and taking of dowry has been illegal in India for many years, there are very few marriages among middle and upper classes that take place without it (Caplan 1985). This long-standing system merely confirms marriage to be like a business deal where parents buy their daughter's way into a family of suitable status as determined by her husband's occupation and income level. A doctor, for example, could now demand over three lakh rupees or 20,000 pounds in dowry (Liddle and Rama 1986:75). Dowry demands are not made only before marriage but during the ceremony and afterwards. Those made after are seen as a prerogative of the groom and his family to express discontent or inadequacy at the amount given earlier (Ghadially and Pramod 1988). The inevitability of high dowry demands has led to a prevalence of amniocentesis tests and terminations if the foetus is found to be female (Desai 1989, Kumari 1989). Female infanticide is not uncommon in a society where girls are looked upon as a financial burden and boys are longed for to guarantee future dowries. Many parents who do have a daughter bankrupt themselves in their anxiety to see her "well settled," for the rapid rate of inflation of all kinds means that calculations made when a girl was young rarely prove sufficient when she is of marriageable age (Caplan 1985).

Dowry deaths are not uncommon in a system where prevailing patriarchal views see women as inferior, and having only themselves to blame for their predicament. There were 999 registered cases of dowry deaths in India in the late 1980s (United Nations 1991), rising to 4,148 cases in 1990 (Ahuja 1994:212). These women are rarely seen as victims of a form of oppression.

Marriage changes the status of a couple greatly. The boy becomes a man, the girl an auspicious person – a married woman, symbolised by a mark on her forehead and also red vermillion powder in the parting of her hair. On marriage women not only renounce all their erotic impulses as well as their loyalties to their parents, but must sever all attachments, both in real life and in fantasy, to all other boys and men they have known during their early lives. Instead, upon marriage, a Hindu woman must direct her physical and emotional tenderness exclusively towards her husband, a complete or near stranger to her until their wedding night. She must also resolve the critical issues of female identity in strange surroundings without the love and support of her family. At this most sensitive and vulnerable period of her development, the presence of feminine figures like Sita is crucial to overcoming this traumatic transition. Her "real" family now becomes her husband's family. Whatever her future fortunes, when she gets married, an Indian girl knows that in the psychological sense she can never return home again (Kakar 1988).

Only those educated middle class brides from urban cities who have had a more liberal and westernised upbringing will spend a short period at their in-laws before setting up home with their husbands to begin a new, independent life. These women are also more likely to seek employment or start a new career, and find more parental help. However, even professional women will, in most cases, place the interests of their families before their own careers (Gaur 1980).

For the vast majority of brides who begin life in a joint family with their in-laws, they occupy one of the lowest rungs in the social hierarchy of their new families (Kakar 1988). Conformity, submissiveness and obedience to the wishes of older women of the family and the mother-in-law especially, is seen as natural. There is minimal, if any communication with the older male family members. The bride is also expected to carry out some of the heaviest household chores without complaint.

A new bride poses a new threat to the unity of the extended family in that she may cause the husband to neglect his duties as son or nephew or uncle, or she may develop a strong husband-wife relationship which may threaten the interests of other family members. Any signs of a growing attachment and tenderness between the couples are actively discouraged by older household members, either by belittling or forbidding any open expression of feelings. Effectively the couple are left alone together to get to know each other well for only brief periods during the night. This is merely often based on a physical relationship.

Some husbands and wives do develop very close relationships with one another, with husbands expressing great solicitude for their wives and vice versa. The ideals of marriage are not such that husbands and wives expect to be companions. On the contrary, the division of labour and norms of sexual segregation tend to mean that men and women have largely separate spheres and interact mainly with members of their own sex (Caplan 1985). Even so, they do participate in some activities together, like going to public or social events as well as to films and concerts.

Norms of marriage are clearly, if frequently and forcibly, stated in Hindu society. The husband has authority over his wife, who should regard him as her master and idolise him, irrespective of his moral value (Kapur 1979). This devotion is obligatory:

> be a husband aged, infirm, deformed, debauched, offensive, a drunkard, a gambler, a frequenter of places of ill-repute, living in open sin with another woman and destitute of honour, still a wife should regard him as a god (Gaur 1980:24).

The wife should do nothing without consulting her husband. She should always put his needs before her own. Couples are careful not to deviate too much from these norms, although they are not kept to absolutely. The resultant husband-wife relationship is, to the modern world, a peculiar amalgam of love and fear, dependence and distrust, sexual partnership and a surrogate of a father-daughter relationship. Even when it is sought to be placed on a new footing indicative of companionship if not equality, this is done at the request of the husband (Ghadially and Pramod 1988).

If the bride comes from a very traditional and conservative family, she is not offered any support. For these women, both physical and psychological brutality is accepted as their destiny by virtue of being a female. Most families discourage a woman from returning to the parental family, even if the husband or his family are brutal (Parikh and Garg 1989). These brides' parents bemoan their loss but remain silent and helpless, unable to make new choices in terms of action.

When relationships do not work satisfactorily, the couple may remain living together, although they may lead very separate lives. A formal separation is seen as bringing shame on the family. The very small minority of brides who do manage to separate themselves and their husbands from the in-laws are often condemned and burdened with guilt at letting their parents down, resulting in turbulent marriages.

Other alternatives today have become available to women, notably those of middle class background with an education, who have the support of their immediate parents. If the husband does not agree to move out of his parents' home, if there is physical or psychological violence, or if new definitions of the husband and wife roles do not emerge, divorce is an option, but not an easy one.

Although legally made possible by Indian parliament since 1955, the actual divorce rate, particularly among rural Hindus, remains negligible (Hiro 1991). Only 0.8 per cent of Indian women aged between 25 and 44 are currently divorced or separated (United Nations 1991:28). For most, formal divorce is out of the question, partly because of the very strong norms against such a step. Social humiliation and remote chances of remarriage also discourage separation (Kumari 1989). As well as disgrace for the woman concerned, divorce results in disgrace for her family too, as the chances of her younger brothers and sisters or her own children making a decent marriage would be "spoilt."

In India widowhood is the main cause of lone parenthood (Bharat 1986). The majority of women are more likely to become widows than to die before their husbands who are usually older than them. Widowhood is considered a great misfortune. Formerly, and to some extent even today, it was thought to be the result of some sin on the part of the woman, perhaps committed in a previous life. Formerly, high caste widows shaved their heads, ate only the simplest foods once a day and observed several other restrictions. Today a widow dons a white sari, dispenses with most jewellery and ceases to use the red powder and forehead mark. However, she is not ill-treated or believed to be a mystical threat. Although widows are no longer burned and unwanted, it is still very rare for a Hindu to marry a woman who has already lived with another husband (Ahuja 1994).

In terms of family acceptance, a young Hindu wife's situation and emotional well-being changes dramatically once she becomes pregnant. In Indian culture there is a very strong belief that marriage is not complete without producing children. Very few couples take any contraceptive precautions at the start of their marriage with the result that children tend to arrive early (Caplan 1985). Those couples who do not produce, and in particular, sons, are often looked down upon and this causes the woman much emotional suffering.

Motherhood is an event in which the culture confirms woman's status as a renewer of the race and gives her a respect not given to her as a "mere" wife. Mothers are expected to put the needs of their children first. The anticipation of motherhood also holds a composite solution for many of her domestic problems. Although Hindu society is not unique in revering motherhood as a moral and religious ideal, the emphasis on the social importance of motherhood encompassing all spheres of life, gives it an indisputable legitimacy in India.

In India love and intimacy develop later in married life, as the couple slowly mature into adult "householders." Parenthood provides the basis for intimacy between man and woman. In middle age the husband and wife bond is seen to evolve out of parental responsibilities, rather than to exclude other family members. Thus, in due time, family solidarity is guaranteed.

Muslim culture

Within a male dominated Islamic ideology, several sets of beliefs relating to the nature of woman establish her status in Muslim tradition and contribute towards determining her role in society. Religion and society are believed to be inter-related and looked upon as a total concept of living (Esposito 1992). Thus, the traditional view of women has its roots in two basic sources of Islamic theology – the Koran and the Sunnah, the collection of inspired sayings uttered by the prophet, Mohammed, and the actions he performed (May 1980).

The Koran says more about the status of women than any other social question (Guillaume 1990:71). Although created spiritually and intellectually equal in the eyes of God, man and woman were also made differently so they would complement one another. This would be reflected in their differing characteristics, capacities and dispositions, and the roles of both sexes in the traditional patriarchal family. According to the Koran, "men are in charge of women because God made one of them excel the other...so good women are the obedient" (May 1980:373).

In Muslim society, marriage is considered the norm for the adult man or woman. A tradition tracing back to Mohammed teaches that marriage is half religion (Jomier 1989). Perhaps in few other societies is entrance into marriage so tightly controlled as it is in a traditional Muslim society (Korson 1979:194). In the socialisation process, a girl is taught to be docile, modest, unassertive and obedient to her elders, especially to the male members of her family. Although patterns of behaviour vary according to region and social class, one of the chief goals in the socialisation process is to instil the psychological feeling of dependence on the male rather than one of self-reliance. Within orthodox homes a girl is severely repressed and prevented from indulging herself in any form of luxury before marriage. She dresses and lives plainly and is brought up to believe that marriage is the ultimate goal in life (Brijbhushan 1980). The excessiveness with which women must be guarded and their virginity protected makes them an almost intolerable burden on the family. This naturally makes it urgent to find husbands for them and to hand them over to their in-laws as soon as possible.

Within Islam there is a basic distrust of woman and her sexuality, emanating from the view that a woman is regarded as "property," rather than as a person (Raza 1993). The safeguarding of women from the sexual advances and aggression of men has always been of paramount importance. According to this concept, through proper behaviour, a woman will bring honour to the men of the family, so their prestige is maintained, if not enhanced. For this reason, if the woman transgresses, it is she who is punished by the men in her family rather than the male transgressor. Any improper behaviour would also weaken a girl's chances of making a good marriage as well as threaten the family's honour and prestige.

In practice most Muslim marriages are arranged, and it is customary for parents to play a major part in choosing their daughters' husbands (Lemu and Heeren 1978). The norm is of the marriage of a Muslim man to a Muslim woman. A Muslim man, however, may marry a non-Muslim woman, whilst the Muslim woman can only marry a Muslim man. The Christian or Jew who wishes to marry her must convert to Islam. The ownership of women is so strong that families may use physical violence against their daughters if they wish to convert to another religion (Raza 1993). Although there may be signs that increasing numbers of educated Muslim women are now exercising their legal rights to repeatedly object to marriage contracts and turn down proposals, the pressure on Muslim girls to accept the husband of their parents' choice remains intense (Horrie and Chippindale 1991). It is not unusual for parents to arrange an early betrothal, frequently before the age of puberty and amongst Muslims in particular, marriage between close kin is common. Despite formally having to give her consent, this clearly shows the social construction of passivity and dependence in Muslim female gender identity. The practical politics of marriage arrangements are reminiscent of any form of transaction, with both parties aiming to achieve the best bargain they can. This atmosphere does not make it easy for a girl to intervene or to disagree when something is to be decided. Whilst girls are supposed to remain ignorant of and detached from the forthcoming marriage, there is no such pressure on boys, who may often object to it, or at the least, put up a struggle (White 1992).

There continues to be no question of a meeting of the boy and girl in orthodox families. Since sexual segregation of women from men who are not related is practised after the onset of puberty, there are very few opportunities for potential marriage partners to meet, and dating, so common in the west, is practically unknown (Korson 1979:195). An approximate idea of the girl's looks and the boy's prospects is obtained through other people who know the family. Although it has been maintained that a fine temperament is more important than looks, a girl's beauty is a considerable factor in attracting a proposal of marriage.

Unlike Hindu marriages which are sacramental, Muslim marriages are more or less precisely defined in simple contracts specifying the obligations and duties of both bride and groom in advance (Abd Al' Ati 1977:50). An important part of the marriage contract is the sum of the dowry pledged by the bridegroom to the bride. It is also part of an institutionalised aspect of insurance for the bride in case of a divorce or separation (Korson 1979). However, the woman may not specify any conditions or size of dowry, or food or clothes to be given. This remains the prerogative of the husband (El Saddawi 1980).

Contrary to western belief, Islam does not impose polygamy as a universal practice. Although a man is permitted to marry up to four wives, monogamy should be regarded as the norm, and polygamy the exception (Lemu and Heeren 1978). In many countries like Pakistan a polygamous marriage requires specific permission from the state (Horrie and Chippindale 1991). Many women, however, if given the alternative, would rather share a husband than remain unmarried. Despite being a dying statistic, polygamy remains to have a psychological effect on the self-esteem of both men and women, by enhancing men's perception of themselves as primarily sexual beings. Polygamy can also be seen as a threat by a man to keep a woman under control, as well as humiliating her as a sexual being by expressing her inability to satisfy him (Mernissi 1985).

There is a sense of radical change at marriage when women move from their familiar home and setting to a household where they have a very different role and expectations to fulfil. The major reasons for entering a marriage are not necessarily romantic love, companionship and the achievement of instant individual happiness, but rather "fertility, permanence and the alliance of two family groups" (Korson 1979:194).

As a new bride, a woman occupies a structurally weak position in the joint family system. She may be very isolated and made to work very hard, taking over many of the heavier tasks under the guidance of her mother-in-law. She is also strictly watched to ensure that her behaviour brings the family no dishonour. The only contact she will have is with members of her husband's household, or at most, their social group. If she encounters any problems she must go to those in authority over her. Although these restrictions are most likely to be at their tightest in richer Muslim households where purdah, the social segregation of the sexes, may be practised, the subordination of new brides is broadly similar across community and class (White 1992).

The primary area for men is in the public sphere. They are expected to protect and support the family, and "deal" with the outside world. This is not only a moral, but a legal responsibility. It is the duty of the husband to command his wife, and to physically punish her if she does not obey him.

The wife is responsible for the care of the home and the family's welfare, and is encouraged to practise her religion. She may express her views and make suggestions concerning all matters, but the best role she can play in keeping the marital tie intact and strong, is to recognise her husband as the person responsible for the running of family affairs. She should obey him even if his judgement is not acceptable to her. This is the meaning of obedience in the context of a Muslim marriage. It recognises that women are subordinate to men by virtue of their more sheltered lives and their protected status.

According to Mernissi (1985), within a traditional marriage the mother-in-law becomes one of the greatest obstacles to conjugal intimacy. The vital factor in the dynamics of the Muslim marriage is the close link between mother and son. Not only is the marital bond weakened and the love for his wife very much discouraged, but the mother is the only woman a man is permitted to love at all, and this is encouraged through a form of lifelong gratitude.

Within the Islamic social order, sexual desire is legitimate only in a marital situation (Rozario 1992). Islam advocates a number of specific measures to reduce the temptations of sex outside of marriage (Lemu and Heeren 1978:24-25). Firstly, all Muslims are advised to marry so their natural desires are legitimate and legal. Secondly, women are directed to cover themselves in modest type of clothing and cast their gaze downwards in public, so as not to attract men. Sex outside marriage is not only a sin, but often punishable as a crime. A wife may also be penalised for her failure to provide sexual services to her husband. By Muslim law a husband may refrain from providing his wife with maintenance, food, clothing and lodging, which are his duties to otherwise provide.

Whilst education and new social responsibilities are recognised, there are also growing pressures to permit the Muslim woman to work, but only if absolutely necessary. This implies that no Muslim woman should be obliged to earn her living unless she has lost her husband through death or divorce and has no other male relatives to provide for her (Jameelah 1983). Even among upper and middle class Muslim males who hold more liberal views about women's right to work, only those jobs guaranteeing segregated employment are acceptable, where women are not confined in their professional contacts with members of their own sex (Youssef 1979). In many cases where the wife is economically independent, the husband automatically loses his role as head of the household. Where the mother does dominate, the children lose all respect for the parents (Jameelah 1983).

The primary aim of marriage is the propagation of children, especially sons who will carry on the family name. Currently, only eight per cent of married Pakistani women practise contraception (United Nations 1991:61). The Muslim woman has a very important role as a mother. The status and value attached to parents is very high. The main duty of the Muslim mother is to make every effort to persuade her children to abide by the teachings of the Koran at as early an age as possible. Her early character training of her children will have a lasting effect on the behaviour and attitudes of the next generation when they reach adolescence and adulthood.

If the bride is a victim of cruelty by the in-laws or her husband, she may flee to her parents' home. As a family tries to use respectability as its basis for keeping the family honour, the expense and risks of having a non-productive young woman at home may be a burden (Abdullah and Zeidenstein 1982). Thus, if the family has very few resources and is in a precarious social predicament, they have no alternative but to send their daughter back to bear the situation.

If a marriage does not work out successfully, divorce is a last resort, discouraged rather than encouraged in Islam. A saying from the prophet states that "of all the permitted things, divorce is the most abominable with God" (Esposito 1992:96). However, the law of Islam does allow divorce, but the emphasis is on reconciliation wherever possible. The husband may divorce his wife at any time and without justification, whereas his wife must prove the validity of her request. The husband can also repudiate his wife in the knowledge that his wife may not do the same to him. Women very rarely initiate divorce. This is partly due to the restraints placed on Muslim women's behaviour, as well as their consequent dependence on men (Rozario

1992). For these reasons the divorce rate amongst Muslim women remains negligible. Currently only 0.5 per cent of Pakistani women aged between 25 and 44 are divorced. For Bangladeshi women the corresponding figure is 1.1 per cent (United Nations 1991:28).

If the reconciliation is unsuccessful, and the wife wants to seek a divorce against the wishes of her husband, she may take her case to court and obtain a divorce this way. Relatively few women are capable of supporting themselves, and following a divorce or separation, return to their own parents' home or that of a brother or other male relative.

Widows and divorced women whose marriages have been legally annulled by law, have also been granted a right to remarry (Abul A'la Maududi 1986). The typically young divorcee who wishes to do so is often subjected to the same family restrictions imposed upon the single girl. In Muslim society, the divorced status is perceived as a temporary one (Youssef 1979). Women are not permitted to see themselves as anything other than "expectant wives," thus reinforcing their traditional status as financial and emotional dependants on their husbands. Once remarried, women are also encouraged to continue their childbearing activities. A widow and her children are expected to return to her family where she is provided for financially. Although she may legally remarry the only activities deemed appropriate for her to pursue are a life of chastity and continence dedicated to her late husband's memory, and devotion to her children.

For the Muslim woman, however, divorce and remarriage take enormous courage. Although Islamic law embodies a number of reforms to protect and enhance the status of women, it must be emphasised that the gulf between the legally available rights and options, and those which are accessible to the Muslim woman is, in reality, very large (Youssef 1979). This is not only because of structural barriers, but also because of prevailing cultural ideals which render many options open to them, totally unacceptable for women. Thus, within Muslim society, strict control in the form of social stigmatisation and punishment for women who try to violate morality taboos, remain far greater deterrents for those women wishing to use the law to their advantage.

In spite of having an education and employed status, this will not liberate the Muslim woman from traditional family restraints. Individualism is not an acceptable concept to the Muslim ethos, since individual ambition and success are translated to mean improving the position of the whole family, whether in financial, social, or prestige terms. For girls, strict seclusion and tight control before marriage instil the idea that only one life exists for the woman. Alternatives to marriage are seen as compromising a girl's sex ethics and as potential threats to her eventual chances of remarriage. Motivation for marriage is stated in society's creation of desires for familial roles, by praising the rewards accruing from the wife-mother status, and by severely censuring spinsterhood. Thus, the consensus regarding the role of the woman in Islam is an overwhelming one. Her value to society remains within the home, and her success as a person is judged solely by her fidelity and obedience to her husband, and the rearing of worthy children.

Sikh culture

Sikhism, a relatively young religion, was born out of Hinduism as a radical breakaway movement. Sikhs form only two per cent of the overall population in India, the majority of whom live in the northern state of Punjab (Hiro 1991). Culturally, Sikhs are akin to Hindus and have always been considered to be a part of the wider Hindu community (Sambhi 1989). According to Jacobs (1988), Sikhism also bears some resemblance to Islam, but it is true to say that it overlaps much more with Hinduism. For these reasons, only the important issues shall be discussed in detail. Where similarities arise, these shall be touched on only briefly.

Values pertaining to the status of women can be seen in the teachings of Guru Nanak, the founder of Sikhism, who lived in the thirteenth century. He highlighted the social importance of women by appreciating their role in the proper development of the family as wives and mothers, and in cementing social ties and relationships (Sambhi 1989). Guru Nanak proclaimed that "it is from women that we are conceived and born. Woman is our lifelong friend and keeps the race going. Why should we despise her who gives birth to great men?" (Sambhi 1989:88).

Like both Hinduism and Islam, Sikhism is a patriarchal culture with emphasis for women to maintain the traditions of the community and to pass on religious teachings from one generation to another (James 1974).

Reverence for the Sikh woman as mother means that she is regarded primarily as a producer of sons. Many parents feel humiliated and deprived if they have not got a male child. The birth of a male child means parties are thrown and ceremonies are arranged. The superiority of the male is carried on throughout life (Kalra 1980:60). Girls are regarded as a liability, mainly because of the economics of the marriage system.

As in both the Hindu and Muslim cultures, social mixing of the sexes is restricted when girls are growing up. Unlike boys, Punjabi girls spend most of their time within the home, and are expected to help their mothers with household chores and cooking, to prepare them for marriage. Parents become very concerned about unfavourable rumours regarding characteristics of their daughters, circulating. Thus the virtues of chastity are pressed upon them, for bringing dishonour to the family must be avoided at all costs.

One of the most important elements in the Sikh community is the family, and emphasis upon family life is such that few Sikhs remain single. Like Hindu and Muslim marriages, Sikh marriages are not private matters between two individuals. Rather, two families become closely connected, and into one family comes a stranger, the wife. Parents and close relatives begin looking for a suitable groom as soon as the daughter has finished her education. Child marriages in the traditional Indian sense have always been repudiated by the Sikhs. Most importantly, a Sikh should marry a Sikh. Other criteria to be met include caste, age and temperament. Dating and courtship are frowned upon, but the couple may see one another in the company of others on numerous occasions when each will be fully informed about the interests and lifestyles of the other (Cole and Sambhi 1978).

An engagement ceremony prior to the marriage is not essential nor religious, but is likely to take place. A dowry is given to the bridegroom's father by the bride's parents. Like a Hindu marriage, a Sikh marriage is defined as a religious sacrament and not as a marriage contract. Neither is the wife to be given any specified money or property if she becomes a divorcee.

The joint family system is the norm, and after marriage the couple are expected to live at the groom's parents' house for as long as they want, or until they can set up their own home. It is the wife's duty to become compatible not only with her husband but to also endear herself to the other family members. A young bride is also expected to mould her habits and attitudes to fit into her new household. Unlike in Islam, purdah, the social segregation of the sexes, has no place in Sikhism (Cole and Sambhi 1978). The householder's life is seen as the norm for the Sikh wife.

A woman in Sikhism is looked upon as a man's helpmate, and as vital to his spiritual growth and morality. She is also expected to obey her husband and show no signs of being independent. Both the husband and wife will work together towards a complete identification of interests, not just through physical contact, but also as a fusion of two souls. Physical demonstrations of love and affection in public between husband and wife are frowned upon. A couple may be compatible, but the sharing of the inner self is not with one's spouse, but with members of one's own sex (Helweg 1986). Having children is a very important event in a woman's life. Contraception among newly weds is rarely practised, since if a child is not produced within the first two years, the parents become anxious.

Divorce is discouraged but possible (Cole and Sambhi 1978). However, it is seldom resorted to, and the chances of a divorced woman remarrying and leading a happy life are very limited. Widows who have led a life of contentment and chastity are respected and allowed to take their full place in the life of the community, where they are surrounded by family and friends.

Conclusion

Although they may be theoretically different, in practice there are many similarities between Hindu, Muslim and Sikh cultures. All three are very patriarchal in outlook, with girls often being regarded as an economic liability. Marriages are arranged and dowries are demanded. The woman's place is in the private domain – she is not expected to take up outside employment. Divorce is frowned upon, and difficult to obtain. All these culture traits are very different to corresponding culture traits of British society today.

Despite the fact that immigrants may adapt and change some of the outward characteristics of their culture, like clothing and diet, to fit in with the host society's way of life, it is far more difficult to change the inner core of cultures such as the norms and values of marriage, divorce and relationships with men. Since they help to explain the very low incidents of divorce in these Asian countries, the themes discussed in this chapter could have important connotations for the research.

3 Methodology and the Sample

The main purpose of this book is to show how Asian lone mothers from the Indian and African sub-continent resolve their two situational difficulties - firstly that of being lone mothers, and secondly that of being of ethnic origin and living in London. A secondary aim of the research is to document the living conditions of the sample and to see how they compare with those of other lone mothers in this country, even though the relevant statistics on Asian lone mothers tend to be partial, over-generalised and based on very small samples. A study of this nature inevitably has implications for policy, and from the appropriate data obtained, the main issues will briefly be discussed.

Prior to the study being carried out, it was surmised that due to their lone parent status the mothers would experience low standards of living through being unemployed and heavily reliant on state benefits, residing in inadequate local authority housing and suffering from poor physical health. A second assumption which underpinned the research was that because Asian culture frowns upon marriage breakdown, the mothers would be stigmatised or rejected by society in general and by their own ethnic communities in particular. This would be reflected in the women feeling ashamed of their single status, leading them to be withdrawn and isolated from both their family and friends as well as from their local communities. Enduring such mental conditions as stress and depression, the mothers' general outlook for the future would be one of pessimism.

Thirdly, because of their immigrant status it was supposed that the respondents would be caught between both the Asian and the British cultures, resulting in their being unable to adjust to life as lone mothers from the Indian and African sub-continent living in London. The findings of the study will reveal whether all these early suppositions have been confirmed or refuted and in what ways.

In order to explore all these primary questions and hypotheses, two literature based chapters have been written. The first chapter traces the theoretical debates concerning the relationship between the immigrant and the host society at large. The second chapter shows how Hindu, Muslim and Sikh cultures disown family breakdown much more than the British culture does.

This chapter will primarily concern itself with examining the various methodology procedures used in the fieldwork undertaken. It will look at the methodological possibilities, advantages and disadvantages of open-ended and closed questions and of random and quota sampling, the importance of pilot studies, the interviewing process itself and the analysis and presentation of the data. The chapter will conclude by briefly presenting a profile of the final sample by revealing such characteristics as type and age of lone mother, country of origin, length of lone parenthood, level of education received, and so on.

Methodology procedures

Methodological possibilities

Once the topic for the research had been chosen, different methodological possibilities were discussed by which to collect the data. Firstly, participant observation was considered, whereby the researcher becomes part of the everyday routines of those he or she wishes to study within its "normal" and "natural" context (Haralambos with Heald 1985). Supporters of participant observation have argued that compared to other research techniques, it provides the best means of directly obtaining a valid picture of social reality at first hand. Using this method, the investigator tries to begin with no pre-conceived ideas about people's roles or positions or what he or she expects to be taking place, but instead, waits for these to be revealed over a period of time (Thompson and Priestley 1996). Participant observation would be useful for generating new hypotheses and "can go in unexpected directions and so can provide sociologists with novel insights and ideas" (Haralambos and Holborn 1991), with the field-worker also being able to follow up any leads that develop in the process of research itself (Giddens 1992).

However, there are many practical disadvantages to this method, which led to its rejection for use in this survey. According to Haralambos with Heald (1985) and Haralambos and Holborn (1991), it is very time consuming, with its success depending initially upon the trust and approval of the investigator by the group to be studied. Once accepted, a major difficulty for the observer is that his or her presence will, to some degree, influence the actions of the sample. This may lead the researcher to actually modify or change the social world of those under investigation. The validity of the data is also bound to be affected by the observer's presence, since the group being studied will not act naturally. Other weaknesses to participant observation include its being a more subjective than objective form of study, and because it is not systematically or rigorously undertaken with its procedures not being made explicit at the beginning, any findings obtained cannot be replicated.

It was felt that participant observation would have been more appropriate for use in an anthropological study and not in a social policy study as this research was intended to be. Because of this, no confidence was felt in using this particular research approach. For an investigation of this size it was also felt that the sample was too large to observe, which would further be compounded by the fact that not all the women were selected from the same source. In addition, not being local to the sample would have meant that this method would have been far too time consuming.

Tape-recording the interviews was also considered, whereby a semi-structured conversation with the women would be conducted. By using this research technique, the sample would be able to talk at greater length about issues which were of concern to them, as well as to communicate their more inner feelings in a more spontaneous manner than if their responses were documented in writing. Thus, the more open the interview, the richer the data obtained (Bechhofer 1992).

This method, however, would also present some difficulties. Some of the mothers may feel uncomfortable being recorded which could be reflected in the unnaturalness of their replies. If the interview is not totally structured, the mothers could also diverge from the more important issues of the topic itself. In addition, with such a large sample involved, this method would be too lengthy to carry out, since following the interviews, the recordings need to be listened to several times, with useful quotes and extracts being transcribed (Thompson and Priestley 1996). Analysis therefore becomes more complex, time consuming and expensive as do the interviews themselves (Bechhofer 1992).

It was finally decided upon to use a structured set questionnaire to obtain the data. Although the designing and wording of the questionnaire may take some time, once in use, the questionnaire can be used to obtain large quantities of data from considerable numbers of people over a relatively short period of time (Haralambos and Holborn 1991). Unlike postal questionnaires, interviewing the sample personally (as in this study) is believed to be a more dependable way of getting questionnaires completed and ensuring that the respondent knows what he or she is expected to do (Thompson and Priestley 1996).

Data from structured interviews are generally thought of as being more reliable than unstructured ones. Because the order and wording of questions are the same for the entire sample, it is more likely that they will be responding to the same stimuli. Therefore, different answers are more likely to indicate real differences between the respondents, and not simply reflect differences in the ways questions are phrased. Thus, the more standardised the interview the easier the analysis of the data becomes (Haralambos with Heald 1985).

There are also disadvantages to using the structured questionnaire method. Firstly the researcher has already decided what issues are important and relevant, and with pre-set questions being asked, imposes his or her framework and priorities on the sample under study (Haralambos and Holborn 1991). Secondly, once a survey has begun, the questionnaire cannot be changed since the main object of using this method is to present all respondents with the same stimuli and so obtain comparable data (Haralambos with Heald 1985). Thirdly, where a questionnaire is to be administered by an interviewer, the latter has to be especially careful not to introduce his or her own views. If a question is not understood and is repeated in a different form, the researcher can easily distort the sense of the original. Fourthly, a properly drawn questionnaire achieves its accuracy at a cost, and what it loses is the chance for individuals to state their own opinions in their own words. Hence, field-work, where open-ended or semi-structured interviews can be conducted, forms a valuable addition and corrective to the numerical data generated by a survey (Calvert and Calvert 1992).

Despite the above drawbacks, the questionnaire method was used to interview the mothers in this study. Given the restraints of time, it was acknowledged that using this procedure would make analysing the findings much quicker, as "the sheer volume of work entailed in analysis must always be considered before data are collected" (Bechhofer 1992:100). However, since assumptions about the sample's lives had already been made before the questionnaire was drawn up, it was also recognised that by using this method not all the concerns of the sample would have been brought to light. Additionally, it could be argued that this approach may lead to a lack of detailed responses to the more personal questions relating to the women's attitudes and feelings which were central to the investigation. In practice, however, this did not prove the case in this project.

Open-ended versus closed questions

In order to test the hypotheses using the questionnaire method, the type of questions to be asked had firstly to be decided. The primary decision about the form of the respondents' choices is between open-ended or free response and closed or fixed alternative questions. Each type of question has both advantages and disadvantages and is more appropriate with some types of projects than with others.

Open-ended questions are presented in a precise form but the answers are left to the discretion of the interviewee, who may reply in a relatively unconstrained way (Madge 1971). Closed questions present a series of answers and allow the respondent to select the choice closest to his or her position (Peil 1982). An alternative "other" is often included, so the respondent is not forced to choose or agree to one of the answers listed. According to Peil, "the advantages of open questions are often the disadvantages of closed questions, and vice versa" (1982:120).

Open-ended questions allow for in-depth interviews. They enable respondents to clarify their standpoints and to explain the factors which influenced them in reaching their decisions (Madge 1971). Unlike closed questions, open-ended questions do not force respondents to choose one of several statements that may appear, to them, unsatisfactory (Judd et al 1991). Open questions produce a greater variety of responses, which are more useful for the researcher in many types of analysis (Peil 1982).

Open-ended questions, however, do depend on many external factors such as general verbal fluency, communicative style and interest in the topic, which may all vary from respondent to respondent. The difficulty of coding and analysing responses is also well documented (Stacey 1969:80, Peil 1982:146, Judd et al 1991:239, Bourque 1992:11).

According to Miller (1983), the advantages of closed questions are that they ensure that the desired topics are covered, as well as providing the respondent with a checklist of possibilities. Pre-set answers may also help the inarticulate to express some view, and give the respondent some control over the classification of his or her response. With sensitive topics such as income, a closed question may get a better response than an open one, because the answer required is more specific. Judd et al (1991) state that asking closed questions speeds up the recording of answers, which are easily coded to produce meaningful results of analysis. Thus, at least on a superficial level results are comparable (Peil 1982).

Miller (1983:16) points to one of the main disadvantages of closed questions. When answering more probing questions, pre-set alternative responses may prompt respondents to articulate feelings and attitudes they do not really possess, or may restrict and channel their answers in ways that that do not reflect their real attitudes. Peil (1982) also adds that although respondents may agree to the same answer one cannot be sure that they all had the same thing in mind. Given the freedom to express themselves, individuals may have produced responses with different shades of meaning.

Sellitz et al (in Stacey 1969) have summarised the way to choose between open and closed questions as follows. The latter should be used where alternative replies are known, are limited in number and are clear cut. Open-ended questions should be used where the issue is of a complex nature, where relevant dimensions are not known and where a process is being explored. According to Judd et al (1991), most researchers today tend to use mainly closed questions in attitude measurement, but with some open-ended questions to obtain reasons or illustrations for attitudes on key issues. They go on to add that "the open-ended response can help in the formulation of new hypotheses and are often quoted to lend interest and concreteness to reports of research results" (1991:240).

With so many different issues being explored in the study, it was neither practical to use solely open-ended nor closed questions. Rather, a mixture of the two were used to obtain the relevant information from the respondent. The section on "Family and Social Contacts," central to the testing of the hypotheses, would require more in-depth answers than the sections on "Material and Living Conditions" or "Future Plans," which are far more clear cut. Despite this, it is true to say that it is the open-ended questions that form the core of this project.

The final questionnaire consisted of 95 questions, split up into eight sections, each one covering a different aspect of lone parenthood. These were "Personal," "The Process of Lone Parenthood," "The Children," "Material and Living Conditions," "The Father," "Family and Social Contacts," "Cultural Issues" and "Future Plans."

Pilot studies

The mass interview or questionnaire properly belongs at the end of a process of elucidation and clarification of a problem (Madge 1971). By the time this stage has been reached, the researcher is expected to have decided what is relevant to his or her hypothesis, and therefore which areas should be investigated by direct questioning. Although the researcher may know the subject matter of the questions to be asked, he or she will need to discover the best means of obtaining the desired information.

The importance of the pilot study to any kind of research project has been well documented over the years (Madge 1971, Youngman 1979, Shipman 1982, Dixon et al 1991, Bourque and Clark 1992). This involves a practice run-through with a small sub-sample of the population under study. As Madge states, "the purpose of the pilot study is quite distinct from that of the main survey" (1971:216).

Stacey (1969) highlights some of its main purposes. The pilot study gives the researcher a chance to check for any ambiguities or resistances which may lead to inadequate or misleading responses. It is also important to examine responses, especially to the more crucial questions, to see that the required data is actually being obtained. Shipman (1982) goes on to state that for closed questions, pilot studies are essential for ensuring that the responses offered as possible answers actually do exhaust all the possibilities. In some cases, open-ended questions may also form a first pilot study, followed by the actual testing of questions in a second stage. Without any pilot stage, the actual research is likely to address unsuitable questions to confused people.

For the purpose of this survey, a trial questionnaire was initially drafted and a pilot study carried out on six lone mothers from the Indian and African sub-continent. One unmarried mother, two divorcees, two separated mothers and one widow were interviewed in the pilot study. The questionnaire was then amended as necessary and then tested out again on three more lone mothers. Following this, the final version of the questionnaire was arrived at, which was used for the main interview.

Random versus quota sampling

An important consideration in the methodology stage was the choosing of the sample. According to Lazerwitz:

> a proper sample should be a small piece of the population obtained by a probability process that mirrors, with known precision, the various patterns and sub-classes of the population (1971:279).

In the social sciences there are two types of sampling procedure - in their most basic forms these are random and non-random sampling (Dixon et al 1991). Random sampling is the ideal method of drawing a sample as it provides the greatest assurance that those selected are a representative sample of the larger group. The sample is usually drawn from sources like the electoral register, doctors' lists, school registers and so on, with every nth name used according to the total size of the sample required (Shipman 1982:61).

This method guarantees that not only has each element in the population an equal chance of being chosen, but it also makes the selection of every possible combination of the specified number of elements equally likely (Dixon et al 1991, Judd et al 1991). One of the greatest virtues of random sampling is that it guards against all kinds of bias of the investigator, without requiring prior knowledge of the significant characteristics of the population under investigation (Miller 1983). The main weakness of random sampling is that if the researcher is looking for an unusual or specialised group whose numbers are small, a very large sample will be initially required from which the final sample can be randomly chosen. This may prove to be an impossibility for the researcher involved.

One form of the non-random sampling procedure is quota sampling, whereby the researcher is able to select groups or individuals on the basis of certain set criteria, such as age, sex and social class (Dixon et al 1991). According to Judd et al:

> the basic goal of quota sampling is the selection of a sample that is the replica of the population to which one wants to generalise - hence the notion that it 'represents' that population (1991:35).

Quota sampling does have its own particular place in social science methodology, and is a method often used due to the pressure of time and budget (Dixon et al 1991). This type of sampling procedure is also thrust upon the researcher by the very nature of the sample under study. Shipman states that "in some cases quota sampling has to be used because it is impossible to find lists from which a probability sample of a population can be drawn" (1982:65).

Dixon et al (1991) point to the usefulness of quota sampling when a particular group or characteristic is relatively rare in the population. Unlike random sampling, quota sampling also allows for the final selection of individuals to be left to the discretion of the field-worker (Madge 1971). Peil goes on to state that a "quota sample can ensure that people with certain characteristics important to the study are included in sufficient numbers to test the hypotheses" (1982:31). However, in comparison to random sampling, there are many flaws to the quota sampling procedure. Field-workers using quota sampling procedures may be biased in favour of approachable individuals. These may be the interviewers' own friends, who tend to be rather like themselves, thereby causing the sample to be potentially non-representative of the overall population. Interviewers may also concentrate on areas where large numbers are available for interview, such as in large shopping centres. This kind of sample would be over-represented by people who tend to congregate in these areas, and under-represented by those who rarely leave their homes. If field-workers fill their quotas by visiting those who live at home, they are more likely to select the more attractive homes, and avoid run-down buildings in dangerous looking neighbourhoods. Presumably this would build a socio-economic bias into the sample (Judd et al 1991:135).

Since the representativeness of the quota is dependent on specific population characteristics such as age, sex, ethnicity, class and so on, if a new and unforeseen variable like occupation becomes of consequence or is revealed later as important during analysis, there is no safeguard that the sample interviewed will be represented in the proper proportions (Madge 1971). Often, characteristics presently studied are dependent on variables that have proven to be significant through prior research in the field (Brewer and Hunter 1990).

In conclusion, research by Moser in 1981 (in Millar 1983:14) has shown that sampling errors are much higher for quota samples, which may need to be at least three times as large as simple random samples to achieve the same accuracy. Even if difficulties of systematic bias can be overcome, quota samples are inherently more variable and less reliable than random samples.

In order to obtain the sample for this study it was decided upon to use the quota sampling procedure. Asian lone mothers from the Indian and African sub-continent living in London are very much a minority group, and because there is not a formal register from which to form a random sample of this group, quota sampling seemed both a necessary and a practicality. Because of this, it was acknowledged that the sample would be far less representative than if it could have been randomly chosen.

The national organisations "Gingerbread" and the "National Council for One Parent Families" were contacted, but neither had any record of lone mothers from the Indian and African sub-continent on their lists. Other sources, however, proved more fruitful.

A good response was found through approaching various Asian women's centres in London, and by taking an interest in the work undertaken there. By building up a good rapport with the lone mothers who attended the centres, many of them were willing to take part in the study.

A second source was found through contacting some general practitioners in the London area, and asking whether they had any lone mothers on their lists. If they did and were willing to assist, their receptionists went through the patients' records and contacted the women in question, explaining to them the situation. An appropriate time was fixed for the interview for those women who agreed to be of help.

A final source was found by locating some of the final sample through social contacts. This involved asking individuals if they were acquainted with any lone mothers who would be interested in being interviewed. Relevant contacts were then made by telephone and appointments to meet were agreed upon.

It was hoped that by interviewing a sample from a wide range of sources, different ideas and opinions about their situations would be conveyed. Because the quota sampling method was to be used, certain pre-determined criteria were decided upon before the respondents were selected in order to correct some of the biases inherent in this procedure. For example, an almost equal number of Hindu, Muslim and Sikh mothers were interviewed, as well as a similar proportion of divorced and separated women. However, other criteria for the sample were not met, resulting in the quota categories not being satisfactorily filled. These deficiencies shall be discussed below.

Despite lone mothers from the Indian and African sub-continent being a minority group, there may also be wide variations between them even within the London area. For example, women living in the more run-down areas of the East End may have very different experiences of lone parenthood to those residing in the other more prosperous parts of the capital. Because the vast majority of the mothers in this investigation were living in west London, the sample was perhaps not as representative as it could have been had more women from the other areas been selected.

Other imbalances inherent within this sample included there being only two unmarried mothers interviewed, since the initial idea to include ten unmarried mothers proved impractical. Less than a quarter of the women were engaged in paid employment, even though the aim was to interview 30 working women at the beginning of the study. There were insufficient numbers of mothers in their twenties (11) with a very large bulk in their mid-thirties to mid-forties (55), with the final sample also comprising of too few women who could not speak English and would need an interpreter.

The "covert" nature of Asian lone mothers from the Indian and African sub-continent living in London, and the time restraints involved, however, made it difficult to adhere to the initially planned quota sample. Thus, it was recognised that a quota sample had not actually been achieved, as the women were ultimately not chosen on the basis of much of the pre-set criteria earlier mentioned, in sufficient numbers.

About ten mothers were, for various reasons, unwilling or reluctant to take part in the research and their decisions were respected. The majority of those asked, however, were enthusiastic to help, understood the importance of the study and were very helpful during the interviews.

The interviewing procedure

According to the source from which the lone mother was obtained, the interview took place either in a spare room in the women's centre, in an unused room in a doctor's surgery or at the interviewee's own home. Each woman was interviewed alone and in confidence, except where an interpreter was used.

The approach was firstly to explain to the mother the purpose of the project, and then to gain her trust and confidence. According to Oakley:

> the goal of finding out about people through interviewing is best achieved when the relationship of interviewer and interviewee is non-hierarchical and when the interviewer is prepared to invest his or her personal identity in the relationship (1981:41).

Judd et al go on to talk about the importance of creating an amiable atmosphere by stating that:

> the interviewer's manner should be friendly, courteous, conversational and unbiased. The idea is to put the respondents at ease so that they will talk freely and fully (1991: 55).

Once the interview began, the usual procedure was to read out the question clearly, and to write down the response as it was given. If the mother did not understand the question, it was reworded in such a manner that it was comprehensible to her, so she was able to reply. Due to their situation, some of the mothers became distressed during parts of the interview pertaining to the more personal questions, and empathy with their experiences was shown. The interviews continued after these mothers had regained their composure. Oakley speaks of how "a balance must then be struck between the warmth required to generate 'rapport' and the detachment necessary to see the interviewee as an object under surveillance" (1981:33).

On the whole, the length of the interview varied from 45 minutes to an hour. As expected, some mothers were more articulate than others and more willing to speak in depth about their situations. But whatever the content of each interview, Judd et al go on to add that "interviewers should take all opinions in stride and never show surprise or disapproval of a respondent's answer" (1991:255).

Once the interview had finished, the respondent stayed behind for a few minutes whilst the questionnaire was checked over to see that it had been properly completed. If there were any incomplete answers, the corresponding questions were asked and the responses written down as required. Some of the mothers stayed on for an informal post-interview chat and any additional statements made by them which may prove useful to supporting or refuting the hypotheses were also noted down.

Analysis and presentation of the data

After the interviews had been completed, the next stage involved analysing and presenting the data. According to Dixon et al (1991), this entails three stages, all of which were undertaken in this study. Firstly, categories must be selected in which the raw data can be summarised. Secondly, once the categories have been chosen, the data are coded, that is, they are sorted into the categories. Lastly, the data are presented in a form which facilitates the drawing of conclusions.

Because of the difficulties of summarising and organising data, much time was devoted to trying out various alternatives until satisfactory categories and coding frames were achieved. Once completed, the data was then cross-tabulated in some way to show the relationship between the responses and different variables which would help to confirm or refute the hypotheses.

The statistics, however, were not analysed by means of a computer package because, although the total of 90 mothers interviewed would have been sufficient for this type of analysis, the actual size of the sub-groups of each category would, in most cases, have been too small. For example, only two widows were working in full time jobs, only three separated mothers in their thirties were owner occupiers and so on. Therefore, it was acknowledged that using a manual method by calculator to achieve the required data meant that the analysis would be very basic, lacking the greater accuracy and complexity of a computer. Although more time consuming, however, analysing the figures in a manual manner did mean that there was more personal involvement in the study from start to finish, which would have been lost if a computer package had been used.

The main aim of this book is to examine the situational difficulties faced by Asian lone mothers living in London within a literature based framework. Although quantitative to some extent, because this study is largely based on the mothers' feelings, opinions and experiences, it is mainly a qualitative form of research. This implies that the data is in the form of words as opposed to numbers, concentrating on the quality of life described through quotations used by those studied, rather than on presenting statistics (McNeill 1982). Qualitative research, like the present study, tries to seek a psychologically rich, in-depth understanding of the individual (Rudestam and Newton 1992). It was essentially felt that the mothers' lengthy responses would give abundant information about their feelings and attitudes in the various areas of their personal lives that were being examined.

Profile of the sample

Usage of the term 'lone' mother

According to Millar (1989:4-5), although the term "one parent family" represents a less judgmental way of describing these families, it does have some disadvantages, namely focusing more attention on the custodial parent than on the "absent" parent. Except in the case of widows and widowers, the other parent does exist and is still a parent. Secondly the child/ren may either live full time with one parent, or live part of the time with one parent and part of the time with the other. In both cases, however, the "absent" parent may still remain emotionally and financially involved. Even if the "absent" parent really is absent, he or less commonly she, still remains the parent, as is the case if he remarries. Thus, in preference to the term "one parent family," "lone parent family" is often used in current literature since it does not appear so singular and will be used in reference to the women in this study.

Ethnic minority lone parents in Britain

Overall, the proportion of lone parent families amongst minority groups in Britain is estimated to be about sixteen per cent, although numbers vary greatly between the groups (Donnellan 1993). Families from the Black ethnic group have the highest proportion of families which are lone parents (HMSO 1996:54). Over half of the mothers in the West Indian ethnic group were lone mothers in 1989-91 (Donnellan 1995). In 1987-89 there were 21,000 Indian, Pakistani and Bangladeshi lone parent families in Britain, making up only 1.9 per cent of the lone parent population (Donnellan 1995). In winter 1994-95 just under ten per cent of all Bangladeshi and Pakistani families with dependent children were headed by a lone parent, compared to just under five per cent of Indian families with dependent children (HMSO 1996:53). These findings thus show the rarity of lone parenthood amongst the Asian population in Britain, and reinforces the notion of the importance of marriage for this group.

Type and age of the mother

A total of 90 lone mothers were interviewed, all of whom had at least one dependent child aged sixteen or under, or a child up to the age of nineteen and in full time education.

As Table 3.1 shows, divorced and separated mothers made up over two-thirds of the sample, with a much smaller number of widows, and only two unmarried mothers. The makeup of this Asian sample differs somewhat from that of the British lone parent population. Where the Asian group is predominantly made up of divorced and separated lone mothers, the British lone mother population contains fewer separated women, with divorced and unmarried mothers making up the two largest groups (Morgan 1995, HMSO 1996). It was very difficult to locate unmarried Asian mothers, which may partly be a reflection of Asian culture and values emphasising the importance of marriage preceding childbearing (Graham 1993). In Britain co-habitation rates are very low for communities of Indian, Pakistani or Bangladeshi origin

(Richards 1995:41). This project will also try to gauge whether the fifteen widows in the sample view lone parenthood in a different light to those separated and divorced.

Table 3.1
Lone parent type by age of mother in years

	Divorced	Separated	Widowed	Unmarried	Total
Up to 19	—	—	—	—	—
20-29	2	6	1	2	11
30-34	7	10	1	—	18
35-39	14	8	3	—	25
40-44	11	9	6	—	26
45-49	3	—	2	—	5
50 +	2	1	2	—	5
Total	**39**	**34**	**15**	**2**	**90**

Table 3.1 goes on to show that over one-half of the sample were aged between 35 and 45, and they tended to be divorcees and widows. There were no teenagers, with the youngest respondent being an unmarried mother aged 24. Only five mothers were aged 50 and over. Because of their age, very few women from this older age group would have a dependent child. This sample has some differences and some similarities with the national picture. In 1992, whilst less than 4 per cent of all lone mothers were under the age of twenty, almost 40 per cent were in their twenties (Donnellan 1995:8). This would suggest that this sample is older than the lone parent population at large, since 51 of the mothers were aged between their mid-thirties and mid-forties. The older age of this sample may be attributed to the negligible numbers of unmarried mothers who would have been more likely to have been in their twenties, and who make up the largest proportion of white lone mothers, thus accounting for the younger British lone parent population.

Reasons for marriage breakdown

The main reasons for marriage breakdown for the 73 divorced and separated mothers were given as violence by the husband (44 mothers), alcoholism by father (28 mothers), neglect of family/irresponsibility of husband (21 mothers), financial problems (20 mothers), difficulties with in-laws (19 mothers) and infidelity by husband (19 mothers). It was found that 25 of the 73 mothers experienced three or more problems in their marriages, implying the extent of their difficulties. The large numbers of mothers citing violence as a reason for divorce is reflected in current trends. According to Donnellan (1993), about one-third of all divorces result from violence by husbands against wives, with 90 per cent of these women's divorce petitions using cruelty on grounds containing evidence of violence.

The decision to terminate the marriage

Forty-one of the 73 divorced and separated mothers said that they themselves decided to terminate their marriages, and were more likely to do so if in a violent marriage. Twenty-nine of these 41 mothers who initiated the divorce or separation were victims of domestic violence. The high percentage of respondents initiating marriage breakdown is in line with the national trend in that "it is predominantly wives who seek to end their marriage by petitioning for a divorce" (Robinson 1991:14). More than two-and-a-half times as many divorces were granted to women as men in England, Wales and Northern Ireland in 1993 - 120,000 compared with 47,000. Where a divorce was granted to the wife, over a half were for unreasonable behaviour (HMSO 1996:59).

Nineteen of the 73 divorced and separated respondents said that their former husbands had decided to terminate the marriage, with another thirteen mothers saying that it was a joint decision.

The children

Lone parents tend to have, on average, fewer and younger children than couple parents (HMSO 1996:55). Twenty-five of the 90 mothers in this study had one dependent child only, and another 29 had only two dependent children. These were more likely to be separated and divorced women. Only twelve mothers had three or four dependent children only. These findings can be compared to the British figures which show that in 1993, families headed by a lone parent had 1.7 children on average compared with 1.9 children in families headed by a married or co-habiting couple (OPCS 1993:8).

Twenty-four of the 90 mothers also had non-dependent children, with the widows being the most likely group to do so. Nine of the fifteen widows gave this response. They also tended to have larger numbers of children over school age per family. These findings may partly be due to the widows' average age being 41 years.

The separated lone mothers were the least likely group to have independent children. Twice as many of them had three or four dependent children only as did the divorcees. In comparison, almost three times as many divorcees had independent children as did the separated. The slightly older average age of 38.5 years of the divorcees compared to 36.7 years of the separated respondents may partly help to explain the difference in statistics.

Sixty of the sample said all or some of their dependent children were aged between five and sixteen. Sixteen said that all or some of their children were under the age of five. Fourteen of the mothers said that all of their dependent children were aged between sixteen and nineteen. This investigation will attempt to show how the numbers and ages of the children may have a bearing on the standards of living of the sample.

Eighty four of the 90 mothers said that all their dependent children were currently residing with them, echoing the national situation. According to Chandler, "women are now awarded custody of the children in ninety per cent of cases and their rights to custody are largely unchallenged for younger children and girls" (1991:25). One mother replied that some of her dependants were living with her and some with her in-laws, whilst another said her only child was currently living with her own family. Two more of the sample said that some of their dependants lived with them and some with the father. Because of circumstances beyond their control a further 2 of the 90 women said that all their dependants were currently residing with the father. All these children had been previously living with their mothers, with a chance of them being reunited in the near future.

Country of origin of the mothers and length of stay in Britain

Table 3.2 shows that an overwhelming majority of the sample immigrated from the Indian and African sub-continent, and because of their socialisation in their countries of origin, may have influenced the responses to the questions regarding the cultural issues. Only two of the mothers were born in Britain. One was a young widow, the other an unmarried mother. Both were in their twenties. Over one-third of the sample originated from India, with lone mothers from Pakistan and Kenya making up the next largest groups. Other countries less well represented included Mauritius, Burma and Sri Lanka.

Almost two-thirds of the sample came to this country during the 1960's and 1970's following marriage in their countries of origin, so 58 of the mothers had been living in Britain for over fifteen years. Just under one-sixth of the women had been settled here for less than ten years.

Table 3.2
Country of origin by length of stay in Britain in years

	Up to 5	5-9	10-14	15-19	20-24	25 +	Total
India	3	3	8	9	7	7	**37**
Kenya	2	1	2	4	7	2	**18**
Pakistan	1	2	6	2	2	4	**17**
Bangladesh	—	—	—	3	2	1	**6**
Tanzania	1	—	1	2	—	1	**5**
Great Britain	—	—	—	—	—	2	**2**
Other	1	—	1	—	1	2	**5**
Total	**8**	**6**	**18**	**20**	**19**	**19**	**90**

The fact that the majority of the sample were immigrants may have important implications for this study. Through their responses, the research will attempt to show whether these mothers have become more westernised in their views towards lone parenthood, or whether they have still retained their values from their countries of origin. Their length of stay in Britain may also be a significant factor, in that those mothers who had been residing in this country for a shorter time may be experiencing a greater dilemma regarding their situation as an immigrant lone parent than those respondents who had become better integrated into the British way of life because of their longer stay in Britain.

Country of education and type of education received by mothers

Table 3.3 shows that only 3 of the 90 women in the study were totally uneducated, with just over one-third being educated up to sixteen, five of whom saying they left school at the age of eleven. Twenty-one of the mothers had a sixth form education, with a large number of the women - a third in all - having been college or university educated. The educational qualifications of the lone mothers of this sample appear to be higher than the national average for lone parents, who tend to be less well qualified than married mothers. Thirty-eight per cent of the lone parent population have no qualifications compared with 25 per cent of other parents (OPCS 1993:9). In 1990 only 20 per cent of lone mothers had A Levels and above (Monk 1993:19).

Table 3.3
Type of education received by country of education

	None	Up to 16	16-19	College	University	Total
India	—	13	6	1	9	29
Pakistan	—	7	4	—	4	15
Kenya	—	3	5	1	—	9
Great Britain	—	4	2	1	—	7
Country of origin & GB	—	5	1	7	7	20
Other combination	—	4	3	—	—	7
Never had education	3	—	—	—	—	3
Total	**3**	**36**	**21**	**10**	**20**	**90**

Two-thirds of the 90 respondents were educated in one country only, and for the majority this was their country of origin. Twenty-seven mothers were educated in two different countries, which may have helped them to gain additional qualifications. Altogether, 27 of the 90 women said they received some or all of their education in Britain, fourteen of whom had gone on to a college or university here.

This study will attempt to show whether the level of education of the mothers had any bearing on their experiences as lone parents. For example, it will examine whether the more highly educated women had an advantage in the labour market, and if they held more liberal attitudes towards lone parenthood than those who left school at an earlier age.

Age at marriage and religion of mothers

Table 3.4 shows a total of 88 and not 90 respondents as the two unmarried mothers are excluded, one of whom was Christian, the other Jain. Thirty-four of the 88 mothers married as teenagers, which may be typical of Asian culture, but not of British culture. Only about six per cent of women who first got married in Britain in 1993 were under the age of twenty (HMSO 1995:58). In Britain there are now later marriages, with the average age of women in England and Wales marrying for the first time in 1993 being 26 years (HMSO 1995:57). The majority of this sample got married at an earlier age. The Hindu mothers were the most likely group to have got married in their early teens, the Muslim mothers in their late teens and early twenties, and the Sikh mothers aged 23 and over.

Table 3.4
Age at marriage in years by religion of mother at marriage

	Hindu	Muslim	Sikh	Christian	Jain	Total
14-16	6	3	5	—	—	**14**
17-19	6	10	4	—	—	**20**
20-22	8	9	7	—	1	**25**
23 +	8	6	11	2	2	**29**
Total	**28**	**28**	**27**	**2**	**3**	**88**

Although not directly asked, it was gauged that the vast majority of the sample had arranged marriages in their countries of origin. Only fifteen of the mothers stated that they had love marriages, reinforcing the Asian tradition of marrying within one's own ethnic group. Only 6 of the 88 women married out of their ethnic or religious group, with three marrying Englishmen. Two of these six were Christian respondents, with only two Hindu mothers, one Sikh and one Muslim mother marrying out of their ethnic or religious group. These six marriages have slightly changed the present religious profile of the sample, in that on marriage these women converted to the religious affiliations of their husbands. Including the two unmarried mothers, the sample finally comprised of 25 Hindu mothers, 28 Muslim mothers, 27 Sikh mothers, 6 Christian mothers and 4 Jain mothers. The findings of this study will also attempt to ascertain whether the religion of the women played any part in shaping their attitudes and experiences of lone parenthood. For example, the Muslim respondents, because of their more conservative and rigid culture, may have faced more adjustment problems towards their lone parent status than the other mothers who belonged to different religions.

Length of marriage of the mother

Table 3.5 reveals the length of marriage of the respondents and excludes the two unmarried mothers, although the latter both had long term relationships with their partners. Just under one-sixth of the sample had only been married for up to five years prior to marriage breakdown, with the largest numbers of mothers becoming lone parents after 5-9 and then 10-14 years of marriage.

The findings of this sample relating to length of marriage are similar to national findings. In 1993 only eight per cent of divorces in the United Kingdom were of marriages that had lasted under three years. At the other extreme less than ten per cent of divorces in the same year were after 25 years of marriage. By contrast, most marriages failed between the fifth and ninth years, accounting for three in ten divorces, and then between ten and fourteen years, making up eighteen per cent of divorces (HMSO 1996:59).

Table 3.5
Length of marriage in years by lone parent type

	Divorced	Separated	Widowed	Total
Up to 5	8	4	2	14
5-9	13	13	2	28
10-14	9	10	5	24
15 +	9	7	6	22
Total	**39**	**34**	**15**	**88**

The widows were the most likely group to have been married for ten years and over. This is not surprising, since these mothers were, on average, the oldest group, and they did not become lone parents through choice. The separated mothers were the most likely group to have been married for between five and nine years, whilst the divorcees were more likely than the other groups to have been married for the shortest time. This could imply that the divorcees had a higher likelihood of experiencing more distressing marriages than the separated mothers, and thus may have wanted to terminate them after a shorter period of marriage.

Last job of father prior to marriage breakdown

The education level of the women appeared to have a bearing on the last type of job the former husbands were employed in prior to marriage breakdown. The arranged marriages of the mothers would imply that the educational level of the husband had been taken into account. A high percentage of mothers were married to partners of a similar educational background, suggesting the accuracy of matches made prior to marriage regarding the educational levels of the couples involved.

Twenty-three of the husbands were in unskilled jobs (twelve of whom were married to uneducated women or mothers who left school at sixteen). Twenty-one of the husbands were self-employed or in business, fourteen were in skilled manual jobs, another fourteen were in skilled non-manual jobs (eleven of whom were married to women educated up to nineteen and over). Only nine of the fathers were professionals (eight of whom were married to college or university educated women). Seven of the fathers were unemployed (six of whom were married to uneducated mothers or those who left school at sixteen).

Almost two-thirds of the mothers had been married to men in manual or unskilled jobs, or else to men who were unemployed, and this may have been a factor in marriage breakdown. According to Morgan:

> the higher the husband's earnings the less likely are couples to part...The close correlation between low socio-economic status and marital dissolution means it is the marriages of the manual working classes and the unemployed that are most likely to be dissolved (1995:58).

Length of lone parenthood for the mothers

Table 3.6 shows the current length of lone parenthood for the 90 mothers, with over half of the sample having experienced marriage breakdown for between one and six years. Just one-tenth of the sample had been lone mothers for under a year, one being a 39 year old Muslim respondent who had only been divorced for under a month. According to Chandler (1991), remarriages now account for a third of all marriages, with the average duration of lone parenthood being between three and five years (Donnellan 1993:2). This sample reveals a third of the women having experienced lone parenthood for over seven years and may suggest that this status is more permanent for Asian than for British lone mothers, who would be more likely to remarry.

Table 3.6
Length of lone parenthood in years by lone parent type

	Divorced	Separated	Widowed	Unmarried	Total
Less than a yr	3	5	1	—	9
1-6	19	21	8	2	50
7-10	9	6	3	—	18
11 +	8	2	3	—	13
Total	**39**	**34**	**15**	**2**	**90**

The divorced and widowed mothers were the most likely groups to have experienced lone parenthood for seven years and over, and the separated mothers for under six years. The shorter length of lone parenthood for the separated respondents may be because these women were in the transition phase before finalising their divorces. This study will try to show whether the mothers who had been lone parents for a longer period were better adjusted to their situation than those women for whom being a lone mother was a relatively new experience.

Conclusion

This chapter has examined the various research methods used in the fieldwork undertaken, and has presented a brief profile of the mothers involved. It should be stressed that the findings and opinions of the sample do not claim to represent those of all Asian lone mothers, since only 90 women from the London area have been interviewed. This study, however, hopes to give a greater insight into a group largely ignored by researchers and policy makers, who have tended to concentrate on the lives of white and to a lesser extent on West Indian lone mothers in this country.

4 Living Conditions of Lone Parent Asian Mothers Living in London

In 1974 the Finer Committee stated that lone parent families "had been forced upon the attention of politicians and administrators of social services as a special group having exceptionally low standards of living" (HMSO 1974:5-6). Although over two decades have passed since this statement was made, there is overwhelming evidence to show that lone parent families continue to remain a significantly disadvantaged group in society (Millar 1989, Millar 1992, Monk 1993, Holtermann 1993, Donnellan 1995).

There is a long-standing association between poverty and lone parenthood, apparent in all poverty studies going back to the pioneering surveys conducted by Booth and Rowntree at the turn of the century (Brown 1985). The Child Poverty Action Group currently defines all those living between 100 and 140 per cent of income support as living on the margins of poverty, whilst those living on and below income support are defined as living in poverty. One in two lone parents are in poverty, compared with only about a fifth of couples with children (Oppenheim 1993:44).

Nine out of ten lone parents today are women and the Department of Social Security shows that three-quarters of lone parent families were living below half the average income in 1992, against less than a third in 1979 (Innes 1995:198). There is now a heightened awareness that a change in family status may be the catalyst for the underlying economic vulnerability of the increasing numbers of disadvantaged women and children in society (Duskin 1990).

Chapter Four is the first chapter presenting and analysing the findings of this study by examining the living conditions of the sample. It will focus on the areas of employment, income, housing and physical health, the main indicators of standards of living, comparing where possible the results of this study with those of national studies. It should be stressed, however, that making such comparisons is particularly difficult, since this sample contains only 90 mothers from the London area.

Employment

Women today form an increasing proportion of the British labour force. From spring 1985 to spring 1995 women's economic activity rate increased from 61 to 71 per cent, representing 43 per cent of the total working force of working age, and 10.8 million workers. Whilst the number of men in employment has risen by 0.1 million since 1985, for women it has grown by 1.3 million over the same period (Labour Force Survey 1995:93).

Despite the encouraging trends, there are variations in figures for employment rates between different groups of women. Over the last two decades the employment situation of lone mothers, in particular, appears to have deteriorated (Monk 1993). Since the Finer Report (1974), the stated objective of government policy towards the employment of lone parents has been that they should have a choice about whether to work or not. Thus, policy should be neutral in terms of encouraging or discouraging employment. Theoretically lone parents are to be helped if they wish to work, but are not required or positively encouraged to do so (Bradshaw and Millar 1991).

Although there are also other more important factors such as the lack of affordable day care facilities and the availability of well paid jobs, this "neutral policy" of the Finer Report may have partly contributed to the gap between the employment rate of lone mothers and that of married mothers in Britain. In 1977-79, 52 per cent of married women with dependent children were actively employed, compared with 47 per cent of lone mothers. In 1991-93, the proportion had increased to 63 per cent of married mothers and only 41 per cent of lone mothers (OPCS 1993:54).

Employment rates amongst lone mothers are also lower in the UK than in most EC countries - 40 per cent compared with the EC average of twelve countries of 54 per cent. In most EC countries economic activity is higher among lone parents than among mothers in general, but the contrary is true in the UK, where lone parents, as stated above, are less likely to be in work than married mothers (Holtermann 1993).

The first section of Chapter Four will concentrate on the employment situation of this sample. It will firstly look at the present working situation of those mothers actively employed, highlighting some of the problems they faced, and will conclude by examining whether the 90 women had any future plans regarding their employment/non-employment situation.

Current employment situation

Thirty-five of the 90 mothers said that they had worked prior to marriage, the vast majority of whom would have been living in their countries of origin at the time, where employment opportunities may have been more restricted. Twenty-eight of these women were married after the age of twenty and hence had a chance to acquire work before they married.

Table 4.1 explores the present employment situation of the 90 mothers in the study, and shows an increase in the numbers of women currently unemployed - from 60 to 73 per cent. Currently over two-thirds of the sample were not working, which is in line with national figures discussed earlier in this chapter.

Table 4.1
Whether the mothers were currently employed by level of education

	Employed	Unemployed	Total
No education	1	2	3
Up to 16	7	29	36
16-19	5	16	21
College (teaching, secretarial)	4	6	10
University	7	13	20
Total	**24**	**66**	**90**

Data from the table suggests that this sample was also more highly educated than lone mothers in the UK generally. According to the General Household Survey (1993:20), 78 per cent of lone parent families either have no qualifications or are educated up to sixteen, compared with 53 per cent of other families. Only four per cent of lone parent families hold degrees compared with fourteen per cent of other families.

Fifty-one of this sample had qualifications equivalent to A Levels and above, compared to Hyatt and Parry-Crooke's study (1990) in which 16 of their 21 respondents were only educated up to sixteen and less, nine of whom had no qualifications. Bradshaw and Millar's research (1991:16) also revealed that over one-half of their sample were without any qualifications.

The results also imply that there is rather a complicated correlation between level of education and employment. One set of findings suggests that there was no difference in the proportion of the uneducated mothers and the university educated who were currently employed. However, when education levels are banded together, the figures may indicate that the likelihood of being employed increases for women who were educated at least to sixth form standard. Thus, some relationship is suggested between length of education received and employment opportunities.

The findings of this project can be compared to those of McKay and Marsh's large scale study of lone parents and work (1994) in which their employed respondents also tended to be better educated on average than those not working. The majority of their employed group had some qualifications, compared with fewer than half of those out of work. However, no more than a third of those with jobs had A Levels or higher, although this was matched by less than a tenth of those not in work.

Although this study of Asian lone mothers contained only 90 respondents, 16 of the 24 employed women were educated at least up to the sixth form stage, as were 35 of the 66 unemployed group. This may imply that, unlike in McKay and Marsh's research, a decent level of education had been received by many of the working and non-working mothers, with the result that education level was not such a strong factor in the employment status of the sample.

Status of current employment

It is well documented that work available to women tends to be low paid, low status jobs in a highly sex segregated labour market (Maclean 1991, Glendinning and Millar 1992, Graham 1993), with Asian women more likely to take up jobs in the more peripheral, underpaid and insecure sectors (Cochrane 1993).

This was reflected in the findings of this study since only 4 of the 24 employed mothers were engaged in professional posts and only three in managerial jobs. The largest bulk of the working group - ten in all - were found in skilled non-manual employment, with seven of the remaining mothers in unskilled jobs. This is echoed by Bradshaw and Millar's findings (1991) which also found that those at work tended to be at the bottom of the labour market in lower paid, routine jobs such as factory work, catering and cleaning.

There appeared to be a connection between the level of educational attainment and status of work, as mothers educated up to at least nineteen were more inclined to be employed in higher status jobs. Professional posts were most likely to be held by university degree holders and included a teacher and a doctor. Managerial jobs were most likely to be taken by mothers who had an A Level education, one of whom was an assistant manager at a day centre, another a shop manager. Skilled non-manual posts such as secretarial and administrative work tended to be the domain of mothers who attended college. In contrast, there was a greater likelihood of unskilled work in traditional "female" jobs like catering and factory work being taken by women who never went to school.

Amount of wages earned

Men tend to be paid higher hourly wage rates than women (Holtermann 1993), despite the introduction of equal pay and sex discrimination over fifteen years ago. Women working full time in 1989 earned on average only 77 per cent of male earnings. Women fared even worse at part time level, where females working part time in non-manual jobs earned only 50 per cent of the male non-manual hourly rate (Payne 1991:62). Even when including overtime, women's average gross hourly earnings in 1992 were only 80 per cent of men's.

Lone motherhood is likely to compound the situation. According to Monk, "the average wage earned by lone mothers is extremely low" (1993:17). Whereas lone mothers in full time employment appear to receive rates of pay similar to married mothers working full time, those lone mothers working part time tend to receive lower hourly rates than their married counterparts (Holtermann 1993).

This study has shown that of the 24 employed mothers, four earned up to £150 per month, nine earned between £151 and £750 monthly, and eleven took home £751 or more a month. The earning power of the Asian sample appears to be somewhat higher than that of lone parents in other recent studies. For example, McKay and Marsh's research (1994:72), conducted at about the same time as this study, found that a fifth of unmarried mothers working for over 24 hours weekly, took home less than £80 a week. Other lone mothers earned a median wage of between

£120 and £130, with fifteen per cent of all the lone mother sample taking home less than £80 weekly.

As expected, a strong relationship was indicated between monthly wages earned and type of employment, in that the higher status jobs paid the better salaries. For example, a divorced professional doctor received £30,000 yearly, whilst a divorced receptionist at an Asian women's centre was earning £6,700 annually. In turn, mothers in the lowest status, unskilled jobs earned the minimum wages, and included a Muslim divorcee of seventeen years who took home £35 weekly as a factory worker.

Closer examination of wages earned in relation to education received suggests a correlation between the two, although not a perfect one. One set of results infers that the university educated mothers were far more likely than the other groups to be earning the better salaries. Another set of findings, however, suggests that a higher level of education is not linked to wages earned, since the proportion of mothers who left school at sixteen were twice as likely as A Level and college educated women to be earning in the top income bracket. One was a separated Sikh respondent in her thirties who left school at sixteen and was now receiving £12,000 yearly as a school administrator. She was earning more than a university educated Hindu divorcee who was only taking home £7,200 annually as an employee for the Department of Social Security.

Whether working part time, full time or unemployed

Recently there has been an overall shift from full to part time employment, coinciding with an increase in the number of women at work. Today, both married women with dependent children and lone mothers are more likely to be working on a part time basis rather than full time, although the differences are greater for the married group. In 1991-93, 41 per cent of married women with dependent children worked part time and 22 per cent full time. Among lone mothers with dependent children, 24 per cent worked part time and 17 per cent full time (OPCS 1993:54). Thus it is noticeable that full time work is very difficult for many lone mothers to sustain, given their domestic responsibilities and the shortage of affordable child care facilities (Glendinning and Millar 1992).

Table 4.2
Whether working part time, full time or unemployed by type of lone mother and age in years

	Divorced			Separated			Widowed			Total
	F/T	P/T	N/E	F/T	P/T	N/E	F/T	P/T	N/E	
20's	1	—	1	—	—	6	—	—	1	9
30's	4	1	16	1	1	16	—	—	4	43
40's	7	2	5	1	2	6	2	1	5	31
50 +	1	—	1	—	—	1	—	—	2	5
Total	**13**	**3**	**23**	**2**	**3**	**29**	**2**	**1**	**12**	**88**

The results of this study seen in Table 4.2 above, however, reveal that 17 of the 24 employed mothers were working full time. This may be due to the very small sample, and thus cannot really be compared to the national trend. Nevertheless, Bradshaw and Millar (1991) also found that a slightly higher proportion of their employed sample were working full time as compared to part time and McKay and Marsh (1994:8) similarly discovered that 23 per cent of their lone mothers were employed for 23 hours a week or more, compared to 11 per cent of their sample who worked part time.

Latest national figures have shown that in 1991-93 50 per cent of divorcees with dependent children were actively employed, 46 per cent of widows, 46 per cent of separated women and 30 per cent of unmarried mothers (OPCS 1993:65), which represents a slight change in the earlier trend where separated mothers were less likely than widows to be in work (Haskey 1993).

The data relating to the employment situation of the mothers in this sample is much in line with the national figures, in that the divorcees were twice as likely as the widows and almost three times more likely than the separated respondents to be employed. Neither of the unmarried mothers had a job, which echoes the low participation rate of this population group (Holtermann 1993). The divorcees were also the most probable group to be in full time work, the separated in part time work and the widows in-between the two. According to Table 4.2, the risk of unemployment appeared to be greater for the separated mothers, most probably because they had more dependent children to care for. Likewise, McKay and Marsh (1994) observed that the divorcees in their sample were the most likely mothers to have a job, with activity rates among the unmarried and widows the lowest, with less than a quarter in paid work of any kind.

Moving on to age of the respondent, mothers in their forties and then in their fifties were the two most likely groups to have participated in the labour market, perhaps due to their having older children than the younger women. Fifteen of the 24 employed mothers in this sample were in their forties, and only one was in her twenties. As Monk has pointed out, "economic activity of lone mothers increases with the age of the mother, with a slight decrease before retirement age" (1993:23). Gregory and Foster's survey into the consequences of divorce for men and women similarly found that the proportion of women who had work increased through the age range, with the maximum rate being reached in the 40-44 age band (1990:34).

Table 4.3
Whether working part time, full time or unemployed by number and age of dependent children

	No. of dependent children				Total
	One	Two	Three	Four	
Works full time					**17**
All/some children below school age	1	1	—	—	
All/some children aged 5-9	2	—	1	—	
All children aged 10 and over	9	3	—	—	
Works part time					7
All/some children below school age	—	1	—	—	
All/some children aged 5-9	1	1	—	—	
All children aged 10 and over	—	3	1	—	
Unemployed					66
All/some children below school age	6	4	3	—	
All/some children aged 5-9	4	13	4	2	
All children aged 10 and over	18	11	1	—	
Total	**41**	**37**	**10**	**2**	**90**

Two important factors affecting women's economic activity are related both to the number of dependent children and whether the youngest child is under or over the age of five (Gregory and Foster 1990). Table 4.3 focuses on whether these were factors in determining work patterns of the sample. The figures suggest that there is a correlation, in that both variables may have been significant in influencing whether the mother could firstly gain employment, and secondly if this was on a full time or part time basis.

Employed mothers were more likely than the non-working group to have only one or two dependent children, with none having four dependants. Full time workers also had a far greater tendency to have only one dependent child, whereas part time workers were more likely to have two. Mothers with three or four dependent children had a higher likelihood of being unemployed, reinforcing the link between number of dependants and chances of working.

The above findings of this study confirm those of Bradshaw and Millar's (1991:37) and McKay and Marsh's (1994:10), in which there was a stronger tendency for those with fewer dependent children to be more economically active than those parents with more.

The results of this study also indicate that the age of the dependent children was a factor in determining work patterns, in that having younger children was a hindrance to being employed full time. The likelihood of the mother being able to do so increased if all her children were aged ten and over. Table 4.3 also suggests that the unemployed women were more inclined than the working mothers to have all or some of their children under school age, helping to partly explain their non-participation in the labour market. Similar findings were revealed in Bradshaw and Millar's study (1991), where not having young children was one of the most important determinants in affecting the probability of the lone mother working full time. McKay and Marsh's investigation (1994:9) also showed how the extent of a lone parent's economic activity was dictated by the age of the youngest child. Only nine per cent of lone parents with a child under five worked full time, whereas half with teenagers had jobs.

Child care arrangements

The increased participation levels in the labour market of women with under fives has seen a large rise in the use of paid child care (McKay and Marsh 1994). Britain has the lowest rates of publicly funded day care of nearly all European countries. Whilst over the period 1980-92 the number of private care places in day nurseries and with child minders has more than doubled, the amount of subsidised local authority provision has only increased by ten per cent to a total of 37,738 in 1991 (Monk 1993:31).

Because of the low earning power of lone parents who work, very few are able to pay for private day care and are therefore dependent on the small number of state subsidised places. Bradshaw and Millar's study (1991:52) revealed that state nurseries were used by only eighteen per cent of those working and with pre-school children but not on Income Support, with only eight per cent of this particular working group using private nurseries. The availability and cost of child care is, thus, an essential factor in influencing the numbers of lone parents who work, and whether this is full time or part time.

The results of this research suggest a strong relationship between the need to provide child care and the age of dependent children for the working mothers. Only 3 of the 21 employed women with some or all of their children aged five and over said they needed to worry about child care. This tended to be for much younger than older children, since many of the mothers had teenagers who could look after themselves. One of the mothers who did need child care took it in turns with a neighbour to share the responsibility, whilst another said her five year old son was collected after school by his grandparents. Just one of these three women paid for child care. She was a 41 year old Sikh divorcee, working as a school administrator for British Airways and earning £200 weekly, and spoke of the arrangements made for her five year old daughter:

I find some friends. It costs fifty pounds and sixty pence for the whole week. I decided to do night shifts, as at night my daughter will be asleep and safe. During the day I'd rather look after my daughter myself, as otherwise I'd be worried.

All three employed mothers with some or all pre-school children had to make child care arrangements for their dependants whilst they were at work and was similarly revealed in McKay and Marsh's study (1994). One of these women in this research, a full time worker in her twenties, said she used family help free of charge. A second mother who worked as a part time playgroup assistant, also for whom cost was not a consideration, said of her four year old son: "I drop him off at the nursery and go to work. At eleven-thirty I pick him up and bring him to the playgroup." The third respondent had to pay for child care.

She was a separated Bangladeshi mother aged 30 and a full time catering assistant. She was earning £150 per week, as well as receiving One Parent Benefit, and explained the circumstances surrounding her two young sons aged seven and three:

> My sister takes my older son to school and picks him up. I leave my younger one with a baby-sitter, and pick him up at four-thirty. It costs fifty pounds for five days. That's two-hundred pounds a month, and the baby-sitter's not even registered.

Other studies of lone parents and child care have produced similar findings. Graham (1993) points out that the formal sector plays a relatively limited role in helping lone mothers faced with the difficulties of finding reliable and affordable child care. Lone mothers often depend on jobs which can be filled around school hours and term times, with irregular hours of work in a flexible labour force. This was the situation faced by many of the employed women in this sample. Other studies by Hyatt and Parry-Crooke (1990), Bradshaw and Millar (1991) and Leeming et al (1994) have all shown that lone mothers have to rely almost entirely on informal child care arrangements through family, friends and neighbours, as was the case for many of the Asian group. McKay and Marsh (1994) also add that those who can afford the more expensive forms of care also tend to be in the better paid jobs.

Future plans for employment

The 90 mothers were asked about their future plans regarding employment. Fifteen of the mothers currently in work were totally satisfied with their jobs. Two of the employed women said they would like to work more hours, and another three expressed a wish to expand their qualifications. One of the latter was a Muslim divorcee, currently working as a part time playgroup assistant. She wanted to gain more qualifications for promotion at her work place, and was currently undertaking a diploma course to become a nursery supervisor. The remaining four employed mothers said they wanted to change jobs, one being a 30 year old catering assistant who wanted to further her ambitions "in computers." Only one of the working mothers expressed complete dissatisfaction with her present job. She was a divorcee in her forties who had been a full time catering assistant for the last six years, and complained of "racial discrimination." However, due to her failing health she was experiencing difficulties in finding other work.

Of the 66 employed mothers, 21 said they were currently available and looking for work. Some of them gave explanations, one being a Muslim divorcee of only a year, who explained that the adverse effects of her marriage breakdown had forced her to give up her seventeen year old job as a cost accountant. Now her divorce had come through, she had regained her confidence and was now actively looking for work in accountancy. A separated mother in her forties, however, was more sceptical about the type of job she would like: "I'm looking now...but on benefit you have to be very careful if you earn a certain amount, so the job may not be worth it."

Eighteen of the 66 unemployed mothers, whose average age was 34, said they would look for work once their children were older. One was a Sikh widow with two young daughters and receiving Income Support and a Widows Pension. She spoke of the lack of affordable child care:

> I would like to work part time but am not looking yet. I've got a two year old daughter to look after, and it's a lot of money with a baby minder - from sixty to seventy pounds a week, which I can't afford.

Seven of the unemployed mothers explained that they would seek work after completing their studies. One was a 24 year old unmarried mother with two young sons, who was about to begin an HND course, which she said would "hopefully lead to a job." Another was a separated respondent from Mauritius currently studying for a City and Guilds diploma which would enable her to become a nursery nurse. Five of the other unemployed mothers gave other reasons for seeking work later, three of whom stating that it was their present housing situation which prevented them from looking for a job.

Ill health and advanced age were the two main reasons which accounted for the fact that eleven mothers had no plans to look for employment. Some of the illnesses included arthritis, asthma, angina and heart problems The remaining four women not in work were undecided about whether to take up a job in the future.

The future employment plans of lone mothers have also been asked in other recent studies, with the main findings echoing those of this sample - that there is a great demand for work among lone parents. Both Bradshaw and Millar's research (1991) and that of McKay and Marsh (1994) revealed that a large proportion of their employed samples said that they were presently seeking work or else would be in the near future. Many of the mothers with younger children also said it was a lack of affordable child care that prevented them from working until their dependants were older.

Income

The second section of Chapter Four will firstly look at the main sources of income, with a discussion on maintenance, before going on to examine whether the women felt their incomes were sufficient in relation to their day-to-day living as lone parents in London.

Sources of income

Because of their high rates of non-participation in the labour market, lone parents are heavily dependent on social security benefits, which has been increasing over the years (Oppenheim 1993). In 1971, 37 per cent of lone parents received Supplementary Benefit, in 1989, 67 per cent received its equivalent Income Support (Holtermann 1993:20) and in 1993, 75 per cent of the 1.4 million lone parent families in Britain were claiming Income Support. Unmarried, followed by the separated mothers were the most likely recipients. Widows were the least likely group (Donnellan 1995:16). This may be because the latter group have benefit rights under National Insurance and are thus better off, without being forced onto Income Support (Pascall 1986). Lone mothers also comprise 40 per cent of all mothers on Family Credit, an income supplement for families on low incomes. Altogether, about 90 per cent of all lone parents are in receipt of a benefit - either Income Support, Housing Benefit or Family Credit - during any given year (Wasoff 1995:82).

Table 4.4 lists the sources of income for the 90 women in this study, with findings similar to those for lone mothers nationally. The results show that two-thirds of the mothers, all of whom were unemployed, relied entirely on government means tested benefits. Only 9 of the 90 respondents were not currently in receipt of state support.

Table 4.4
Sources of income for the lone mothers

Benefits only (excluding Child Benefit)	60 mothers
Benefits and wages only	13 mothers
Benefits and maintenance only	6 mothers
Benefits, wages and maintenance	2 mothers
Wages only	6 mothers
Wages and maintenance only	3 mothers
Total	**90 mothers**

Of the 24 mothers in employment, only six earned enough to manage on their incomes alone. These were all full time workers at the top end of the pay scale and included a doctor and a psychiatrist. Thirteen of the remaining women in work also received benefits such as Family Credit and Housing Benefit to boost their incomes. These included both full time and part time workers, many of whom were in low paid, low status jobs such as catering and factory work, which merited their taking up benefits.

Maintenance payments

In recent years the numbers of lone parents in Britain in receipt of maintenance payments from ex-partners has fallen, and has been associated with rising levels of social security expenditure (Chandler 1991). In 1990, only 30 per cent of lone mothers received regular maintenance payments, with the average weekly amount awarded per child being £16, and only £12 per child if there were more than three children. Two in five lone parents experienced at least one period when the absent parent failed to pay. Arrears paid in full or in part in the magistrates court was compensated in only nineteen per cent of cases (Monk 1993:22). Despite this, British Social Attitudes have found that 90 per cent of men and 95 per cent of women are in unanimous agreement that a father should be made to support his child (1992-93:108). Although in 1993 the Child Support Agency came into operation to pursue absent fathers to recoup some of the costs of state support, the general picture still remains somewhat discouraging, as reflected in the findings of this research.

Table 4.4 shows that a very low percentage of the 90 mothers received maintenance payments from their former partners. Twenty-two of the women were not eligible to claim - fifteen were widows, five of the mothers said their former partners had since died, and two mothers pointed out that their dependent children were currently living with the father.

Fifty-seven of the 68 respondents who were eligible for maintenance did not receive any form of payment. Compared with McKay and Marsh's study (1994), which found that one-third of their sample were in receipt of maintenance, this research has reinforced the low take up rate of this form of income for the lone mothers. One reason for the low figures may be attributed to the ignorance on the part of some of the women who may not have heard of maintenance. Additionally, the reality for many lone parents is that as all maintenance is deducted pound for pound from benefits received, there is no financial gain by going to court (Glendinning and Millar 1992, Collins 1992). During the course of the interviews it also came to light that many of the mothers had lost contact with their former partners, some of whom had gone back to their countries of origin, some of whom had remarried.

Evidence from other recent studies on maintenance have shown that many mothers choose not to be financially dependent on their ex-husbands, preferring to make a clean break (Bradshaw and Millar 1991, McKay and Marsh 1994). This was illustrated by a respondent in this project whose former partner was a mechanical engineer with a good salary: "I didn't want any more involvement with him. I didn't want to ask even though friends told me I'm entitled to maintenance."

However, twelve respondents who did want maintenance payments for their children explained that their previous partners were currently unemployed, a common problem faced by many lone mothers (Bradshaw and Millar 1991, Collins 1992). Walczak (1984) also adds that "many men temporarily give up work or do not declare their true earnings" to avoid having to pay maintenance. An instance of this was illustrated by an unemployed separated mother in her thirties with two children:

> My husband's not working. He's now unemployed. He was advised not to work for a year by his family so he wouldn't have to pay maintenance by the courts. He was an accounts clerk with a good salary. I'm trying to get maintenance, but he's got no job so he's not interested.

Attention will now be focused on the eleven lone mothers in this study who claimed maintenance. Other findings have revealed that certain characteristics often help to determine which mothers stand a greater chance of receiving payments, and these shall be compared with the eleven Asian lone parents.

According to McKay and Marsh's analysis (1994), maintenance was most commonly received by divorcees, owner occupiers and those in work, especially if not claiming Income Support. These employed lone parents also got larger amounts. The findings of this study are only partially similar to McKay and Marsh's. Whilst seven of the eleven mothers in this sample were divorced and only four separated, only two of the recipients were home owners. One was staying with friends, with the remaining eight living in council property.

Only five of the eleven mothers in this study were employed, three of whom were earning over £10,000 annually. Two of these three women were not receiving any benefits, and two were claiming regular maintenance. One mother was receiving over £50 weekly for her son, and the other two £16-20 per week per child. The remaining two employed respondents on lower incomes were both receiving irregular payments of up to £10 per child weekly. Looking at the six unemployed mothers, three received payments regularly, and three irregularly. Three of the unemployed women were only getting up to £10 weekly per child, two were in receipt of £11-15 and only one received over £20 a week.

Maclean (1991) and McKay and Marsh (1994) have both observed that well qualified women find it easier to get work on their own account, and to claim maintenance from their typically well qualified and better paid former partners. Four of the eleven mothers who were in receipt of maintenance in this research were university educated and another four were educated up to A Level standard. This suggests that their higher level of educational attainment may have helped in their awareness to claim their rights, or else they had married men with professional jobs who were willing and able to pay. For example, one divorcee with a university degree who had been married to an engineer was receiving £200 monthly through the courts.

In this study, seven of the eleven mothers were receiving payments for only one dependent child, indicating the advantage of having a small family when claiming. Only three of these eleven mothers had three dependants to claim for, and only one of these respondents was paid regularly.

Not all the women who received maintenance were satisfied. One, a separated mother from Kenya said the £10 her son received weekly from his father was deducted from her Income Support, a problem touched on earlier. Other women spoke of the reluctance of their former partners to pay. Chandler confirms this by stating that maintenance payments "are vulnerable to irregularities in the husband's work and his co-operation" (1991:100), an example of this being given by Sikh mother of two daughters, whose former husband was a casual worker:

In the past seven years I've only received six months maintenance, and only through dragging him to court. The last cheque was at Christmas. It was supposed to be twenty pounds for both children per week. In the last seven years I've only been paid six-hundred to seven-hundred pounds.

This particular mother did not appear optimistic about recouping any money, and this was also echoed by many of the respondents of Collins' study (1992:185) in which only one-third of men whose payments fell into arrears paid off the amount owed to the mothers and children.

Other women in this research made it clear that the maintenance payments they received were not enough. The amounts mentioned earlier show payments not only to be small, but often irregular and an unstable form of income. As well as this, divorce rates are higher among men in semi-skilled and unskilled occupations (Parkinson 1987, Graham 1993), thus accounting for their inability to pay their former wives a decent amount. One such mother to complain about the meagre maintenance her two sons received was a 43 year old divorcee from Kenya whose ex-husband was a factory worker:

> I get maintenance now and then, not regularly. I get twenty pounds per week at the moment, but it's not enough as inflation is rising and maintenance doesn't keep up with it. As my husband's got remarried it's not really very helpful. He was supposed to pay for both the children, but now he only pays for one. He says he can't pay for both as he's on Income Support.

Whether the mothers felt their incomes were sufficient

The literature so far has shown that it is the state and not the labour market which is the major income provider for lone parent families. Leeming et al's study (1994:66) revealed that most of their mothers had a much lower disposable income following separation than when they had lived with their husbands.

Table 4.5 shows that over two-thirds of the 90 participants felt that their incomes were insufficient. Despite the fact that widows are generally regarded as the most well off lone parent type, twelve of the fifteen widows in this study expressed dissatisfaction with their incomes. Some studies, such as those by Pahl (1985) and Bradshaw and Millar (1991), have found that some lone mothers, usually between a quarter and a third feel they are better off as lone parents than as married women, because being on their own means they have sole control over their income and resources. Although almost a quarter of this sample did express satisfaction with their incomes, this did not imply that they felt better off than when they were married. On the contrary, the majority of the respondents echoed the sentiments of lone mothers in Bradshaw and Millar's study (1991:31) who said that living on benefits made them feel "inadequate" or "hard-pressed."

Table 4.5
Sufficiency of income by number of dependent children
and whether employed or unemployed

| | Number of dependent children | | | |
	One	Two	Three/Four	Total
Income sufficient				23
Employed	8	3	—	11
Unemployed	8	2	2	12
Income insufficient				67
Employed	5	7	1	13
Unemployed	20	26	8	54
Total	**41**	**38**	**11**	**90**

Evidence from McKay and Marsh's study (1994) denotes that families with more than two young children and who only have benefit or benefit level incomes, experience material difficulties not faced by other families. Likewise, the data from Table 4.5 suggests a clear correlation between feelings of sufficiency of income and numbers of dependent children. This can be seen by the mothers having only one dependent child as being almost twice as likely to be satisfied with their incomes as dissatisfied. Vice versa the mothers with two or more children were twice as likely to have been dissatisfied as satisfied.

Table 4.5 also goes on to indicate a relationship between employment and sufficiency of income. Employed respondents in this study were far more likely to have only one or two dependent children, with only one working mother having three. The employed women satisfied with their incomes were also more likely to have only one dependent child than two, whilst the dissatisfied working mothers tended to have two or more dependent children. Unemployed women with only one dependent child were more inclined to be satisfied with their incomes, whereas those non-working mothers with two or more dependants were more likely to be dissatisfied.

Some of these unemployed mothers with large families related the difficulties they experienced on a low income. A Muslim divorcee with four sons aged between seven and thirteen said she did not use the heating "to save money for the children." Another respondent, separated for two years with three daughters aged twelve, ten and eight explained how she was forced into finding alternative ways of boosting her income:

> I've had to borrow from friends. I've had to sell my necklace, earrings and gold bangles to get money. I've also had to sell my shawls, saris and Pakistani dresses at lower prices. I've made about two-hundred pounds. I need uniforms for the children, but I can't get a grant. I've had to spend forty pounds for their school uniforms and clothes alone.

Further analysis regarding sufficiency levels does imply a relationship between this and working patterns, in that mothers most likely to be happy with their incomes were those in full time work and in high status, well paid jobs, such as medicine and teaching. Only two of these women also received benefits to help raise their incomes. Those mothers working full time and who expressed dissatisfaction with their incomes tended to be in low status, low paid work, suggesting that it was not so much being in full time employment that influenced sufficiency of income, but status of employment. For example, a low paid full time catering assistant said of her meagre income: "It's not enough. I need a thousand pounds a month and that goes on the mortgage."

Part time workers were twice as likely as full time workers to feel that their incomes were insufficient, and these women were found in less well paid jobs such as factory and reception work. Only one of the seven part time workers was happy with her income. The analysis also implies that income made no difference to feelings of sufficiency at part time level, since part time workers and those who were unemployed had similar feelings about the sufficiency of their incomes. These findings are in line with those of McKay and Marsh's study (1994) which revealed that out of work lone parents were the worst off group, whilst the best off were the moderate and highest income lone parents for whom severe hardship was almost unknown.

Commodities the mothers cut down on/went without

Although women are more likely to have more scope to make decisions about coping with poverty if not in two parent households, this does not necessarily make their task any easier. For women, poverty draws on their skills as a manager and a good housekeeper. However, whereas "better off households typically budget by the month and use a bank account, low income households budget by the week and deal in cash" (Graham 1993:153).

Most women in Leeming et al's study (1994) identified the family budget as their greatest problem, given their substantially reduced income. However, as time goes by, lone parents learn to develop a range of coping strategies through which they can come to be "better off poor" (Crow and Hardey 1992:151). Recent studies (Bradshaw and Millar 1991, Leeming et al 1994, McKay and Marsh 1994) have all shown how lone parents have to cut back or go without essential basics like food, fuel and clothing in order to cope on their very tight budgets. Cutting out personal items and services, going without luxury items and avoiding impulsive buying are also common of families on low incomes.

The findings of this study confirm those mentioned above. Table 4.6 shows that an overwhelming number of the sample said they had to economise in some way, the majority of whom were unemployed or on low wages. A 39 year old Sikh mother with two children and currently looking for work, summed up the feelings of 24 other women who had to economise generally:

> You can't afford to live on your income. If you get a low paid job they cut your benefit. You have to cut down on everything. You have to think about budgeting before you go anywhere and buy anything. You have to do without things.

Even some of the respondents who had earlier expressed satisfaction with their incomes said they felt "the need to economise ...and watch the pennies" as a separated shop manager put it. Hence, the sentiments of the women in this study were similar to the image of a "struggle" given by many of the separated mothers in Leeming et al's research (1994:67) to describe their budgeting methods.

Table 4.6
Commodities the mothers cut down on/went short of

No need to cut down/could manage	**12 mothers**
Economised on everything generally	**25 mothers**
Economised on clothes mainly	**12 mothers**
Economised on clothes and/or presents & food mainly	**25 mothers**
Economised on luxuries only	**2 mothers**
Economised on other combinations	**14 mothers**
Total	**90 mothers**

Over a third of this sample stated having to economise on clothing. Two widows in their forties said they never bought clothes, their parents sending them from abroad instead. A Sikh divorcee with three children explained that she bought "clothes and shoes in the sales all the time" and could "not ever afford to buy them at their original prices." Even being employed did not guarantee being able to afford clothing, with a part time administrator claiming she was forced to "pick up bargains and go to sales."

Having to buy presents was a source of worry for some mothers, and as one of these, an unemployed Sikh divorcee with three children, put it: "I only get presents if they're useful to us as a family." About a sixth of the sample mentioned having to cut down on food, a recurrent theme in studies of poor households. A separated mother spoke of her embarrassing experiences at the supermarket: "I go to the check-out and have to put things back. I have to budget but am surviving." A few of the women also spoke of no longer being able to afford a social life. One said she had to sacrifice going out for the sake of the children's well-being: "I have no social life to spend money. I first have to think of the important things I need, especially for the children."

Only twelve of the sample said they did not need to economise at all, seven of whom were in highly paid, full time work such as psychiatry, medicine and management. The remaining five women who did not economise were all unemployed, and included an unmarried mother who lived with her parents, and a 25 year old widow who received help from her "wealthy and very well off" family.

Worries about paying the bills

Seventy-one of the 90 respondents said they worried about paying their bills, ten said they did not, and nine replied that they did not have to pay any bills. Leeming et al's recent study (1994) also found that their separated mothers expressed continued worries about meeting payments for large bills, and this remained a predominant concern as to whether they could cope quite well, or just survive.

In this research there appeared to be a correlation, although not a substantial one, between being employed and worries about bill payments, with the unemployed mothers being more likely than those with jobs to express anxiety. Examining the figures more closely, part time workers followed by the unemployed were the most probable groups to have worries, although proportionately there was very little difference between the two. This suggests that income received from part time work was probably no better than government benefits. Many of these women were in low paid jobs, as was a playgroup assistant earning £12 weekly who complained about the consequences of not keeping up with payments: "The poll tax gives me a headache. If I don't pay the bills I get cut off sometimes." Some of the unemployed respondents also expressed their concerns, one being a separated Muslim mother in her thirties who said she sometimes could not sleep at night because of excessive worry.

Not unexpectedly, respondents who worked full time were the least likely group to worry about paying bills. They also tended to be receiving good salaries, one being a mother in management earning £17,000 annually: "There are no worries. All the money goes on the accounts." Those who did not have to pay their bills tended to be employed rather than out of work. Most of them also lived with friends or relatives, implying that the bills were paid for by other family members or friends.

Access to a car

In 1994-95, 69 per cent of households in Britain had access to a car (CSO 1995:138). National statistics for 1994-95 show that 42 per cent of one adult one child families and 38 per cent of lone parent families with two or more children had access to a car. This compares with 86 per cent of married couples with one child and 92 per cent of those with two or more children (CSO 1995:138). Gregory and Foster (1990) also claim that fewer lone mothers have access to a car than do lone fathers.

Only 39 of the 90 women in this study had access to a car, a lower percentage than the national average for lone parents. The majority of these women had either bought them themselves or had been given them as gifts. There appeared to be a relationship between access to transport and employment, in that the working mothers were more likely to have a car, as was the case for 18 of the 24 employed group. The mothers' incomes earned from their jobs may have helped pay for the cars, or else the women may have needed a form of transport to get to work. Leeming et al's study (1994) similarly showed how those few separated respondents using a car were exclusively in employment and considered it essential to travel to work as well as to take their children to child care facilities.

In this study unemployed mothers were the least likely group to have access to a car - only 11 of the 66 women did - which suggests that this form of transport was not affordable for those who relied solely on benefits.

The divorcees were also twice as likely as the separated mothers to have a car, perhaps because almost three times as many divorced as separated mothers were in employment, enabling them to afford the running costs. Widows were the second most likely group to have the use of a car, also with more numbers proportionately in paid work than the separated respondents. The unmarried mothers were the least likely women to have access, and were the most likely to be unemployed.

Holidays

A survey carried out in 1994 showed that only one-third of lone parents were able to go on holiday once a year, with one in five lone parent families never taking a holiday (Donnellan 1995:7).

As anticipated, only 12 of the 90 mothers in this study said they could afford a family holiday. Not surprisingly, the full time workers had a higher likelihood than the part time workers and the unemployed mothers of being able to afford the expenses. These women were also working in high status, well paid jobs, such as teaching and medicine, as well as having only one dependent child to care for. Being unemployed or working part time made no difference to being able to take a holiday, indicating that income earned from part time, low status jobs was insufficient and no different to living entirely on benefits.

Heavy debts

Debts on the community charge, housing fuel and other household expenses account for two-thirds of all debts in the UK. Lone mothers are known to be particularly vulnerable to debt and to multiple debt (Parker 1992, Graham 1993). Leeming et al's survey (1994) showed that fifteen months after separation, the majority of their sample were repaying debts, encompassing housing and fuel arrears. Most of the debts faced by those on low incomes are thus not through excessive consumerism, but rather because of week-to-week budgeting problems (Oppenheim 1993).

Forty-eight of the 90 mothers in this study said they had, at some point, incurred serious debts. For some lone mothers debt is a problem inherited from their previous relationship (Graham 1993), and they may be left to carry responsibility for arrears incurred before marriage breakdown (Parker 1992, Leeming et al 1994). This was illustrated by a Sikh respondent in this sample who said her present heavy debts were attributed to her former husband leaving her with all the mortgage arrears on her home. She was finding it hard to keep up repayments and look after four dependent children at the same time. None of the eight women who stayed with family or friends had faced heavy debts, suggesting that they may have had less financial responsibilities living in someone else's home.

Berthoud and Kempson have identified three "debt-inducing" factors, these being age, number of children and level of income. They found that any two of these factors brought a higher risk of debt. Lone parents, especially, had three times the number of difficulties as single people without children (Oppenheim 1993:80).

Analysis of the data for this research do indicate a correlation between risk of debt and number of dependent children in that the mothers with only one dependent child were less likely to have ever been in serious debt than those women with two, three or four children, and vice versa. This suggests that the respondents with fewer dependants would have reduced family expenses and be less inclined to borrow money than those with larger families. For example, a Sikh divorcee with three dependent children said she owed money for new carpets for her home, as well as for her parents' air tickets and other household expenses.

The mothers employed full time were the most likely group to avoid running into heavy debt, and they tended to be in highly paid posts such as management and psychiatry, and so could keep up with payments. In comparison, being unemployed or working part time in low paid jobs did not really make any difference to the mothers' replies. It would, therefore, appear that high income and small numbers of dependent children were significant factors in determining debts and arrears.

Housing

In 1974 the Finer Committee stated that "second only to financial difficulties...housing is the largest single problem of one parent families" (Rimmer and Rossiter 1983:59). Present housing policy, however, continues to be based on the notion of the nuclear household, where the head of household is still assumed to be the man, even if his wife is working (Morris and Winn 1993), and on the assumption that women and ethnic minorities should fit into existing structures and organisations which have been developed by and for white males (Balchin 1995). However, recent years have seen a change in family formation, with the proportion of families headed by a lone parent increasing from nearly 8 per cent to 22 per cent in 1993 (HMSO 1995:54). In comparison, the proportion of households containing a "traditional" family of a married or co-habiting couple with dependent children fell from 32 per cent in the early 1980's to 24 per cent in 1993 (OPCS 1993:5).

The separation of two partners almost inevitably involves a change in housing circumstances. In 1991 it was estimated that an extra 80,000 new homes were needed to keep up with the demand created by the current rate of divorce (Utting 1995:36). The upheaval and expense involved in finding alternative accommodation and moving into it can be a source of stress experienced by lone parents. The situation of lone mothers, in particular, is further compounded by the operation of the British housing system where all other tenure, apart from "traditional" family accommodation, is defined as "special need" housing (Austerberry and Watson 1986).

The third section of Chapter Four will focus on the housing situation of the 90 mothers in this study. It firstly examines the type of housing in which the women were residing, whether it was of satisfactory physical condition and if it contained the usual amenities. The section will conclude by looking at whether the sample had any future plans to improve their housing situation.

Type of housing

Housing is an area in which lone parent families are disadvantaged compared to two parent families. Lone parents in Britain are far more likely than other families to rent their homes from local authorities (57 per cent compared with 17 per cent), and less likely to be buying their homes with a mortgage (28 per cent compared with 70 per cent) (OPCS 1993:8-9). The proportion of lone parents in privately rented accommodation is very low - only seven per cent, compared with four per cent of other families (OPCS 1993:20).

The prime importance of council housing for mothers facing relationship breakdown is the fact that the public rented sector provides access to housing on need rather than on ability to pay (Morris and Winn 1993). Council homes are now increasingly female headed, with 40 per cent of council rented households being headed by a woman (Graham 1993:64). Asian women facing marriage breakdown tend to be in low status, low paid jobs, and therefore may face more difficulties in acquiring private sector housing, unaware of options available within the public sector, especially if English is their second language (Balchin 1995).

Table 4.7 looks at the distribution of housing type amongst the sample, showing the results for 87 and not 90 women. One newly separated respondent in her thirties explained that she was staying in temporary bed and breakfast accommodation, whilst of the two unmarried mothers, one was living in council housing and the other with her parents. The findings of the table correspond with those of the national picture which show that lone parents have a higher likelihood of living in council properties. Over half of the respondents in this study were residing in public sector rented properties, 41 of whom were in council housing. Just under a third of the mothers were owner occupiers, with much smaller numbers in privately rented accommodation. These results appear to echo those of Bradshaw and Millar (1991:89), who found that 57 per cent of their sample were local authority tenants whilst only 28 per cent owned their homes.

According to Table 4.7 the widows were the group most inclined to be owner occupiers, followed by the divorced; vice versa, the separated mothers were the most likely group to be living in rented accommodation, followed by the divorcees. This may be a reflection of the differing situations of the mothers. Widows are more likely than the other lone parent types to remain in their matrimonial homes (Chandler 1991) as well as to be able to maintain independent accommodation (Pascall 1986). The high proportion of lone parents who are public sector tenants is not just through relationship breakdown, but also because public sector tenants are more likely to divorce (Morris and Winn 1993). This would also partly help to explain why the widows are under-represented in local authority housing, compared with the other groups. On the other hand, separated mothers tend to be residing in more "insecure" housing, such as with family and friends, than divorcees, whose status and housing is more secure in the long term. The housing tenure in this study pertaining to the divorced and separated mothers differs somewhat to that observed by Bradshaw and Millar (1991), who found that the two groups were accommodated in very similar types of accommodation.

Table 4.7
Type of housing by type and age of mother in years

	Owner Occupied	Council Housing	Privately Rented	Housing Assoc.	Family/ Friends	Tot.
Divorced						39
20's	—	1	—	—	1	
30's	6	13	1	1	—	
40's/50's +	7	8	—	1	—	
Separated						33
20's	1	3	1	—	1	
30's	3	8	2	2	2	
40's/50's +	3	4	—	1	2	
Widowed						15
20's	1	—	—	—	—	
30's	3	—	—	—	1	
40's/50's +	4	3	2	1	—	
Total	**28**	**40**	**6**	**6**	**7**	**87**

Further analysis regarding housing "security" indicates that the widows were the most likely mothers to have been living at their present addresses for eleven years or more, the divorcees for between six and ten years and the separated group for only under a year, implying that length of residence is related to lone parent type and in turn to housing type.

Table 4.7 also examines whether age was a factor in determining type of accommodation, with the findings suggesting that the owner occupiers were more inclined to be in their forties and fifties. These mothers would have older and more non-dependent children, be better settled and thus be more able to pay for their homes. Women in council housing tended to be in their thirties and then in their twenties. Whilst age did not make much difference to those in privately rented and housing association accommodation, mothers staying with family or friends had a higher likelihood of being in their twenties. For these well less settled women with very young children, their accommodation was more likely to have been of a temporary nature whilst they looked for their own homes.

A relationship between housing type and income received was also indicated in the analysis. A report on the Family Expenditure Survey showed that owner occupiers with a mortgage have the highest average weekly gross income (£530), as well as the highest proportion of income from wages and salaries (CSO 1994-95:123). Similarly, in this study owner occupiers were more likely than the other groups to be acquiring an income through wages only or through a combination of wages and benefits, and less likely to be claiming benefits alone. Those women who could afford their own homes solely on their employment incomes tended to be working in professional jobs, and included a GP earning £30,000 and a psychiatrist £20,000 annually.

According to Graham, "council housing is increasingly becoming a residual sector for those who do not have the money to buy into owner occupation" (1993:57). A report on the Family Expenditure Survey has revealed that those renting unfurnished property from local authorities or from housing associations, had the highest proportion of income from social security benefits (CSO 1994-95:123). Likewise, the mothers in this research living in rented accommodation, the majority of whom were in council housing, were more likely than the other respondents to be unemployed and therefore be receiving benefits and maintenance or benefits only. They were far less inclined to be wage earners only. The one mother receiving income solely from work was a divorcee employed by the Department of Transport earning £13,000 yearly.

Attitudes towards physical condition of housing

It has been well documented in social policy literature over the years that lone parent families live in the worst physical housing conditions compared to other families (Walczak 1984, Austerberry and Watson 1986, Chandler 1991, Morris and Winn 1993). Table 4.8, however, shows that about three-quarters of this sample expressed satisfaction with the physical condition of their accommodation, although the likelihood of this differed according to tenure. The owner occupiers in this project were the most likely group to express satisfaction with the physical condition of their housing, followed by those mothers staying with family or friends. The English House Condition survey reveals that 30 per cent of private tenants and 28 per cent of local authority tenants are unhappy with the state of repair of their dwellings (HMSO 1993). Likewise, in this study of Asian lone mothers, the council house tenants were the most likely women to be dissatisfied with the physical condition of their properties, followed by those in privately rented and housing association accommodation. Home owners were the least disposed group to express disapproval.

Table 4.8
Attitudes towards the physical condition of accommodation by tenure

	Satisfactory	Unsatisfactory	Central heated Yes	No
Owner occupied	25	3	26	2
Council housing	29	12	30	11
Privately rented	4	2	6	—
Housing association	4	2	1	5
Family and friends	6	2	6	2
Bed and breakfast	1	—	1	—
Total	**69**	**21**	**70**	**20**

The main complaints made by the dissatisfied mothers in this research were damp, overcrowding and a lack of hygiene, and included a separated respondent living in council housing who disapproved of the state of uncleanliness: "It's not good. The carpet's very dirty, and downstairs is a mess. I've been to the homeless department two or three times but they don't want to help me. I'm still waiting to hear." A second tenant, an unemployed divorcee, said the bedrooms were in bad physical condition because the roof was leaking, causing damp and was thus a "risk to health."

Since very few households now lack the basic amenities such as a bath or shower and inside toilet, central heating is a better indicator of a household's standard of accommodation. Whilst the proportion of households in Britain with central heating has increased from 47 per cent in 1975 to 84 per cent in 1994-95 (CSO 1994-95:136), fewer lone parents have central heating (78 per cent) compared to other families (88 per cent) (OPCS 1993:20). In 1994-95 over 85 per cent of home owners and just under 80 per cent of local authority tenants had full or partial central heating. In the privately rented sector this falls to three-fifths in unfurnished and two-thirds in furnished accommodation (HMSO 1996:181). The figures from Table 4.8 show that the majority of the 90 mothers said their homes were centrally heated, and this was across almost all tenures. More importantly, the proportion was very similar to the national picture, with the likelihood being greatest for owner occupiers and those in the privately rented sector. This may partly be explained by their choosing to live in heated properties. The women most likely to be without central heating were those in housing association accommodation, followed by council housing tenants and then mothers staying with family or friends. Due to their low incomes, these women may have been forced to live in cheaper forms of housing where having no central heating may have saved them money.

Ownership of telephone, television and washing-machine

The presence of dependent children in a household tends to indicate that it is more likely to have certain consumer durable goods. One person households, like pensioners, are far less likely to have consumer durables than other household types, including lone parent families. National figures have shown that 97 per cent of lone parents have a colour television, 93 per cent a washing-machine and 83 per cent a telephone (HMSO 1996:119), amounting to a high proportion of the lone parent population. However, in this study it was found that only 73 of the mothers said they had a television, washing-machine and a telephone. Fifteen of the women had either one or two of the commodities, and only two had none, one of whom was currently in bed and breakfast accommodation.

The analysis indicates that the owner occupiers were the most likely group to own all three durables, followed by those in rented accommodation, amounting to 26 of the 28 home owners and 41 of the 54 mothers in rented properties. Some women in the latter housing type explained the importance of having a telephone, one of whom was a separated Christian respondent with a ten year old daughter: "I must keep a phone. I know I can't afford it, but I'm forced to keep it as I'm a single parent." Another was a Muslim divorcee with four young sons whose social worker had advised her to have a phone installed in case of any unforeseen problems. Those in rented properties were the most likely mothers to have either none or one of the commodities, perhaps because they could not afford the costs on low incomes or benefits. For example, a Hindu divorcee who owned a telephone and TV set explained that her telephone received incoming calls only. Those staying with family or friends were the most likely group to have access to two of the three durables, which may not be surprising since sharing "usually gives access to better amenities" (Balchin 1995:148).

More significantly, perhaps, a separate analysis of the data showed that all 24 employed mothers owned all three commodities, strongly suggesting that their earning power enabled them to buy and utilise them.

Future housing plans

The 90 mothers were asked whether they had any future plans regarding their housing situation, with 47 stating that they did not and 43 saying that they did have plans. As anticipated, the owner occupiers were the least likely group to want to change their housing situation. The most common response, and given by a quarter of the heads of households in the 1994-95 Survey of English Housing as to why they had moved in the last year, was because they wanted bigger or better accommodation (HMSO 1996:185). Likewise, 21, or just under a quarter of this sample of Asian mothers gave this response as to why they would prefer to move.

Lone parent families are more likely than other families to be in accommodation which is at or below the bedroom standard, an indicator of overcrowding (OPCS 1993:20). Twenty-six per cent of lone parent families live in overcrowded conditions compared with only nine per cent of two parent families (Morris and Winn 1993:131). In England, about a third of households living in rented accommodation below bedroom standard are dissatisfied (HMSO 1996:180). Research carried out by the Institute of Housing in 1992 showed a tendency to offer lone parent families smaller sized properties than to two parent families. Almost one-fifth of local authorities would require a lone mother and child to share a bedroom (Donnellan 1995:7), whereas larger three bedroomed properties are far more likely to be given to couples with one child than to a lone parent with one child (NCOPF 1995:8).

The council house tenants in this study were more likely than the other mothers to want to move into bigger or better accommodation or else buy their own homes. Seven of the women living in flats said they wanted to move into houses, preferably with gardens. One of these mothers, separated and with three young daughters, also cited overcrowding as a major problem: "I'm hoping now to change from a two bedroomed to a three bedroomed place. My older and middle daughters now want their own rooms." This was also reflected by Walczak's investigation (1984) in which the children of divorcees gave importance to having their own bedrooms for privacy and a place to bring friends. A smaller proportion of the council house tenants in this research wanted to buy their own homes, one being a divorcee with three children and full time receptionist who said it "would be an asset for the children."

Mothers in privately rented accommodation were more inclined to either want to buy their own homes or move into permanent council housing. One of the former was an unemployed Sikh respondent in her thirties who wished to buy her own home one day because "it's a sense of having your own property, and a sense of belonging." Women in housing association accommodation were more likely than the other mothers to either want permanent council housing or bigger and better properties. One was a 33 year old respondent whose present housing, although in good condition, was temporary. However, it has been documented that ethnic minority families have to wait longer than other families to be rehoused if they are not happy (Graham 1993, Mason 1995), leading the mother to make a complaint: "The council said it will be another two to three years. I can't do anything to the house, or settle in properly as I know I'll be moving."

According to Balchin (1995), the most popular solution to racial harassment in the social rented sector is to transfer the ethnic household rather than take legal action against the perpetrator. Another housing association tenant in this study, an employed divorcee with three children who cited racism as one of the main reasons for her having to move to a better area, spoke in some detail of her family's ordeal:

> I'm not happy in a flat with no garden. I've been put in a block with all elderly people. There's a lot of racism. Some of the old people are set in their ways...there had never been a Black person on the estate before. I then started getting threatening phone calls telling me to go back to where I came from, and that they didn't want us here. I'm not happy and am hopefully going to move.

Women staying with family or friends tended to either want to be rehoused in permanent council housing or else buy their own homes. One was an unmarried mother living at home for four years, who said she would welcome some extra support: "I now want to get my own council house and will have go to the Citizen's Advice Bureau, and get someone else to do the talking for me. You don't get anywhere on your own."

Physical health

The quality of health, and the freedom from medical problems can provide an important indicator of living standards, in addition to potentially affecting life chances. Recent literature has shown that low income households have a higher risk of experiencing poor health than other family types due to their more disadvantaged circumstances. Popay and Jones (1990), analysing General Household Survey data, found that lone parents generally felt themselves to be in poorer health than did parents in couples, with more lone mothers reporting poorer health than lone fathers.

The final section of the chapter on living standards will examine the physical state of health of the mothers. It will firstly focus on their own perceptions of health, before discussing the types of illnesses suffered and their possible connection with the sample's lone parent status.

The mothers' perceptions of their state of health

The mothers' own perceptions of their state of health in relation to lone parent type and age are presented in Table 4.9. The two unmarried mothers have been omitted, both of whom said they were in very good health. The overall findings show that one-third of the sample said they were in very good health, one-half were in average health and one-sixth were in poor health.

Table 4.9
Perceptions of state of health by type and age of mother in years

	Divorced	Separated	Widowed	Total
Very healthy				29
20's	1	4	—	
30's	9	6	2	
40's/50's +	4	1	2	
Average health				44
20's	1	2	1	
30's	11	8	1	
40's/50's +	6	9	5	
Poor health				15
20's	—	—	—	
30's	1	4	1	
40's/50's +	6	—	3	
Total	**39**	**34**	**15**	**88**

Concentrating on lone parent type, the results may indicate that the divorced followed by the separated mothers were the two most inclined groupings to feel they were in very good health. Those women in average health were more likely to be separated and then widowed. Likewise, widows followed by the divorcees were the most likely groups to perceive themselves as being in poor health.

The findings relating to the impaired health of the widows and divorcees correspond to the perceptions of Chandler (1991), who has stated that the trauma and grief experienced by widows erodes feelings of good health and makes them more susceptible to mental health problems and physical illness. Divorce, too, according to Chandler, undermines feelings of well-being and these women are more likely to experience health problems.

Table 4.9 goes on to suggest a correlation between age of respondent and her perception of health. Mothers in their twenties were more likely to be unmarried or separated and in very good health. Those in their thirties were more likely to either be divorced or separated and in very good or average health. Likewise, women in their forties and fifties tended to be widows rather than divorcees or separated, and in poor followed by average health.

The findings of this study partly support those observed by McKay and Marsh's research (1994:43). Although they found a larger proportion of lone parents to be in very good health (58 per cent) and a smaller proportion in average health (27 per cent), the percentage of those in poor health was similar to that of this study (14 per cent). In addition, the differences in health perceptions between this and McKay and Marsh's study may have been more marked because the 1994 study contained more unmarried mothers as well as lone fathers, both of whom tended to be in generally good health.

According to Mason (1995), levels of health can be linked with housing status. A survey of low income households carried out by Hunt et al in 1988, pointed to a gradient of ill health, with the proportion of mothers reporting a range of symptoms, including coughs, blocked noses, high blood pressure and nausea, increasing in line with the levels of damp and mould in the house (Graham 1993:69).

This study has also implied a relationship between levels of health and physical condition of housing. As Table 4.8 has suggested, the owner occupiers and those staying with family or friends were the most likely groups to be satisfied with the physical condition of their housing, and they were more inclined to be in average and very good health respectively. Vice versa, the women in rented properties, being the most likely mothers to be dissatisfied with their housing condition, were the most likely group to be in poor health.

One may expect the perceptions of health to improve in line with the length of lone parenthood as the mothers become more settled in their single status. Further analysis, however, implies that there is no correlation between the two, since the very healthy mothers were more likely than the other groups to have only been lone parents for between one and six years. Women in average health tended to have experienced lone motherhood for under a year, and those in poor health for eleven years or more. It would appear that age rather than length of lone parenthood determined the respondents' replies, because the lone mothers of the longest duration were more likely to be older, thus accounting for their poorer health, whilst the lone parents of a shorter period were in better health due to their younger age.

Growing evidence has emerged regarding the clear links between ill health and unemployment (Oppenheim 1993, Mason 1995). However, for the respondents in this project, being actively employed in the labour market was not a factor in influencing perceptions of health, since one in six of both the employed and unemployed women felt that their health was poor, with only a slightly higher proportion of mothers who were in good health having jobs.

Types of physical illnesses suffered by the mothers

Fifty-three of the 90 mothers said they suffered from at least one physical illness. The most common complaints were as follows - arthritis (fifteen mothers), asthma (twelve mothers), back problems/slipped disc (twelve mothers), migraine (six mothers), anaemia (four mothers), heart problems (four mothers), high blood pressure (four mothers) and pre-menstrual tension (three mothers). Other less common responses were varicose veins, ulcers, hernias, sinus and kidney problems. Thirty-seven of the 90 respondents stated that they did not suffer from any physical illnesses. These mothers tended to be younger, with an average age of 34.5 years, and to perceive themselves to be in very good health.

Ten of the women who said they were of average health did not suffer from any maladies. The median age of those in average health who did endure illnesses was 38 years, with the most common conditions being arthritis, asthma and back problems. One of these was a separated Muslim mother who said her back and hernia problems were a direct result of looking after her three children, and especially through lifting her handicapped son who needed physiotherapy at hospital. Another separated respondent explained how her spinal problem had been caused by the cruelty of her husband's family:

> I've got my back problem from working over sixty hours a week at my in-laws' rest home. They said I was lying about my back, and didn't listen. At the time I couldn't stand, sit or lie down. Because of my situation I tried to overdose. Luckily one of my sons stopped me.

Not unexpectedly, all fifteen mothers who said they were in poor health also suffered from physical illnesses, many of which were of a serious nature. The average age of these women was 41.5 years, with the more common illnesses endured being arthritis, asthma and heart problems. One of these who had arthritis was a 41 year old widow who needed to have weekly injections at hospital to ease the pain. The less common complaints made by these women included epilepsy, ulcers and sickle cell disease. In their research, McKay and Marsh (1994:43) found that a small proportion of their sample (fifteen per cent) said they suffered from long-standing illnesses, with the widows and divorcees, older on average, being slightly more likely than the separated mothers to report this. It would appear that the lone mothers in this study endured more illnesses than the respondents in McKay and Marsh's survey, although it was not directly asked of the Asian group as to the length of time they had been suffering.

Thirty-six of the 53 mothers who complained about physical illnesses also said they were connected to their lone parent status, with 27 of these 36 women claiming that all their illnesses developed after their marriages had ended. One was in her forties and suffering from poor health and said her asthma, arthritis and heart problems were triggered off following her divorce ten years previously. A second respondent in her forties explained that her anaemia and arthritis began after the death of her husband six years ago when "everything became too much to handle."

Seven of the 36 women claimed that all their illnesses endured whilst they were married increased following lone parenthood. For example, one respondent in her thirties said that her asthma became more severe after her divorce, whilst another in her forties remarked that the diabetes she already suffered from flared up so badly following the stress of her separation a year ago, that her consultant was forced to prescribe her with insulin. The remaining 2 of the 36 women said they had suffered from some of their conditions prior to experiencing lone parenthood, with others developing afterwards. Seventeen of the 53 mothers who currently suffered from at least one physical illness said that their maladies were not connected to their lone parent status, but were developed through other causes. For some of these respondents, their illnesses such as sickle cell disease, were of a hereditary nature.

Conclusion

The Finer Committee's claim of lone parents having "exceptionally low standards of living" can be applied to the Asian lone mothers in this study (HMSO 1974:6). Although only 90 women were interviewed, many parallels can be drawn with the living conditions of lone parents on a national level.

Chapter Four has painted the picture of living standards of Asian lone mothers in London, and corresponds largely with other recent studies undertaken. The majority of this sample were unemployed and living solely on benefits, with those who were employed tending to work in low paid, low status jobs with no opportunities for promotion. These findings were also observed in research referred to throughout this chapter. Again echoing other investigations, the women in this survey were also more likely to be living in rented rather than in owned accommodation, with many women expressing dissatisfaction with their housing. Many Asian lone mothers continued to suffer from a range of physical illnesses, the incidence of some of which followed family breakdown. The chapter also shows that many of the disadvantages suffered by the women often reinforced each other.

5 The Mothers' Attitudes Towards Marriage, the Family and the Position of Women

As Chapter Two has shown, Asian culture places much more value and emphasis than does British culture on marriage and the family, with women playing a more subordinate role. This chapter will explore the attitudes of the 90 mothers in this study regarding these three areas, since their responses may have important implications for their status as lone parents living in London. Much of the respondents' narrative will overlap and be repeated across the three sections, and this is perhaps unavoidable, given that the issues of marriage, the family and the position of women are intertwined in many ways. Additionally, many of the mothers will have stereotyped and misconceived perceptions of British culture, which may be inevitable between any two different ethnic groups.

The mothers' attitudes towards marriage

According to Boyden (1993), in many non-western countries, marriage is virtually a certainty. In India, if a woman is not married, it is more often because she has missed her chance, rather than due to a deliberate desire to remain a spinster or a liberated, independent female (Khanna and Varghese 1978). Likewise, in Islamic culture, there remain very few lifelong niches for a single woman, and as far as society is concerned, she is always a future wife until she is clearly too old to be marriageable (Minai 1981).

Table 5.1 examines whether the 90 mothers felt that there were differences in marriage values between British and Asian cultures. Not unexpectedly the results show that over two-thirds of the sample believed that there were disparities, and interestingly there were almost as many mothers preferring the western rather than the Asian approach to marriage. Only a sixth of the respondents claimed that there were no differences between the two cultures.

Looking at the findings in relation to the three most popular responses, the data suggests that the mothers from India were the most likely group to reply that Asian marriage values were superior to British ones. A 27 year old separated respondent who preferred the Asian approach spoke of the lack of commitment within a western marriage: "The English choose their own partners but I don't approve because I'm Indian, and Indians have more serious relationships." A second mother from India, aged 40 and working for the Department of Transport claimed that the British did not try hard enough to keep their marriages together: "There are English people who don't give marriage time. One minute they don't get on, they part. Indian women tolerate marriage and expect to put up with men whether they like it or not."

Table 5.1
Whether mothers felt Asian and British values regarding marriage were different and which values were superior by country of origin

	India	Pak.	E.Afr.	Bang.	Other	Total
I *Asian and British values diff.*						69
Asian values better	13	2	7	4	3	29
Western values better	9	6	7	2	1	25
No opinion	7	4	4	—	—	15
II *Both values the same*	6	4	5	—	2	17
III *Don't know*	2	1	1	—	—	4
Total	**37**	**17**	**24**	**6**	**6**	**90**

According to Table 5.1, the women who originated from Pakistan were more inclined than the other groups to say that they approved of western rather than Asian marriage values. This may have been because many of the Muslim mothers were dissatisfied with the Islamic marriage laws "which allow a man to repudiate his wife with relative ease" (Minai 1981:189). The irrevocable pronouncement of divorce dissolves the marriage on its utterance (Ahuja 1994), and the husband does not even have to tell his wife about it (Minces 1982). This was the explanation given by a separated respondent with three daughters from Pakistan, whose former partner had left her for another woman:

I like the English law on marriage a lot. It supports you more, and your children too. The Pakistani law on marriage is bad. In Pakistan, a husband can give you a divorce any time with no notice. A man can get remarried three or four times without a divorce. In English law, divorce is not made easy. You can have just one wife, and need to divorce first and remarry if you want to. The wife in Pakistan doesn't even know her husband has remarried; her friends and relatives tell her of it before her own husband does.

Asian marriages are arranged by families within a socio-religious conception of a "right" marriage, often with very little regard to the couple's prior ideas and personal wishes (Reynolds and Tanner 1995), and was the reason why a 35 year old mother from Pakistan favoured western marriage values:

I don't believe in arranged marriages any more in our society because of what I went through. The woman should know the person and go out and get to know him first. I was forced into my marriage. It's a matter of a whole life and not just a few days. I got to know the bad things when it was too late. It's better to know good and bad before your marriage.

By comparison, the respondents from East Africa were the most likely group to believe that there were no differences between British and Asian marriage values today. This could be attributed to their having been brought up in more multi-cultural societies, which may have given them a more liberal outlook before settling in Britain. A more westernised view was held by a separated mother from Kenya, who said:

There are older English people who talk like our Asian people and say that they never did this or that in their day. This new generation of English and Asians have different values to the older generation. The Asians today are more open-minded and have come out of their shells in many ways. The English have always been so. Even my father sees changes. About seven years ago he would have been different and wouldn't want to know my partner if we were just living together without being married.

The table goes on to imply that the women from Bangladesh were more inclined to prefer the Asian marriage system , whilst those who originated from the smaller countries to either favour the Asian approach or else believe that both British and Asian values were the same.

Table 5.2 tabulates the findings for marriage values in relation to the age of the mother, and may indicate that the latter did make a difference to their perceptions. Those in their twenties had a higher likelihood than the other women of believing that both British and Asian marriage values were similar, suggesting that the youngest respondents would be less interested in cultural traditions. This was pointed out by a 25 year old divorcee: "Marriage depends on people and how they keep it. It's up to people involved and not the religion or culture, because they never teach bad things." Mothers in their thirties were more likely than the other groupings to hold a preference for British marriage values, perhaps because the younger generation are now "widely exposed to western notions of love and marriage" and place greater emphasis on sharing common interests (Gardner and Shukur 1994:157).

Table 5.2
Whether mothers felt Asian and British values regarding marriage were different and which values were superior by age of mother in years

	20's	30's	40's/50's +	Total
I *Asian and British values diff.*				**69**
Asian values better	3	13	13	29
Western values better	—	16	9	25
No opinion	2	8	5	15
II *Both values the same*	6	5	6	**17**
III *Don't know*	—	1	3	**4**
Total	**11**	**43**	**36**	**90**

There has always been a strong economic element with a "sense of competition" involved in an Asian marriage as to which family can give more dowry (Devandra 1985:111), provoking the disapproval of a separated Sikh respondent in her thirties:

We maintain the old way of getting married without realising it is no longer accepted by the incoming generation. For example, the dowry system. English people get married for love. It's different and better to be married for the right reasons. For us, it's an economical consideration as to who gives more dowry.

In many instances in an Asian marriage it is the wife who has to maintain the stability and harmony through tolerance, willingness to adjust, compromise and sacrifice (Dhagamwar 1987), which was not acceptable to two more of the women in their thirties. The first spoke in favour of the equality she saw within a western marriage:

> In an English marriage you share things. It's give and take. There's commitment on both sides. In Asian marriages the man has the say all the time. The wife is expected to listen to him all the time.

The second respondent, a Hindu aged 37, blamed the callous behaviour of many Asian husbands:

> Indian men treat their wives like servants and keep them under their thumbs. They don't understand the meaning of marriage.

Table 5.2 suggests that compared to the younger mothers in their twenties and thirties who appeared more liberally-minded, the older women were more inclined to hold more traditional attitudes. This can be seen by the respondents in their forties and fifties being more likely than their younger counterparts to approve of the Asian rather than the western marriage ideology. This finding is somewhat predictable given their upbringing in their countries of origin at a time when very conservative values were accepted as the norm.

A 56 year old divorced doctor argued that the lack of compromise within British marriages led to a higher incidence of marital breakdown:

> For Asians, marriage is a very important part of life. It should be taken seriously and you should try to make the marriage work. Well, I did try, and tried to go along with what my husband wanted, to keep the peace and stability in the marriage. For the English, it's a far more casual approach. They're not so family oriented. That's why they have so many divorces.

Some of the older women defended the arranged marriage system, the whole rationale of which is that the boy and girl are too immature to make the necessary judgement themselves (Sharma 1980). Adults argue that marriages are better arranged by cool-headed parents than by an infatuated couple (Jeffrey 1976). This was the sentiment expressed by a divorced mother aged 47 in this study, who said:

I respect Asian values. The parents are more experienced in arranging marriages for their children. The English choose their own partners but they're too young and can't choose someone suitable.

Fruzzetti claims that "a love marriage is a one-sided affair as it unites two people but separates them from their caste brothers and close relatives" (1990:16), with the result that if it fails, one may lose the love and support of the family (Wilson 1978). This particular disadvantage of having a love marriage was illustrated by a separated respondent in her forties, who spoke from experience:

The English think arranged marriages are forced, sort of alien. For Indians it's just a way of life. It'll always be like it. I'm for it. At least your parents come to your aid if your marriage breaks down. I had a love marriage to a South Indian man and couldn't fall back on anyone when my marriage broke down.

According to Khanna and Varghese (1978), better educated Asian girls tend to become more selective and conform less easily to traditional marriage patterns, preferring to marry only if they approve of a person. Even if their parents have already made a selection, they would rather wait and marry someone they liked than marry for the sake of marrying. However, a separate analysis of the findings suggests that there is no link between the level of education received and the attitudes of the respondents towards marriage in this study. Mothers who never attended school and those who were educated up to nineteen were the two most probable groups to favour western marriage values, whilst those who left school at sixteen and women who went to college were the most likely groups to claim that both British and Asian marriage values were similar. Despite receiving a university education, these mothers, however, were the most inclined to feel that Asian marriage values were superior to western ones. They also tended to be in their forties and over, reinforcing the relationship between age and attitudes towards marriage as seen in Table 5.2.

The mothers' attitudes towards losing the family honour

The significance of the family unit in Asian culture has been well documented in literature over the years (Anwar 1979, Caplan 1985, Ahuja 1994). According to Kalra, "the family is the most basic and powerful institution in the Indian way of life" (1980:40), whilst Joly argues that "the family as an institution is...the most solid tenet of Pakistani beliefs about a desirable form of existence" (1995:166). In Asian culture, family well-being and success are not seen to be advanced by the concentration of the development of personal characteristics, abilities and ambitions of individual members (Stopes-Roe and Cochrane 1990). Upholding the"izzat," the Asian equivalent of family honour is, therefore, an integral part of the Asian culture.

Table 5.3 focuses on whether the 90 respondents felt that marriage breakdown meant a loss of family honour and whether this was a greater problem for Asian rather than British lone mothers. The data appears to reconfirm the literature quoted above, in that for over two-thirds of the sample, loss of family honour was a problem following marital disruption and that this posed more of a dilemma for Asian lone mothers than it did for their British counterparts. More significantly, none of the 90 women replied that British lone mothers faced additional difficulties with loss of honour through marriage breakdown, and only three respondents claimed that loss of family prestige was not an issue for either groups of mothers.

Table 5.3
Whether the mothers felt that marriage breakdown meant a loss of family honour and whether this was a greater problem for Asian than for British lone mothers by religion

	Hindu	Muslim	Sikh	Chri.	Jain	Tot.
Yes, greater problem for Asians	14	27	19	4	3	67
No, no problems for either group	2	—	—	—	1	3
Depends on family involved	3	—	5	—	—	8
Don't know/unsure	6	1	3	2	—	12
Total	**25**	**28**	**27**	**6**	**4**	**90**

Many of the mothers gave explanations for their responses, one being a Sikh divorcee who spoke of how western culture placed far less value on family priorities:

The English have their culture but it's not as deeply set. They don't have such closely knit families, and aren't bound by old fashioned myths and honour. You're judged as an individual.

Another separated respondent from India expressed fears for her eighteen year old daughter's future arranged marriage prospects because of her own status as a lone mother:

It is a problem for Asian single parents, especially for marriage later. People could think my daughter is bad as she has no father. It's difficult to get a girl married as the boy's family would want to know about my family background. For the English, there's no problem as they let their girls become independent at sixteen. They can marry who they like.

According to Jeffrey, Asian:

kin sometimes fail to live up to the expectations held of them and their relatives may try to bring them back in line. If all else fails, ostracism may be tried, which both puts pressure on the deviant to conform and also protects the izzat of his relatives (1976:125).

The greater risk of family rejection for an Asian lone mother as compared to her British counterpart was illustrated by a separated respondent of eighteen years, who said:

There's definitely a difference. Asian families do think you've brought shame, especially at the beginning. Many relatives and in-laws don't want to know you, like you are an outcast. English lone parents get more help from their families. They don't mind if you are a single parent. There's no shame. They don't disown you and are more understanding.

Table 5.3 also suggests another dimension to the notion of family honour, with all but one of the 28 Muslim women replying that this was not only a problem caused by marriage breakdown, but also that it affected the Asian lone mother more adversely than her British counterpart. The Muslim respondents in this sample were also far more likely than either the Hindu or the Sikh mothers to give this answer, and may partly be explained by their greater tendency to marry within the kin group, thus the tightness of the family unit, and the greater control over its members' actions. As culture intertwines with religion, the whole family honour can be thrown into disrepute by a daughter's behaviour (Joly 1995).

A number of the Muslim respondents explained how being an Asian lone mother affected other family members. One of these was a divorcee in her thirties who said that many parents tried to hide the status of their daughter if she was no longer married: "Pakistani parents feel ashamed to mix with other relatives if their daughter is divorced. Sometimes they don't tell people as they wouldn't be looked upon with respect." An Asian lone mother's reputation being passed on to her daughter was the reason given by a second respondent: "People will think that because her mother's divorced, she too will divorce."

In contrast to the western system, an Asian marriage is not expected to be a primary emotional investment; often an individual's ties with parents, siblings and children are more important (Shaw 1988). A Muslim mother in her thirties and separated for only seven months said that her parents wanted her to put their interests before her own through pressurising her to reconcile with the partner:

> My own family are telling me that I should sacrifice my life for the family honour and get back with my husband. The English don't have this problem to my knowledge. Their thoughts are, if you don't get on, what's the point of living together?

Table 5.3 implies that the Hindu women were the least likely group to believe that Asian lone mothers had more problems with losing the family honour, with just under a quarter of them replying that they were unsure or else did not know. Wilson explains that this may be because the notion of izzat does not have the same impact for Hindus as it does for Muslims:

> Despite Hindu and Muslim ways of life in the Indian sub-continent, there is no exact analogy for izzat among the Hindus. There is reputation, one's good name and so on, but these are extensions or corollaries of izzat and rather than the thing itself (1978:42).

Additional analysis of the data also implies that the level of education received by the sample did influence their attitudes towards loss of family honour. This can be seen by the higher likelihood of women who never attended school and those who left at sixteen of believing that loss of honour through marriage breakdown posed greater difficulties for Asian rather than British lone mothers. This may be due to their having more conservative opinions through their limited education, as reflected in the words of a separated respondent who was only schooled until the age of sixteen: "The family is an important part of the Asian culture. You have to think of them first and how anything bad will affect their standing in the community. That's why I feel so bad." Mothers who were educated over the age of sixteen did appear to hold more open-minded views regarding the family. Whilst those taught up to sixth form level were more likely than the other groups to say that disgracing the family was not a problem, college and university educated women had a higher tendency than the other groups of replying that the extent of shame depended on the family involved. For example, a Sikh doctor in her fifties explained how her relatives had taken a broad-minded approach to her marriage dissolving:

> It can be a problem if you do not have a good, understanding family who will support you, like my family did. These families are not bothered about their own honour but are more concerned about you and how you will cope.

The mothers' attitudes towards the position of women

The position of women in India has changed considerably since the 1950's, where both structural and cultural changes have provided equality of opportunities to women in education, employment and political participation. Additionally, women have been encouraged to develop their own organisations which take a keen interest in their problems (Ahuja 1994). However, despite the increasing incidence of higher education amongst both males and females and rapidly increasing urbanisation and industralisation changing the family structure and social values (Kalra 1980), the general attitude towards women is not greatly changed (Pothen 1987).

Table 5.4 examines whether the respondents felt that there were differences between Asian and British values regarding the independence of women, and shows, as anticipated, that the vast majority of the sample held the opinion that Asian women were less independent than their British counterparts. Significantly, none of the mothers replied that Asian women had greater independence. These results echo those of other studies over the years (Jeffrey 1976, Wilson 1978, Stopes-Roe and Cochrane 1990, Joly 1995), which have produced similar findings regarding the position of Asian women.

Table 5.4
Whether mothers felt there were differences between Asian and British women regarding the independence of women by level of education of mothers

	None	Up to 16	Up to 19	Coll.	Univ.	Total
Asian women less independent	2	30	18	7	15	72
Asian women same independence	1	4	2	3	4	14
Depends on circumstances	—	2	1	—	1	4
Total	3	36	21	10	20	90

Many of the sample gave explanations as to why they thought Asian women had less independence than British women. Asian men's obligation to control women and their power throughout all stages of their lives (Wadley 1988) was the reason given by a respondent from Kenya for the dependent state of women:

Indian women are generally not very independent because if they are not married, their parents control their lives. When they are married their husbands control their lives so they have no choices. English women are independent and more in control.

Whereas the popular image of marriage in the west is that a husband and wife set up home together, an Asian bride very often moves into the home of the husband's family, where the older, traditional women often implement patriarchal values by controlling younger women and enforcing qualities of docility, obedience and submission (Desai and Krishnaraj 1987). This form of oppression of the Indian woman was illustrated by the response of a separated mother with a three year old daughter:

Indian women will never have independence as long as they are living with their in-laws and are fed by dowries. They will never grow up as they will have no contact with the outside world. Their mothers-in-law will never let the wives do what they want, only to obey and serve them. English women love independence, have it and can cope with it. They don't need their parents. They have grown up and are not controlled by other people.

According to Chowdhury, "if a woman is seen to be assertive it is the husband who is declared to be weak," with any woman even slightly voicing an opinion rather than meekly accepting male orders, inviting ridicule and denigration. Thus, culturally valued authority continues to reside with the man (1994:277). Similarly, a separated Sikh mother in her thirties from India pointed to the lack of confidence that contributed to an Asian woman's subordination:

> Independence doesn't exist in our culture as far as women are concerned. That word is not relevant at all. They are supposed to do as they are told. English women have full independence. The women I've met are in full control of their lives. Our women are inarticulate as they are not allowed to be an individual. Others make statements on their behalf, especially men. They have no chance to speak for themselves.

Looking more closely at the data in Table 5.4, there appears to be a partial relationship between the mothers' attitudes towards the position of women and the level of education they received. On the one hand, there is no correlation since those who never attended school were more likely than the other respondents to believe that Asian women were as liberated as their British counterparts and the least likely group to say that Asian women were less independent. However, when the uneducated group are omitted from the analysis, a much clearer correlation emerges, which shall be discussed below.

Of the mothers who attended school, those who left at sixteen and those who left at nineteen had the highest likelihood of holding the opinion that Asian women were less independent than western women. This was perhaps because, having left the education system at an earlier age, they had less broad-minded attitudes towards the position of women generally. For example, an unmarried mother who was taught until the sixth form stage spoke of how even the higher level of education received by Asian women today made no difference to their liberation:

> An Indian woman's place is still at home looking after the children. Very few Indian women are career-minded in comparison to English girls, even if they have been well educated. Once they have finished school, English girls can also leave home without their parents refusing. This is not on for Indian girls, so English girls have more opportunity to be independent.

A 40 year old widow who left school at sixteen explained how the Asian woman's subjection included her having no say in important issues that affected her personally: "There is certainly an upper hand to make decisions for the life of a woman in the Asian community. The woman always follows the man to avoid any conflict."

Table 5.4 goes on to imply that of the mothers who had received an education, those who attended college and university were the most likely groups to believe that Asian women had as much autonomy as their British counterparts. These respondents would probably have regarded their higher level of learning as an expression of self-independence, since "with the advent of higher education, Asian women have started realising the advantages in the new system and are making efforts to achieve it" (Pothen 1987:140). The opportunities in education now open to Asian women to give them increasing levels of freedom was reflected in the words of a separated respondent in her thirties who attended college: "Everyone is educated now. There are not many uneducated Indian women now, even from overseas." She went on to add they were also now participating more in the labour market: "Most Indian women do work, even if they are in low paid jobs."

Further investigation of the findings suggest that the Muslim and Hindu respondents were the most inclined mothers in the sample to claim that Asian women were less liberated than their British counterparts. This can probably be attributed to these particular respondents belonging to the two oldest and most deeply rooted of the major Asian religions. One of these was a separated mother of two young sons, who explained that whilst British women were allowed to go out and socialise, Muslim women, in particular, were expected to be more based in the home:

> English women go out to nightclubs, drink and get out and about. We can't stay out later than five or six. It's our Islamic culture. I wanted to go out sometimes on my birthday. My husband told me no. Before I was married, my parents didn't let me out either.

A second Muslim respondent, aged 60, went on to speak in favour of Asian women playing a more subservient role. She explained:

> They have respect for their husbands. They listen to them. If the men don't want their wives to work, they won't. English women are more liberated and probably too much. They can do anything they want and don't listen to their husbands.

A Hindu widow in her forties from Kenya argued that Asian culture was not seen to be equated with a woman's emancipation: "Being a male dominated society, people say an independent woman is out of hand. Men feel they are losing their power." According to Khanna and Varghese, "the Indian girl is tutored to play her role as wife and mother from a very young age" (1978:12), and this was the reason given by a separated Hindu mother as to why an Asian woman knew what was expected of her:

> English girls do what they like at sixteen. Their parents don't mind. They go out and have boyfriends. Indian girls learn from their parents how to behave from childhood. They learn respect. They are dependent on their family, will have an arranged marriage and take care of their homes and husbands.

The analysis goes on to indicate that the Sikh and Jain women were the most likely groups to hold the view that Asian and British females had equal independence. This may partially be due to their being affiliated to the younger and less rigid of the Asian religions, enabling them to have more liberated values. According to Kalra, "Sikhs pride themselves on their relatively progressive attitudes to the position of women in society" (1980:42), and this was confirmed by a Sikh divorcee in this study: "Everyone's changed. Indian women are copying the English now and are just as independent."

Table 5.5 looks at whether being a member of a social organisation or being employed made any difference to the sample's attitudes towards the position of women. It appeared that club membership was not a factor in the mothers' attitudes, since those who belonged to an organisation were only very marginally more likely than the non-members to say that Asian women were as liberated as the British. Vice versa, non-members were only slightly more likely than the members to feel that British women had greater independence.

Moving on to employment, the data suggests a relationship, since mothers who had a job were more inclined than the unemployed group to argue that Asian women had now achieved autonomy to the same extent as their British counterparts. This was probably because the mothers who worked were earning their own incomes, and thus felt independent themselves. A 42 year old Sikh factory worker explained how being self-supportive had nothing to do with culture: "Both English and Asian women are as independent as each other. They both need financial sufficiency to be independent. The key is money," whilst a divorced receptionist said that Asian women had parity with British women in expressing their opinions: "Asian women have equality to English women. They can fight for their rights in Britain, are educated and are standing on their own two feet."

Table 5.5
Whether mothers felt there were differences between Asian and British women regarding the independence of women by whether member of social organisation and whether employed

	Employed	Unemployed	Total
Asian women less independent			72
Member of organisation	9	35	44
Not a member	9	19	28
Asian women same independence			14
Member of organisation	2	7	9
Not a member	3	2	5
Depends on circumstances			4
Member of organisation	—	3	3
Not a member	1	—	1
Total	**24**	**66**	**90**

In comparison, the unemployed mothers had a higher likelihood than the working group of believing that Asian women were less liberated than their British counterparts and this may be because of their more traditional outlooks, since they did not have jobs. One was an unemployed Sikh respondent in her thirties with three sons who pointed out how one's duty in marriage, whatever the circumstances, meant that any independence for an Asian woman was lost: "No one wants to give independence to women in our culture. They think once you are married it's your job to listen to your in-laws and husband, even if your husband is treating you badly." A separated Muslim mother with three daughters explained how Asian men did not trust their wives if they worked or wanted an education and spoke from her own experience:

It's a very narrow-minded, uneducated view that the woman should stay at home. The men feel that if the wives work, they'll be independent and go out with other men, so they don't allow them to work. They're not even allowed to go out to study. The women must finish their studies before marriage. I wanted to study after marriage but my husband didn't like it. He didn't allow me to work either.

This view, especially held by Muslim men, is confirmed by Anwar (1979), who has argued that the Islamic religion does not approve of wives and daughters working. This is because it is believed that Muslim women may learn too much about liberty and other permissive ideas in western society, which would threaten men's authority over them.

Conclusion

In Chapter Five, the responses of the 90 mothers have echoed the findings of the literature which claim that British culture differs from Asian culture regarding marriage, the family and the position of women. ,,hilst British culture promotes individualism, a right to autonomy and personal responsibility, the male dominated Asian literature prescribes control and subordination of their women, with "limited scope for individual inclinations and initiatives" within the family (Shaw 1988:74). Thus, the oppressively patriarchal Asian culture pre-supposes that "girls and women have no sphere of their own, no independent livelihood and activity, no area of family and community responsibility and dominance, no living space apart from that of men" (Kakar 1988:49).

These observations also appeared to be confirmed by the majority of this sample and through their replies one may presume that the mothers would therefore disown lone parenthood as an acceptable status within their culture. It is primarily with this issue that the next chapter will concern itself.

6 The Mothers' Attitudes Towards Marriage Breakdown and Lone Parenthood

Chapter Two has shown that Hindu, Muslim and Sikh cultures are very different to the British culture regarding the issues of marriage, the family and the status of women, and this has been reconfirmed through the responses of the Asian mothers in Chapter Five. British culture is more accepting of lone parenthood in its various forms, paralleled with the existence of over one million of such households in this country, numbers of which are rising (Crow and Hardey 1992). Between 1991 and the year 2025, the official projections of the UK population have shown that up to 40 per cent of new marriages will end in divorce (Kiernan and Wicks 1990:43). In contrast, Asian literature points to the importance of the traditional family, so it may follow that it would disown lone parenthood as an acceptable status. It is with this issue that Chapter Six will now concentrate, by focusing on the mothers' attitudes towards marriage breakdown and lone parenthood within the context of relevant existing Asian literature.

The chapter will firstly look at the sample's attitudes towards marital dissolution prior to and following breakdown, before going on to examine whether the mothers felt that people in general looked down on lone parent families compared with the traditional two parent family. The remainder of the chapter will be devoted to exploring themes specifically related to Asian culture, which may have significant implications for the 90 respondents' experiences of lone parenthood in London. These topics are whether or not lone parenthood is accepted by the Asian community, if loss of marital status created a problem for the women, and whether or not shame and betrayal of culture were factors in shaping the mothers' perceptions of themselves. Inevitably some of the areas discussed will overlap due to their being related issues. It must also be stressed again that many of the respondents had preconceived ideas about some aspects of British culture, which is inevitable, given the separateness of the two cultures.

The mothers' own attitudes towards marriage breakdown and lone parenthood

Hinduism has traditionally considered marriage as sacrosanct and therefore indissoluble and until the mid 1950's Hindu law did not permit divorce (Ahuja 1994). However, the Hindu Marriage Act 1955, amended in 1976 and 1981, provides for judicial separation and divorce by mutual consent. It is only when two years have elapsed since the date of marriage that a petition for divorce may be filed (Ahuja 1994:177). Legally Hindu women now have the same rights as Hindu men in matters of marriage, divorce and maintenance (Siganporia 1993).

In comparison, the Koran considers marriage as a civil contract, and therefore divorce among Muslims is easier for husbands to obtain and is more frequent than generally thought (Hiro 1991). Since no justification for divorcing a wife is demanded by the Koran, the husband can do so without any reason other than his own whim (Reynolds and Tanner 1995). The Koran, however, does regard divorce as a last resort and strongly recommends reconciliation and forgiveness. If this is not possible, a divorce can be resorted to, providing certain other conditions are observed (Fadhlalla Haeri 1993).

Estimation of lone parent families is a difficult task in India as in many other developing countries where the census does not report data on heads of household by sex, marital status, age and economic activity. It thus becomes problematic to estimate the number of families headed by males and those by females, and whether they are widows, widowers, divorced or never married. This may be due to defining heads of households in cultural terms, since in most patriarchal societies, the oldest male is considered the head of the house, irrespective of his economic function and age in comparison to the oldest women in the house (Bharat 1986). Widows, divorced and single women thus tend to become absorbed into extended family households (Boyden 1993), although it may be they who are earning and supporting the family. Hence, it is very difficult to identify lone parent families and ascertain their incidence, and more so because a majority of these are women headed (Bharat 1986:57).

With these difficulties in mind, the literature points to a low incidence of marriage breakdown in India and Pakistan. It is generally known that divorce is rare in Pakistan, and it has been especially difficult to obtain any figures or studies from this country. Although "there is a dearth of research in India" (Bharat 1986:55), it has nevertheless proved much easier to obtain some data and literature. The 1981 Census has indicated that there were 25.9 million widows, divorced and separated families in India, making up 8.5 per cent of the total female population. In contrast, there were only 8.4 million widowers, divorced and separated men, or 2.7 per cent of the total male population (Sinha 1992:95). It is significant to note, however, that in India in over 80 per cent of cases, death of a spouse is the major cause of lone parenthood (Bharat 1988:227). This shows that the number of divorced persons in India is relatively low (Pothen 1987, Ahuja 1994).

The mothers' attitudes towards lone parenthood before marriage breakdown

Table 6.1 explores the mothers' attitudes towards lone parenthood prior to marriage dissolution or the birth of the first child for the unmarried mothers. Not surprisingly, perhaps, the data shows that almost two-thirds of the sample said that they held no specific views about lone parenthood before their own marriages failed and the mothers who originated from Pakistan and then from India were the two most likely groups to say this. As suggested earlier in this chapter and in Chapter Two, the rates of divorce and separation in these traditional countries are very low and so a great many of the mothers growing up there may not have been aware of lone parenthood as a phenomenon. Therefore, they would not have been likely to have any opinions regarding the issues, or else believe that they themselves would never experience marriage breakdown. This was the reason given by a 37 year old Pakistani divorcee: "I didn't know about it then. No one was a single parent. Everyone was married. I never thought it could happen to me." Another of these mothers, aged 25 and from India, spoke of how being trapped in her marriage caused her ignorance of lone parenthood:

> I never knew about anything because my husband and mother-in-law never wanted me to speak with anyone. They didn't want me to know about the outside world. They never sent me anywhere.

Table 6.1
The mothers' attitudes towards lone parenthood before marriage breakdown by country of origin

	Sympathetic	Unsympathetic	No views	Total
India	10	3	24	37
Pakistan	1	1	15	17
East Africa	8	2	14	24
Bangladesh	4	—	2	6
Other	2	1	3	6
Total	**25**	**7**	**58**	**90**

Mothers who originated from East Africa were the most likely group to have been sympathetic towards lone parenthood before their own marriages were dissolved. This can partially be explained by their having been brought up in multi-cultural countries, in which they would have been more widely exposed to lone parenthood. This was illustrated by a respondent who had come from Tanzania fifteen years previously: "I used to be involved in a women's group for social gatherings. There were some single parents there. I respected them and helped them. I didn't look down on them."

Only 7 of the 90 mothers said that they held unsympathetic opinions of lone parents before their marriages ended. One of these women spoke of her family's disapproval of divorcees and unmarried mothers at the time:

> My family didn't have any lone parents. We always looked down on them, thinking they were naughty enough not to try hard enough, and to bring a child into the world just like that.

Further analysis indicates a relationship between employment prior to marriage, and attitudes towards lone parenthood before breakdown. Mothers who were employed were more likely than those without jobs to have held a view, whether sympathetic or unsympathetic, regarding lone parenthood. This may be due to the working group having been more greatly exposed to its existence through social interaction outside the home, as illustrated by a separated respondent who worked as a catering assistant: "I knew there were lone parents who were suffering. I felt sorry for them. My friend, a girl at work, was divorced before me. She told me how she felt and why she divorced."

In comparison, the mothers who did not work before marriage had a higher likelihood than the employed women of holding no specific views regarding lone parenthood, implying that their more sheltered lives may have been a factor in their ignorance. This was the point made by a Sikh divorcee aged 30: "I had no ideas. I was very simple in many ways."

There appeared to be a complicated correlation between level of education received and attitudes towards lone parenthood prior to marriage dissolution, since, on the one hand, the likelihood of mothers holding no opinions was the same for the uneducated women as it was for the university educated. One reason for this may have been because those who went to university tended to be older, and since divorce rates were even lower at the time, there may have been a lack of awareness on the topic. For example, a Sikh divorcee in her fifties who had trained to be a doctor echoed this by saying:

> I had never heard of the word 'divorce' in my day, and never imagined that I'd be a divorced woman. I was family oriented and single parents had just started in Britain then.

Women who were sympathetic towards lone parents tended to be educated up to nineteen, or else college educated, suggesting that the higher level of education may have helped in their recognition of the plight of a-typical families. Mothers only educated up to sixteen, who were perhaps more traditional in outlook, were more likely than the other groups to have held unsympathetic views and this was illustrated by a separated Muslim respondent: "It was wrong to be single. It was no life for a woman, especially if you had daughters."

There seemed to be some relationship between the sample's attitudes to lone parenthood before marital disruption and their length of stay in Britain. Respondents only living in Britain for nine years and less had the highest likelihood of not holding views, which may be due to their shorter length of residence in this country. Mothers residing in this country for ten years or over were more likely than the other groups to have held opinions, and to have been more sympathetic. Having lived in a western society for a considerable period of time, these women would have been more accustomed to the phenomena of lone parenthood and the problems faced by these families, as explained by a divorcee in Britain for 25 years: "I knew they existed. I felt very bad for them and knew that they'd be going through hell." Similarly, a young, unmarried mother in this country for 23 years, spoke of how she had been directly affected by marriage breakdown before her two sons were born: "I knew about the situation as my own parents split up when I was doing my O Levels. They'd been through a hard time and I sympathised with them."

The mothers' attitudes towards lone parenthood following marriage breakdown

Table 6.2 examines whether the women's attitudes towards lone parenthood had changed since their own marriages had broken down. The two unmarried mothers have been omitted from the table, one of whom was now unsympathetic, whilst the other held no specific views.

Table 6.2
Whether mothers have changed their attitudes towards lone parenthood following marriage breakdown by type and age of mother in years

	Divorced	Separated	Widowed	Total
Change to sympathetic				60
20's/30's	20	10	3	
40's/50's +	14	5	8	
Change to unsympathetic				2
20's/30's	—	1	—	
40's/50's +	—	1	—	
Still sympathetic				24
20's/30's	3	12	2	
40's/50's +	2	3	2	
Still no views/unsympathetic				2
20's/30's	—	1	—	
40's/50's +	—	1	—	
Total	**39**	**34**	**15**	**88**

The findings show that over two-thirds of the sample had changed their opinions since experiencing lone parenthood, with an overwhelming majority of the women presently sympathetic. This may not be surprising since:

> attitudes towards marital dissolution or out-of-wedlock births shift as more people become involved in these trends...divorced and remarried people have more tolerant attitudes to separation and divorce, as do unmarried mothers for rearing children without fathers (Morgan 1995:91).

Additionally, the vast majority of the respondents in this project ended their marriages in Britain where divorce and separation are far more acceptable, as opposed to in their countries of origin, where lone parenthood is much more frowned upon. Only 4 of the 90 mothers currently disapproved of non-traditional families, with a further two women holding indifferent attitudes.

Looking at the data in relation to lone mother type, the divorcees followed by the widows were the two most likely groups to have changed their attitudes and become sympathetic towards lone parent families. This may partially be explained by these women being the oldest in the sample with previously held traditional views. According to Gibson, "prejudice should have diminished as more people, either directly or by association become acquainted with the world of divorce" (1994:147). One of the mothers in this situation was a 40 year old divorcee who had once disapproved of lone parenthood, but had now become sympathetic, and even more so since she began working at a day centre for women:

> Since I've become a lone parent, I've given extra support and done counselling for single parents. I can relate to them. My counselling is moral, and I use my own example to tell women how they can stand on their own two feet and support their own families. I tell them they don't need support from a man and can be self-reliant. I make other women feel confident and assertive.

Table 6.2 suggests that the separated mothers were more likely than the other respondents to have still remained sympathetic, perhaps because they were younger than the widows and divorcees. Somewhat unexpectedly, neither of the unmarried mothers advocated lone parenthood as an acceptable status.

The figures of the table appear to confirm that there is a connection between the age of the mother and her change in attitudes. This can be seen by those in their forties and fifties being more inclined than the younger age group to now approve of lone parenthood from formerly being unsympathetic or holding no specific views. This may be because they were previously more conservative about marriage being a permanent status, and they had only changed their minds following the failure of their own relationships. For example, a 41 year old separated mother who had once been indifferent explained:

> Now I can understand because I'm in the same position. I feel sorry, especially for those girls who have no relatives here, girls who come from India and who have poor parents in India who cannot help their daughters. They need more support. They're the ones who are worse off than me.

The younger generation of women in their twenties and thirties had a higher likelihood than the older respondents of always having empathised with lone parents. Compared to the more traditional, older group, these mothers may always have been more liberal-minded due to their age, as a separated Hindu respondent aged 38 pointed out: "I feel even more sorry for them now. I understand the feelings of these women and how they suffer handling the responsibility of home, work and children."

Age can also be regarded as a determinant towards approval or disapproval of divorce in Indian society. According to Whyte and Whyte (1982), opposition to divorce is found amongst older people, irrespective of social class. The senior generation still expect a wife to put up with an impotent, insane or diseased husband, whilst younger people, being more aware of the obligations by both partners, believe that if a marriage is disharmonious, it is in the interests of both husband and wife, and children, that they should feel free to part.

The mothers' attitudes towards how others perceived them as lone parents

This section will examine how the 90 mothers felt others perceived them as lone parents, by firstly looking at this issue in a general setting, before focusing specifically on the reactions of the Asian community. The findings will be compared, wherever possible, to literature and studies on divorce in India.

Whether the mothers felt that people generally looked down on lone parent families compared to two parent families

According to Stopes-Roe and Cochrane:

> although British society may have come to accept divorce, the underlying attitude is still, as it is for Asians, that marriage is a permanent contract and when it fails this is a 'breakdown,' and not simply a 'change' (1990: 28).

This preference for the nuclear family as opposed to the lone parent family is reflected in the data from Table 6.3, which clearly indicates that most of the sample believed that people did frown more upon the latter family type. Only six of the mothers said that society did not disapprove of lone parenthood, and these tended to be younger women. The table has left out the two unmarried mothers, the first of whom said that people looked down on the female side of the partnership, whilst the second felt that opinions depended on the individuals involved.

Table 6.3
Whether the mothers felt that people generally looked down on lone parents compared to two parent families by lone mother type

	Divorced	Separated	Widowed	Total
I *Yes, people do look down*				72
Yes, espec. in Asian culture	12	15	3	30
Yes, because of social pressures to be married	6	3	7	16
Yes, as it affects children	6	6	1	13
Yes, people frown upon woman	7	2	1	10
Yes, because of ignorance	2	—	1	3
II *People do not look down*	4	2	—	**6**
III *Depends on individual*	2	3	1	**6**
IV *Don't know*	—	3	1	**4**
Total	**39**	**34**	**15**	**88**

According to the table, one-third of the respondents felt that the Asian community, in particular, objected to lone parent families, which may infer that, in comparison, they saw the British as being more accepting. The separated mothers were the most likely group to believe that Asians, especially, frowned upon lone parenthood, and they were twice as likely as the widows to say so. This may partly be attributed to the fact that the separated sample had not yet completely broken away from their marriages and were thus still facing hostility from their communities.

Two of the separated women gave the reason for this as being embedded in Asian culture itself, where it is believed that even today the ideal wife is "one who under any sort of trial and temptation will stick to her husband" (Pothen 1987:197). The first mother to speak was aged 33 and whose husband had been unfaithful to her: "The Asian community believe you should stick to your husband and treat him like a God." This sentiment was echoed by a second separated respondent who was a school administrator: "Asian society believes you should be your husband's servant and should stay with your husband when married, and live on his terms and not suggest compromising."

Table 6.3 goes on to suggest that the widows were the most likely group to believe that society placed great pressures on couples to remain married. Due to becoming lone parents through circumstances beyond their control, the widows may not have felt so stigmatised by the Asian community as they would have been if they were separated or divorced. A 43 year old Sikh widow of six years spoke in more general terms:

> If you have a husband no one can touch or tease you. You can be protected by him. He is the head. He can do anything. But lone mothers are on their own and are worrying alone and getting no help.

Both the divorced and separated respondents were equally as likely to hold the opinion that people condemned lone parents families because of the adverse effect marriage breakdown had on the children. This is not unexpected since the outcome for children is one of the most forceful arguments against divorce (Ahuja 1994).

The quality of lone parenting is often assessed in terms of its equivalence to an ideal model of the "normal" family. Using this yardstick, any difference is seen as a deficit, and lone parenting is looked upon as a poor substitute for proper parenting (Chandler 1991). According to Morgan, over 70 per cent of people believe that a child needs both parents to grow up properly (1995:82). The proportion of the British sample who agreed that a child needs a home with both a father and mother to grow up happily increased from 67 to 73 per cent between 1981 and 1990 (Burghes 1994:14). The consequences of lone parenthood for the children involved in lone parent families will be discussed in more depth in Chapter Seven.

Some of the mothers in this study who felt that people judged them because they were bringing up children alone gave examples of the effects of marriage breakdown on their dependants. The first was a 38 year old separated Muslim respondent with three dependent children who herself also felt that a child needed both parents:

> People think that the children need both parents. If you can live together it's good for the children. I feel shouting and fighting is no good for the children, but there is something missing. Children need a man's role. When my children see two parent families they get upset and think, why are mum and dad not together? But it's not possible.

A second mother was a 56 year old doctor from Burma who spoke from experience of how her daughter had become withdrawn as a result of her divorce:

> My own daughter didn't want to go to university at first as she didn't want people to say she was from a broken family. She was so affected. She wanted to go to Oxford University but totally gave up. She couldn't face society and stayed at home for three years.

The divorcees were more inclined than the other groups to feel that people tended to frown especially upon the female side of the partnership. Although lone mothers, on the one hand, may be urged to go out, meet people and enjoy themselves, on the other hand, if they do they are seen as loose (Chandler 1991), and this was experienced by a 39 year old Muslim mother in this research: "People think you're a criminal or just single to want your freedom deliberately. Now if I talk to a man people think badly."

One of the respondents who felt that society did not look down on lone parent families was a Hindu divorcee from Tanzania who said that people "look at you as a person," whilst a second divorcee of Muslim origin claimed that opinions depended on the individual: "Some people do, some people don't. People are two-faced. Some say they like single parents but they don't."

*Whether the mothers felt that the Asian community accepted lone
parenthood less or the same as British society*

Table 6.4 focuses on the issue of whether the sample believed that the
Asian community accepted lone parenthood to the same extent as did
the British. The two unmarried mothers have been omitted from the
table, both of whom acknowledged that the Asian community were
less sympathetic towards lone parenthood.

As anticipated, the figures reveal that over two-thirds of the
mothers said that Asians were less accepting of lone parenthood than
were the host society. Perceived cultural differences between the two
groups was a major reason given by many of these women.

Table 6.4
**Whether the mothers felt the Asian community accepted
lone parenthood same as or less than the British by
lone parent type and religion**

	Hindu	Muslim	Sikh	Chri.	Jain	Total
Asians more						
unsympathetic						**70**
Divorced	8	10	10	1	2	
Separated	9	7	7	2	1	
Widowed	5	5	3	—	—	
Asians accept the same						**7**
Divorced	1	—	2	—	—	
Separated	1	1	—	—	—	
Widowed	—	1	1	—	—	
Depends on individual, D/K						**11**
Divorced	1	1	3	—	—	
Separated	—	3	1	2	—	
Widowed	—	—	—	—	—	
Total	25	28	27	5	3	**88**

A 29 year old unmarried mother pointed out that the older
generation did not expect their children to adopt more liberal attitudes
towards marriage breakdown:

Maybe it's the way Asians are brought up. It's a very strict culture, and parents expect their children to carry on their traditional way of thinking. They never see their children as having western views.

This may be because the weakening of traditional ways, family discipline and social structure and loss of opportunity to pass on the culture is a threat to ethnic identity (Stopes-Roe and Cochrane 1990).

A 40 year old employed divorcee with two daughters argued that domestic violence was still seen as an acceptable part of Asian culture, thus preventing many women from seeking a divorce:

> The issue of divorce and domestic violence is not addressed openly in our society, but is still very much hidden. For the English, divorce is part and parcel of their lives now. I still see Asian women who put up with violence and abuse. They genuinely believe it is part and parcel of the culture and tradition, and put up with it.

This sentiment reflects the common practice in India where a woman is viewed as someone's sister, daughter, wife or mother, and never as a citizen in her own right who also needs to live with dignity and self-respect (Desai and Krishnaraj 1987). It is socially acceptable that the man is the master and the woman is inferior to him, and where domestic violence is seen as a natural occurrence to justify a man's need to "tame" his wife into accepting her traditional role as a submissive and subordinate partner (Kakar 1988).

According to Dhagamwar (1987), a wife who reacts, who wishes to leave her marriage, does not fit into the traditional pattern. It is a crisis not envisaged by society at all. One gets married and remains so, and this was echoed by the thoughts of a 24 year old unmarried mother: "Divorce and remarriage is shunned, as the vows taken by Indians is 'till death do us part, regardless of circumstances.'"

Unlike western cultures where both spouses make adjustments and meet halfway, in Indian culture it is the wife who has to bear the entire burden of adjustment (Pothen 1987). She should preserve the marriage partnership without magnifying the problems (Khanna and Varghese 1978), as expressed by a 40 year old Pakistani widow in this study:

> If a person is divorced our people don't like it. It's not such an open society, like the British, who can easily move out of a marriage. We can't, even if the husband is a bad person. The woman has to cope. In our culture, when married, the woman has to look after the husband in every sense of life, whether good or bad.

If the woman deviates a little, she is then considered to be at fault, with society disapproval more towards female than male divorcees (Pothen 1987). This view was confirmed by a 38 year old separated respondent from Bangladesh who explained:

> Lone parenthood is very rare in our society. Women have to tolerate everything. If she can't, it's her fault and shows she's incapable. The view in our country and culture is that the man is the boss of the family and is always correct, with the woman having no voice.

Fourteen of the 72 mothers who believed that the Asian community was more disapproving of lone parenthood than the British also qualified their replies by stating that Asian society was now slowly becoming more accepting of marital breakdown. Seven of these women were of Hindu religion, two were Sikhs and only one was Muslim and could imply that of the three major Asian religious groupings, "Hinduism is far more tolerant" (Stopes-Roe and Cochrane 1990:207).

Although divorce, in itself, may not better the position of a woman, it is accepted that it will ease, to some extent, her mental torture and intolerable existence (Ahuja 1994), as recognised by a 38 year old Hindu respondent:

> Asians are becoming more and more accepting. Because it's a different culture to the British, it doesn't come easily. Indian culture thinks, what's the use of becoming fully westernised? But many Asians don't want the woman to suffer any more. It's better to get out. We're gradually seeing more and more single parents in the community.

A second Hindu mother in her thirties and divorced for six years remarked that the Asian community was more accepting of a lone parent if she could prove her worth to them. Speaking from her own experience, she said:

> Indians don't accept you at the start. You have to prove it to them to be accepted. At first I got dirty looks at the temple, but if you show your talents, such as by singing, the people then accept you. Before that, they don't. Our people are at first shocked when they find out you're divorced.

As anticipated, only a very tiny minority of the women - seven in all - said that the Asian community approved of lone parenthood as much as the British did, one being a Sikh respondent in her forties who explained that Asians were now far more open-minded than they had been in the past: "Now it's a different generation. People from the first generation have now come to terms with lone parenthood, unlike before when it was a stigma. Generally, people are more liberal."

The findings of this project relating to Asian attitudes towards lone mothers can be compared to some of those carried out in India. An unpublished study by the YWCA of India of 200 urban based divorced and separated women aged between 20 and 48 from different income groups, found that about two-thirds of the sample reported being perceived negatively by society after breakdown (Bharat 1986:60). Nevertheless, according to some more recent research, "it has been found that in India divorce does not invite social disapproval" (Ahuja 1994:195). There is evidence which indicates that divorce is now becoming less of a stigma and that couples as well as society are now accepting that marriages can break down (Siganporia 1993).

Bharat's study of 28 lone families and a comparative sample of 28 intact family mothers (1988:234) found that, although most of the women were widows, about 89 per cent of the lone mothers said they were not looked down on because of their single status. Siganporia's survey of 100 divorced Muslim women in Bombay and Pune (1993) discovered that except in a few extreme cases, the women did not have to deal with harassment from their social support system, perhaps indicating the growing acceptance of divorce as an alternative to an unhappy marriage.

The mothers' attitudes towards loss of marital status in the Asian community

Whilst Table 5.2 referred to marital breakdown leading to a loss of family honour, Table 6.5 takes this issue a little further by relating it more personally to the women themselves.

Table 6.5 investigates whether the sample felt that losing one's marital status within the Asian community was a greater problem for Asian lone mothers than it was for their British counterparts within their society. Somewhat as predicted, the results reveal that over two-thirds of the women felt that loss of marital status did affect Asian lone mothers more than white lone mothers. Only seven of the sample said that loss of status did not cause any difficulties for either sets of women.

Some of the respondents who supported the view that Asian lone mothers encountered more problems, gave explanations. Within Asian culture the "woman is an advocate of traditional behaviour, even at her own cost," where divorce is considered right if a woman misbehaves but not if a man does (Whyte and Whyte 1982:95). This point was illustrated by a separated mother of ten years, who said:

> People do treat you differently in Indian society, like you couldn't stick to the rules provided. They blame the woman, but not the man. For the English, even if a couple split up, they still stay friends. For us, friends don't want to know you.

Table 6.5
Whether mothers felt loss of marital status in the community was a greater problem for Asian lone mothers than for British lone mothers by lone parent type

	Divorced	Separated	Widowed	Unm.	Total
Greater problem for Asians	33	19	10	2	**64**
Not a problem for either	2	5	—	—	**7**
Depends on circumstances	1	5	4	—	**10**
Don't know/unsure	3	5	1	—	**9**
Total	**39**	**34**	**15**	**2**	**90**

Many friendships of the formerly married turn out to have depended on their marital status, in that they no longer participate with the couples in evening sociability, and this view was confirmed by an employed divorcee in her twenties: "It is a problem since you don't tend to get invitations anymore to parties, since you'll be the odd one out." She went on to add:

> For Asians, you've only got an identity if you've got a man. For the English, the women will always have been independent since childhood. A woman's a person in her own right.

Other Asian women are often very quick to make accusations, feeling they can make their own position safer by emphasising their commitment to social norms (White 1992). This was one of the dilemmas faced by a 40 year old Sikh divorcee:

> You go through the stage when you're single when you always feel like a second class citizen, especially by your own community. The women, especially, like to talk. You feel quite vulnerable to their attitudes and behaviour as you don't have that security of a man, a horrible way of putting it. The English are quite proud of using their own maiden names. Even though I'm progressive I've still got my previous husband's name because I'm very conscious of isolating my children, and really from people questioning why my surname's different to my children's. For the English it's quite normal to have children out of marriage. For me it isn't.

A lone mother is often regarded as fair game, making the establishment of new relationships with men more difficult (Chandler 1991). A fourth respondent in this study explained that it was Asian men in particular who took advantage of a woman's single status:

> In the Indian community, if a man found out I'm a lone parent, he'll think it's an open door to sleep with me. It's very difficult to make friends. English men don't think in the same way, they like me for what I am and not that I'm a good catch as I'm by myself.

Looking at Table 6.5 in relation to lone parent type, the divorcees were the most likely group to feel that loss of marital status had greater implications for the Asian lone mother population than for the corresponding white group. This is perhaps because the divorced respondents, having made a complete break from their marriages, were more vulnerable to the disapproval of the Asian community. For example, a 35 year old Muslim mother with two teenagers spoke of the inherent differences in being married and being divorced for an Asian woman:

> This is an Asian problem. As a lone mother you feel that you were once married, and now you're not, and that maybe you will not be able to marry again. There's a difference between being a married and a divorced woman, in that you don't feel very proud if you're divorced. You feel low in other people's eyes. I myself feel like that. The English feel normal; they don't feel anything.

The separated sample had a greater tendency than the other groups to express the view that Asian lone mothers had no dilemmas regarding loss of marital status. Since their relationships had not completely been dissolved they may not have felt the affects as strongly as the divorcees.

The widows were more inclined than either the divorcees or the separated mothers to believe that experiencing a loss of status depended upon the circumstances of the individual involved. These women could have made a distinction between being divorced and being widowed, as did a respondent who had lost her husband nine years previously: "For Indians there is a different approach to different situations. The community is always helpful and sympathetic towards a widow, whilst it is not so willing to help a divorcee." Not surprisingly, because they had had children out of wedlock, the two unmarried mothers said that the Asian community would frown upon them.

There also appeared to be a correlation between the age of the mothers and their attitudes towards loss of status, with those in their twenties and thirties being more inclined than the older groups to not perceive this to be a problem. Six of the seven respondents who gave this reply were in the younger age bracket, and thus may have held more westernised attitudes, as did one 30 year old separated mother: "If the marriage was bad, people think it's good if it's finished." Whilst women in their forties had the highest likelihood of saying that difficulties with losing one's status depended on individual circumstances, mothers aged 50 and over tended to feel that Asian women were affected by becoming lone parents. One of the reasons for the oldest group's responses could be because of their more deeply rooted beliefs towards marriage, as reflected in the words of a 60 year old mother, married for 26 years before her separation:

> The aim of all Asian women is to get married. Once you are divorced or separated you do lose your status. People don't want to know you any more. In the English community, there are less family values and no shame for them.

Additional investigation indicates that the Muslim, followed by the Jain and Sikh respondents were the three most likely groupings to maintain that loss of status affected Asian lone mothers more adversely than British lone mothers, with the data relating to the Muslim women partly being attributed to their more rigid approach to the family.

Weiss (1975) has put forward the opinion that same sex friends of the separated fear the loss of their spouses, whilst friends of the other sex fear their own impulses. The reputations of lone women may also be closely scrutinised and guarded by other women, thus reducing fellow feeling and heightening suspicion (Chandler 1991). This was illustrated by a 42 year old Muslim respondent, working as a psychiatrist:

> Some single parents are not even accepted in some people's houses. You are seen as a threat, and this is two-fold. You are seen as a threat to other wives in that you are available to their husbands. Secondly, you are a threat to the husbands who think you are young, good looking and can teach their wives the tricks of divorce.

Religion did not appear to make any difference to those who said that there were no difficulties regarding loss of marital status, whilst the Christian followed by the Jain women were the two most likely groups to believe this problem was dependent upon circumstances. For the Christian mothers this may be due to their more open-minded attitudes in comparison to the respondents who were affiliated to the more traditional faiths.

The mothers' attitudes towards their being lone parents

The findings, so far, have indicated that Asian culture places far greater importance on marriage as an institution than does the British culture. The fourth section of Chapter Six will explore how the 90 mothers perceived themselves as lone parents in relation to their more conservative Asian culture.

Whether the mothers felt they were betraying their culture becoming lone mothers

Table 6.6 examines whether the respondents felt they were betraying their culture through becoming lone parents. The fifteen widows have been excluded from the table since they did not become single through choice.

Just over one-half of the sample said that they were not betraying their culture and values through marriage breakdown. Given the weight of literature against lone parenthood as an acceptable status within Asian culture, this finding is, perhaps, very unexpected. One of the reasons for this may be because there is a view in Asian culture that claims that "the causes of divorce lie with individuals and not with the institutions of family or marriage" (Ahuja 1994:195). This standpoint was supported by a mother in her twenties and a victim of domestic violence: "It has nothing to do with culture really when a relationship between two people goes wrong." As they were now lone parents themselves, many of the women were probably now more accepting of this single status as a growing phenomenon. As a separated respondent from Kenya put it: "These things now happen in each family." Other women also made it clear that the welfare of their children came before any thoughts of betrayal of culture, since they "should not entail unnecessary hardship and degradation" (Ahuja 1994:194). This was the explanation given by a separated mother in her thirties with three dependent children: "I haven't lost my culture and become an English person. I had to think of the children and not ruin their lives."

Table 6.6
Whether or not the mothers felt they were betraying their culture and values becoming lone parents by religion and length of lone parenthood in years

	Hindu	Muslim	Sikh	Chri.	Jain	Total
Yes, betraying their Asian culture						26
Up to 1 yr	1	2	3	—	—	
1-6	1	4	8	1	2	
7-10	—	1	—	—	—	
11 +	—	2	1	—	—	
No, not betraying culture						49
Up to 1 yr	—	1	1	—	—	
1-6	14	8	1	2	1	
7-10	3	3	4	3	1	
11 +	1	1	5	—	—	
Total	20	22	23	6	4	75

Data from Table 6.6 indicates a relationship between the mothers' attitudes and their length of lone parenthood, in that the women who had experienced marriage breakdown for six years and less were more likely than the other groups to hold the view that they had betrayed their culture. These women were perhaps not yet used to their new single status and thus still had negative feelings about their situation, as pointed out by a separated respondent of only five months:

> I don't trust many people. If I'm lonely I go to the temple but not to friends or relatives. I do feel I'm going against the culture because of what some people may say. I don't want to hurt myself by listening to them.

The lone mothers of seven years or more had a greater likelihood than the other women of believing that they were not going against their culture through marital disruption. This group would have been more accustomed to their lone parent status and were maybe less affected by the expectations of their culture. A divorcee of fifteen years and with two daughters echoed Chandler's claim (1991) that children of lone women may become the mothers' main or only source of personal meaning through emotional compensation, by stating:

> It's good if you divorce. It's good to know that our children know we care about them. It's better to live in a happy environment together than stay in a bad marriage for culture's sake. I now have a good relationship with my children. They're like my best friends. We are very close.

According to Table 6.6, the mothers of Sikh and Muslim religions were more inclined than respondents who belonged to other faiths to say that they had gone against the ethics of their culture through divorce or separation. This could reflect the more rigid ideologies of these religions compared to Hinduism. For example, a 47 year old Muslim divorcee with sixteen year old twins spoke of the importance of upholding the family: "Our culture is very different. It's very important to be part of a family unit, and especially for me, since everyone in my family is still married." A Sikh respondent pointed out that she had broken her marriage vows, giving her a sense of betrayal: "In a Sikh marriage, you can't think of divorce. I hate this word for my name. That's why I tried hard to save my marriage."

Those who felt they were not betraying their Asian culture were most likely to have been Hindu or Christian. For the latter group, the results may partially be attributed to their having more liberal opinions, as illustrated by a 40 year old mother with a teenage daughter: "My grandfather is English so I have a westernised culture. Therefore, coming to England was not a shock and so I expected that my situation would arise."

There appeared to be a complicated correlation between attitudes towards betrayal of culture and the level of education received by the 75 mothers. At one level the uneducated women were as likely as those who attended university to not have any sense of betrayal, which is surprising given that one may have expected the former group to have been more traditional.

However, when analysing the figures in relation only to the mothers who had received some kind of education, a connection could be found. This was seen by the university and college educated women being the two most disposed groups to feel that becoming lone mothers was not contrary to the Asian culture and may be because approval of divorce is linked with the educational level of women. As the education level increases, so more and more women approve of divorce if conditions of married life are not congenial (Khanna and Varghese 1978).

Broad-minded attitudes towards their situation were revealed in the responses of some of the highly educated mothers in this study. One was a 32 year old Hindu divorcee who spoke of how attending a British college of Further Education had enabled her to become more westernised in her thinking:

> I don't feel as though I am going against my culture as I have really been brought up and educated here, and although the Indian tradition is still practised to an extent, the pressure is not as heavy as it would have been had the same question arisen in India.

A university educated respondent pointed out that becoming a lone mother was not related to culture: "Our culture is good. There are no drawbacks in our culture. It's more to do with people, and if they are narrow-minded you can't change them."

Women who said they were betraying their culture tended to have had a sixth form education or else left school at sixteen. They were perhaps more conservative in outlook than the mothers who had received a higher level of education, and this was confirmed by a Sikh respondent who was educated up to sixteen: "It's not a done thing. It ruins the family honour and also makes it hard for the children."

There was also an indication that the mothers in their twenties and thirties had a greater tendency than the older age groups to feel that they had been disloyal to their Asian culture through lone parenthood. This result may not have been anticipated, given that the younger women should perhaps have been more liberal-minded and less influenced by their culture than those in their forties and fifties.

On closer examination, this finding could firstly be explained by these mothers having been residents in Britain for less time than the older group, and secondly, by their having only experienced lone parenthood for a relatively short period. Therefore, with these contributing factors, the younger respondents would have reason to still retain much of their original culture and therefore feel a sense of betrayal through marriage breakdown. On the other hand, the mothers aged forty and over were more likely to have been lone parents for longer as well as to have been living in Britain for a greater number of years. Thus they would, perhaps, have now been less concerned about their lone parent status being culture related.

Whether or not the mothers had ever felt ashamed of their lone parent status

Table 6.7 investigates whether the sample had ever felt ashamed of their lone parent status, with the two unmarried mothers being excluded. One replied that she once felt ashamed, whilst the second said she still felt so.

Table 6.7
Whether or not the mothers had ever felt ashamed of their lone parent status because of their Asian origin by lone parent type and country of origin

	India	Pak.	E.Afr.	Bang.	Other	Total
Has never felt ashamed						52
Divorced	13	3	6	2	—	
Separated	7	3	2	4	—	
Widowed	4	3	4	—	1	
Once used to feel ashamed						20
Divorced	5	1	4	—	—	
Separated	3	2	3	—	2	
Widowed	—	—	—	—	—	
Still feels ashamed						16
Divorced	1	1	2	—	1	
Separated	4	2	1	—	1	
Widowed	—	2	1	—	—	
Total	37	17	23	6	5	88

This finding may well be foreseen in the light of the Asian community's condemnation of single motherhood as an ever greater stigma than divorce or separation. The overall findings show that 73 of the 90 women currently felt no shame, although 21 of them admitted to having experienced this in the past. Altogether, of the 90 respondents, 38 had been remorseful at some time, with just under a fifth of the sample still affected.

As with the unexpected results of Table 6.6, it may be surprising to discover that over one-half of the sample had never been ashamed of their lone parent status. In this case, the mothers may indeed have felt self-reproach in the past, but had not admitted to it, or else they had genuinely forgotten their earlier experiences. Secondly, some of these women could have felt they had done nothing wrong becoming unmarried, as reflected in the response of a divorcee from Tanzania: "If a marriage is broken, it's a personal problem. We should enjoy ourselves with our friends, whether male or female, like two parent families do."

Not surprisingly, the widows were more likely than the other lone parent types to have never felt ashamed of their status since, for them, marriage breakdown was not through choice.

The divorcees had a higher likelihood than the other mothers of either saying they had never been, or else had once felt shame. Those divorced women who had previously been affected may have now rebuilt their lives following a period of turmoil. For example, one of these respondents explained how she had overcome her sense of shame with the help of her family's support:

> Generally, because of Indian culture Indians do tend to feel too guilty about their situation and won't open up to anyone. But I've tried not to let it get to me. In the past I was ashamed and never left the house, but my parents said I've done nothing wrong and gave me a lot of help.

Dhagamwar's Indian study (1987) also found that the "fear of society" factor posed more difficulties for the lone mothers rather than disapproval from their families, who were generally more supportive.

Table 6.7 goes on to imply that the separated women were more likely than the other groups to say that they used to feel or else still felt ashamed of being a lone parent. Unlike the divorcees, the separated mothers had a less finalised status and this could have led to feelings of shame being recalled. One such respondent who presently felt grieved was a Hindu lone mother of two years in her mid-thirties, who claimed that the on-going gossip of her local Asian community was still affecting her: "I don't want to meet my own people as they will ask personal questions. They'll say it serves me right and will laugh at me as they won't think of me as one of them."

According to the data regarding country of origin, the mothers from India and Bangladesh were the two most likely groupings to have never felt ashamed of their lone parent status, which may be surprising, given the traditional natures of these countries. Respondents who had initially felt shame were more inclined to have come from East Africa and the smaller countries, even though they had been brought up in more multi-cultural societies where lone parent families would have been less hidden.

More significantly, perhaps, the Pakistani women were the most likely mothers to still feel inflicted by their single status, and were twice as likely as the Indian women to give this response. The reason for this could partially be attributed to the more dominant and insular Islamic cultural ideology, which tends "both to preclude adoption of other customs and contact with other ways of thinking and living" (Stopes-Roe and Cochrane 1990:207). A Muslim respondent in her fifties in this study spoke of the very conservative Islamic marriage values inherent in her culture: "When I go out alone to meet families with a mother and a father I do feel ashamed because Muslim culture, especially, places so much emphasis on having a partner." A second Pakistani divorcee in her forties went on to remark how the Muslim community contributed to her feelings of remorse in a social world of couples "where lone women feel marginalised and uncomfortable" (Chandler 1991:72). She explained:

> I feel shame as I'm the only lone parent in my family. I have to go to weddings as a lone mother and see other women wearing nice clothes and jewellery. I don't go much to weddings or parties as many there will ask me why I haven't got a husband.

Further analysis implies some correlation between feelings of shame and the length of marriage breakdown. Respondents who had never been badly affected were the most likely group to have experienced lone parenthood for seven years or more. This may be due to their being more used to their status and hence their lack of concern, even though some of these mothers may actually have once felt ashamed. Although taking on new responsibilities and doing unfamiliar tasks with little social support are not easy for lone parents, the experience of making decisions and mastering tasks forms the basis of a new, more satisfactory self-concept (Kohen, Brown and Feldberg 1979). The women who had experienced lone parenthood for a longer time would perhaps be more inclined to be in a position to analyse their positive achievements, as did a divorced employee whose marriage had dissolved nine years previously:

> I can say that I do feel quite brave and proud that I have managed very well bringing up the children on my own. I have built up my career. Work has not changed my beliefs and culture but has made a better person of me.

Women who previously felt ashamed were more inclined than the other groups to have only been lone mothers for up to six years, suggesting that their shorter length of lone parenthood may have enabled them to recall their earlier experiences. The length of marital breakdown, however, made no difference to those seventeen respondents who still felt ashamed of their single status.

Conclusion

This chapter has shown that although most mothers were largely ignorant of lone parenthood prior to marriage breakdown, they were presently overwhelmingly sympathetic. However, 72 of the 90 mothers did feel that people generally frowned upon lone parent families compared to traditional families, with a third of these women mentioning that the disapproval was mainly embedded within Asian culture.

As anticipated, 70 of the 90 women felt that the Asian community had not yet accepted lone parenthood at the same level as British culture, with over two-thirds of the sample stating that loss of marital status did pose more problems for an Asian woman than it did for her British counterpart.

Given the weight of literature pointing to the importance of marriage in Asian culture, the results pertaining to the mothers' perceptions of themselves as lone parents were rather surprising. Only 26 of the 90 mothers felt that they were betraying their culture through marriage breakdown, whilst 52 of the respondents said they had never felt ashamed of their single status. One reason for these unexpected replies may partly be explained by Morgan, who puts forward the view that lone parents, "in an attempt to justify or make the best of their own experience...are more likely to denigrate the traditional family" (1995:82).

Despite the differences between British and Asian cultures regarding the attitudes towards lone parenthood, evidence from this study would suggest that only a small minority of the mothers currently expressed feelings of guilt or remorse regarding their marriage breakdown.

7 The Mothers' Experiences of Lone Parenthood

Chapter Five has highlighted the differences between British and Asian values pertaining to marriage, the family and the status of women. This has further been confirmed by the findings of Chapter Six which strongly suggest that the Asian culture rejects lone parenthood to a greater extent than does the British culture. These cultural dissimilarities, therefore, may have important connotations for the mothers' experiences as lone parents, which may be hostile in the light of their marginal situation. Chapter Seven will focus on the sample's relationships with the father, their family and friends and with social organisations, comparing them, wherever possible, with both British and Indian literature. A section on the effects of marital breakdown on the children and their relationship with the father has also been incorporated into the chapter.

The mothers' contact and attachment with the father

Divorce does not mark the end of family life and structure but instead, is the starting point in a particular family's life which will continue in another form. For many couples, contact and communication is maintained because of the presence of the children and family kin. In addition:

> marital relationships do not disintegrate overnight and the feelings of being closely bound up with another person are not easily withdrawn and placed elsewhere (Parkinson 1987:121).

Despite this, however, most discussion in the literature tends to focus on the contacts between the child and the non-custodial parent, whilst the on-going relationship between the former spouses is rarely studied (Chandler 1991:117).

The first section of Chapter Seven examines whether the mothers in this study had retained any contact with their previous partners, before going on to look at the extent of emotional attachment.

The mothers' contact with their former partners

Table 7.1 focuses on whether the sample currently saw the father and shows a total of 70 and not 90 mothers since fifteen of the respondents were widowed, whilst a further five said that their former partners had since died. According to the findings, the vast majority of the women said they did not see their ex-husbands, with only nineteen mothers having any such contact.

Table 7.1
Whether mother sees former partner by lone parent type and length of lone parenthood in years

	Never sees			Sees regularly		Sees irregularly		Total
	Div.	Sep.	Unm.	Div.	Sep.	Div.	Sep.	
Under 1 yr	3	4	—	—	—	—	1	8
1-6	16	10	1	1	5	2	4	39
7-10	7	4	—	1	1	—	1	14
11 +	5	1	—	1	1	1	—	9
Total	**31**	**19**	**1**	**3**	**7**	**3**	**6**	**70**

These results appear to be dissimilar to other research carried out both in Britain and in India in the sense that in most of the other studies (Lund (1984) in O'Brien and Lewis 1994, Ahrons and Rodgers (1987) in Chandler 1991, Bradshaw and Millar 1991, Leeming et al 1994), many parents kept in touch with one another, even if it was only on a minimal level. Literature from India also echoes these findings. Although Choudhry's investigation of 125 cases of divorce showed that only 24 per cent of his sample saw their ex-spouses following marriage breakdown (Ahuja 1994:187), Pothen (1987:194) discovered that a larger proportion of his respondents - 59 per cent in all - did have some kind of contact with the father.

Some of the 51 mothers in this project who never saw their former partners gave explanations for this. A number of them said that the fathers were now living in another country, or had gone back to their countries of origin. Another reason put forward was that the father had remarried or was now involved in another relationship. A 34 year old divorcee of five years, whose husband had committed adultery during their marriage illustrated this by saying:

I've never seen him since he left. I asked him whether he wanted me or her. He said he wanted the other woman. Since then there's been no contact by either side.

Sexual abuse by the father against his daughter was another explanation for no further contact given by a divorcee aged 39 and married for nineteen years and who was still very bitter: "I don't ever want to see him again. He's dead for me now."

According to Table 7.1, the women who had experienced lone parenthood for over eleven years were just as likely to see their former spouses as those whose marriages had broken down for between one and six years, thus refuting any link between the length of lone motherhood and an on-going relationship between the partners. This is somewhat different to Bradshaw and Millar's findings (1991) which showed that, although not very marked, the proportion of mothers who had no contact with the father tended to increase with the length of lone parenthood.

The data from this research does positively suggest, however, that the separated respondents were more likely than the divorcees to currently see the father. This would indicate the finality of divorce as opposed to the uncertainty of separation and corresponds with Bradshaw and Millar's survey findings (1991). One of the separated Asian mothers of five years in this study explained that she only saw her former partner because her children wanted to see their grandparents, with whom he was living: "I visit him because of my in-laws. He meets me about once a week when I go to his parents but he doesn't talk to me." A second separated respondent, aged 39 and whose ex-husband was presently in America, said that although there was some contact, she would like to see him more because he was still the father of her two children:

> It doesn't bother me, but the children should see their father regularly. They haven't seen him for a year now. It makes a lot of difference. He doesn't realise he's moving away from them.

One of the principal reasons given by the women in this study for the regularity of seeing the former partner was that the father still lived in close proximity. One was a separated Muslim mother whose ex-husband lived "five minutes away with his mother," whilst a divorcee of sixteen years said of the father: "He lives across the road. For the last six years I see him at least daily." A third respondent who still saw her former partner everyday explained that she only did so because they still worked together in their shop.

From the women's narrative it was clear that those mothers whose contact was only infrequent or irregular, made no effort to do so. A few of these respondents said the father was now living abroad, one of these being a 39 year old separated Sikh mother: "He's overseas in the States. He comes over when he wants. He must be working over there." Other women spoke only of seeing their ex-partners "now and then," "whenever he feels like it" and "on the streets now and then."

When asked how they felt about not seeing the father regularly, five of the nine mothers who only had irregular contact replied that they no longer cared, or were happy about the present arrangements. For example, a separated respondent whose former alcoholic and violent husband had now returned to Mauritius, said that he still came back to see her and "reappears as if nothing has happened." She then went on to express her disapproval: "I'd like to know he's not going to get in touch with me. I'd like him to disappear without telling me."

Only one of the women expressed a wish to see the father more regularly for personal reasons. She was a separated Christian respondent whose ex-partner was now in Italy, from where he visited every two years. Although there was telephone contact, the mother explained that she would like to see him more often because they still remained friends.

The mothers' emotional attachment to the father

Recent studies on lone parenthood, both in Britain and India, have pointed to a general state of emotional detachment for couples following separation and divorce. For example, Leeming et al (1994) discovered that their separated sample's feelings towards the fathers had grown more formal, distant and cold over time. Likewise, Pothen's Indian study (1987:198) found that although the divorced men and women expressed a wide range of sentiments for their ex-spouses such as "still love," "repentant," "no ill-feeling," "bitter feelings" and "hate intensely," the vast majority of them - 65 per cent of the husbands and 78.5 per cent of the wives - articulated unfavourable emotions.

Evidence from this investigation of Asian lone mothers is consistent with the findings of the above research, in that 57, or two-thirds of the sample stated that they were no longer attached to the father. Thirty of the respondents replied that they were still emotionally attached, whilst three said they were unsure of their feelings. These results may well be predicted in the light of so few of the divorced and separated mothers actually having any present contact with their former parents.

The divorcees in this survey were the most inclined group to express adverse sentiments, perhaps because of their more finalised status, as well as the fact that:

> divorcees are already emotionally estranged, since it is the resolution of this that is the whole purpose of the divorce. Emotional detachment is intrinsic to the whole purpose of divorce itself, not a sad, but inevitable by-product of loss, as in death (Chandler 1991:63).

One Sikh mother whose previous husband had behaved irresponsibly during their marriage, now spoke bitterly of him: "I've no feelings left. I'm very relieved. I feel as though I put up with it for too long." A second respondent, divorced and in her forties, expressed even more hostile feelings: "I despise him still. I'd be angry if I saw him now."

Not unexpectedly, fourteen of the fifteen widows said they continued to be emotionally attached to their husbands. Chandler claims that this is a natural reaction:

> It is not that the anguish is smoothed away as memories fade, but confronted in the repetition of poignant memories...marital history is rewritten as husbands are idealised and marriages are remembered as happier than they were (1991: 61).

The separated group, by virtue of their not having completely terminated their marriages, were the second most likely mothers to have retained positive feelings for the father, as recalled by a Sikh respondent in her thirties: "Yes, I still have feelings, and only remember the good times."

Further analysis implies that the women still attached to their ex-partners had a higher likelihood of having experienced lone parenthood for six years and under than the other groups. Because of the newness of their single status, the fathers may continue to be in their thoughts, as was illustrated by a separated Hindu mother of only three years, who still had fond memories of her former partner: "I miss the company. He was like a friend, and I miss the companionship." Vice versa, those women no longer attached were more likely to have been lone parents for seven years or more, suggesting that negative emotions intensified in line with the length of the separation. As Weiss has put it: "In general...as each member of the couple establishes a new life and a new identity, the other spouse becomes less important" (1975:124). This was echoed by a Sikh divorcee of nine years who said of her previous husband: "I hate him and don't want to see him in this lifetime," and a Muslim divorcee of sixteen years who uttered similar sentiments: "I've forgotten all that's happened. I've no feelings left."

A connection between the mother's fondness for the father and the length of time she had been married to him was evident. Respondents who had been married for ten years and over were the most inclined women to have remained attached to their former spouses, whilst those who no longer had any feelings tended to have only been married for up to five, and then for between five and nine years. This may denote that the briefer time spent together contributed to a lack of affectionate emotions, as expressed by a 34 year old divorcee, whose marriage had only lasted for three years:

> I don't want to be attached to him. I have no feelings now. For the first two years I had mixed feelings and felt bad. But now if I saw him on the street I won't care. For me, he's completely dead.

The above relationship can be matched to the results of Choudhry's study in 1988, which similarly revealed that those partners who had lived together for a longer period had more sympathetic feelings for each other than those whose marriages had been terminated earlier (Ahuja 1994:187).

Table 7.2 will explore, in greater detail, the emotional feelings of the 73 divorced and separated mothers towards the father by looking at several factors which may have influenced the extent of their attachment. The data suggests that domestic violence did make a difference to their attachment to the father. Those women who had positive feelings were less likely to have experienced a violent marriage, and vice versa, those who expressed negative sentiments were more likely to have been victims of domestic violence. A number of the respondents said they would now find it difficult to have any emotional attachment to their ex-husbands. One was a Hindu divorcee in her thirties, whose former partner had once poured kerosene over her and set her sari alight, and she said of him: "I can't tell you how much I despise him, he was the most terrifying person I knew." Another Hindu divorcee of six years, whose ex-husband used to beat her viciously in front of her children, called him "the worst person in the world" and then added a warning: "The day will come when he'll regret what he's done."

Table 7.2
Whether divorced and separated mothers were still emotionally attached to the father by whether violence in marriage and whose decision to terminate marriage

	Attached	Not attached	Unsure	Total
Violence in marriage				73
Yes	8	35	1	44
No	7	20	2	29
Decision to end marriage				73
Mother's	11	29	1	41
Father's	2	16	1	19
Joint decision	2	10	1	13

The way the decision to separate or divorce was reached also appeared to determine, to a degree, the mother's feelings towards the father. Women who still had an attachment were more inclined to have initiated the marriage breakdown themselves, which may suggest that since it was their decision, there was less anger directed at their spouses. One of these was a separated respondent in her forties from Kenya who had left her husband because of experiencing difficulties with her in-laws: "I still love him inside. It's not his fault but his parents' and he had to listen to them."

Mothers who were now detached had a greater tendency to claim that the father had ended the relationship, which may partly be explained by these women not wanting to terminate their marriages. A case of this was illustrated by a 31 year old Sikh divorcee: "I hate him because of everything, even after I co-operated with full heart. I tried to save the marriage."

The mothers' relationships with family and friends

This section of Chapter Seven will focus on the mothers' relationships with their family and friends, by firstly examining whether they knew of the women's lone parent status and their reaction to this. It will then proceed to look at whether the sample received any social, emotional and material support from these networks, and if the attitudes of family and friends towards them had changed in the light of their situation.

Whether the family and friends knew of the mothers' lone parent status

Despite the shame marriage breakdown can bring on the family concerned, as confirmed in Chapter Six, 71 of the mothers said that their relatives and friends had been told of their lone parent status, whilst another 16 women stated that a mixture of family and friends were aware. It was found that the latter group had experienced lone parenthood for an average of five years, with nine of the sixteen mothers having only been single for less than a year. These women, therefore, may still have been in the process of relating the news to other relatives and friends. Only 3 of the 90 respondents had told neither family nor friends of their situation, and being separated as opposed to divorced may have made their status easier to hide.

The reactions of family and friends on learning of lone parent status

Although the reaction of family and friends can vary so much on learning of the marriage breakdown, "the divorced woman attracts less sympathy than the widow, and divorce, unlike death by natural causes, is seen as somebody's fault" (Chandler 1991:63). Despite its rising phenomenon, unmarried motherhood may also evoke unsympathetic feelings within the family, as discovered in Phoenix's study of young, single women under the age of twenty. When told of the pregnancy by the daughters, almost one-half of the mothers and three in ten of the fathers were reported to have expressed nothing but displeasure at the news (1991:86).

Table 7.3
Reaction of family and friends on hearing of lone parent status of mother by lone parent type

	Div.	Sep.	Wid.	Unm.	Total
All family sympathetic	29	26	13	1	69
All family unsympathetic	2	4	2	1	9
Family - mixed reaction	8	1	—	—	9
No family know of status	—	3	—	—	3
All friends sympathetic	29	27	15	2	73
All friends unsympathetic	—	—	—	—	—
Friends - mixed reaction	8	1	—	—	9
No friends know of status	2	6	—	—	8

Table 7.3 focuses on the reaction of the family and friends on hearing of the mothers' lone parent status. Overall, it was found that 64 of the 90 women had a sympathetic reaction from both family and friends. Looking at a breakdown of the results as presented in the table, over two-thirds of the sample stated that the reactions of their families were favourable while the corresponding proportion for friends was 80 per cent. Only nine mothers said that none of their immediate kin group were supportive, and interestingly, no respondents felt this way about their friends' attitudes.

As predicted, the widows had the highest likelihood of receiving a sympathetic reaction from their families, one of whom was aged only 25: "My family are all very upset and want me to get remarried." An almost equal proportion of separated and divorced women replied that their relatives had been understanding. A 41 year old separated mother who had experienced domestic violence explained that her parents had already doubted the husband's morals: "My family told me to separate. They knew he wouldn't change. They were right behind me after I tried to commit suicide." Some of the respondents admitted to have been pleasantly surprised by the favourable attitudes of their families and this was confirmed by a Sikh divorcee of six years:

> Much to my surprise my mother was someone who encouraged me to take the positive step as she saw me suffer and become homeless three times. She told me to get a job and do things for myself. I was surprised, especially since I didn't have an arranged marriage. I felt guilty that my mother would turn around and say 'you chose him, so it's your problem.'

The separated group, however, were more inclined than the divorcees to receive a negative response from their relatives, which may partly be ascribed to their more "insecure" status, in addition to the pressure some of them may have been under to reconcile with their husbands. One such mother, aged 32 and only separated for seven months following a fourteen year marriage, said of her family:

> They were bloody angry, not sympathetic. They just want me to get back with my husband. I wish they would disown me. We're always arguing and I'm fed up.

Another separated respondent in her thirties attributed her parents' disapproval to her having married an Englishman: "My family said I made the wrong choice and should have married someone from my own country."

Somewhat unexpectedly, two widows also felt that they had unsympathetic families, one explaining that they spared no time for her: "They're not really bothered. They're always busy and ask me why I'm always worried. 'Your husband died ten years ago,' they say. But I do worry." One of the unmarried mothers similarly faced hostility from her relatives. With her former partner presently serving a prison sentence, she said she felt abandoned at a time when she most needed their support:

> There's been no communication between me and my family. My mother's not even seen my children and doesn't want to know me. My boyfriend gave my relatives a lot of hassle, but they don't realise I'm a victim too. I didn't put him up to it.

Table 7.3 signifies that a slightly higher proportion of respondents said that their immediate friends had reacted more sympathetically towards them than their families had done. None of the sample reported facing adversity from all of their friends. Perhaps because they had not finally terminated their marriages, a greater percentage of separated than divorced mothers explained that they had not told their friends of their situation.

The separated and divorced women were almost equally likely as each other to say they had sympathetic friends, one being a college educated, separated respondent whose friends had not judged her in any way:

> My friends never interfered and told me what to do; what they thought was right. They respected my decision. My friends said I would know more than anyone else what the problems in the marriage were.

Additional examination of the data indicates that the religion of the sample did make some difference to the attitudes of their families, with Hindu, Christian and Jain respondents being the most likely groups to receive favourable reactions. This may be due to the more liberal-minded approaches of these faiths as compared to Islam and Sikhism. For example, a 25 year old separated Hindu mother of seven months and a victim of domestic violence, explained how her family now felt guilty about the whole situation:

> They feel very sorry for me and were very happy because my life is now safe as my husband and his family were beating me. They realise now that they should have found out about the boy's family first.

In comparison, the Muslim mothers were the least likely group to receive an amicable response from their families, perhaps reflecting their more rigid and traditional ideology towards marriage. Unlike the Hindu respondent, a 50 year old Muslim divorcee whose former husband had also been violent, was confronted by a completely different reaction from her relations: "I didn't see my own relatives after the divorce. They didn't care and didn't like it, so they haven't accepted it." A second Muslim respondent in her forties claimed that her family were not happy after her separation because she had gone against their wishes:

> I had no idea. He was handsome, talked well and lived twenty years in Britain. He had a nice personality. It was a love marriage. My family blame me as he was my choice. They wanted me to marry someone of their choice.

The Muslim women were also the least likely mothers to gain sympathy from all their friends, and instead tended to have received only a mixed reaction from them.

Evidence from the figures also implies that the choice of partner who initiated the breakdown was a factor in determining the responses of family and friends, since they were more inclined to be sympathetic towards the mother if the husband chose to terminate the marriage, and then if it was a mutual decision. In one case, a 34 year old respondent whose former partner ended their fourteen year old marriage pointed out that her family now blamed themselves for her misfortune:

> My parents were very upset. My mother was especially, because when I got married, she told me my husband was okay. My mother feels guilty now that he's bad. I've got a big family who are all understanding, as are my friends.

Another mother aged 30, who jointly agreed to dissolve her marriage and gained universal support, explained that her ex-husband had never been popular anyway:

> My family were very happy. They didn't like his bad behaviour, especially since he's got a permanent stay in Britain. My friends feel bad for me that I have to cope alone with two children, but they're glad he's gone.

On the other hand, family and friends were least likely to have approved if the mother decided to end the marriage, and may reconfirm the notion of the Asian woman having to tolerate the marital conditions, however serious. This was further illustrated by a 31 year old respondent who, despite experiencing domestic violence in her thirteen year old marriage, said her relatives condemned her separation two years ago:

> They were shocked and didn't accept it. I told them I had three choices. I could commit suicide, separate or have a nervous breakdown. I knew I would go mentally mad if I stayed any longer with my in-laws. My family couldn't stop me as they were in India, but they didn't encourage any choices. They thought I'd go back to my husband in the end.

Choudhry's Indian study produced similar results to this research, in that in three-fifths of the 54 cases where female women had taken the initiative in filing the petition for divorce, their decision was disapproved by their relatives, and in about one-half of cases, by their friends. In comparison, the male divorcees who filed for divorce were reproached by their families in only a quarter of cases, and by friends in only a third of cases (Ahuja 1994:188).

Types of support given to the lone mothers by family and friends

The dissolution of a marriage disrupts and changes kinship and friendship networks, but family and friends are also sources of informal support (Chandler 1991). For women in low income households, most help tends to come from other female relatives and female friends. Their mothers often play an important part in this informal economy of care, providing both practical assistance with child care and material support, typically in kind than cash, such as through gifts of food, children's shoes and toys. Generally, families can also be an important source of financial help in emergencies (Graham 1992).

Evason's 1980 study of lone parents in Northern Ireland found that a third of the sample reported that they received some economic help from family or friends, although this tended to be small, intermittent and unpredictable. Over a half of the women in paid employment said that they relied on the unpaid services of friends and relatives to achieve a working wage (Graham 1993:109). A more recent study by Phoenix (1991) also showed how relatives, especially the unmarried women's mothers, were more likely than anyone else to provide them with practical, emotional and material support.

The importance of informal social support and networks has also been recognised in the absence of formal social services for lone parents in India (Siganporia 1993). Siganporia's findings (1993:360) showed that the most frequent source of assistance for the Muslim lone mothers came from parents and then siblings. This took the form of providing accommodation and meals, as well as providing post-divorce emotional help, whilst friends were mainly available for social and leisure activities. Pothen (1987:192), however, discovered that only one-third of his divorced sample were helped by their parents immediately following marriage breakdown. Thirty-five per cent of the divorced wives had to support themselves, with nineteen per cent getting little or no assistance from any source.

Table 7.4
Types of support from family and friends by type of lone mother

	Div.	Sep.	Wid.	Unm.	Total
1 Social and emotional help only from family and friends	20	11	8	—	39
2 Social, emotional and material help from family and friends	10	8	4	1	23
3 No support from family, support from friends	3	5	2	1	11
4 No support from friends, support from family	5	6	1	—	12
5 No support from anyone	1	1	—	—	2
None know of situation	—	3	—	—	3
Total	**39**	**34**	**15**	**2**	**90**

The mothers who took part in this study were asked about the types of support they received from their families and friends, the results of which are presented in Table 7.4. As mentioned earlier, a large number of the sample said that their close family were living abroad, which may have limited the extent of help that could be given. According to the data, however, practically all the mothers said that they got some kind of support, and this corresponds largely with the findings of other research outlined above. The most frequently mentioned forms of help were letter writing, social visits, telephone conversations and emotional support. Over two-thirds of the women said they were receiving assistance from both family and friends. However, only a quarter of the respondents received all three types of help - social, emotional and material - from both their friends and relations.

Table 7.4 shows that almost one-half of the sample received social and emotional support only from both family and friends, with widows and divorcees being the two most likeliest recipients. One was a divorced Hindu mother with a five year old son who said that family co-operation enabled her to work full time: "The grandparents of my son help with looking after him in the school holidays and after school." She went on to add of her friends: "They basically give me moral support." Although she tried not to impose on them too much, a 44 year old widow of twelve years mentioned the types of social and emotional help she accepted from her relations, some of whom were residing overseas:

> My family write from Africa. I tend not to call them unless I have to. They've got their own problems and I don't want to add to them. They're always there and we help and visit each other. If I'm depressed, they help me.

A 25 year old divorcee of only a year explained how her friends, especially, had become her principal form of support:

> I mainly speak on the phone to my parents. I'm too lazy to write. With my friends, it's like I don't feel they're outsiders. They're like my sisters or family. We plan and do things together.

Of the 23 women who acquired social, emotional and material help, the divorced, separated and widowed mothers were almost all equally likely to receive it. The smaller number of respondents who accepted material support may have been attributed to the fact that asking family for this kind of help undermines the moral base on which relations with kin are built. Requiring help transgresses the ethic of independence which governs many families, especially Asian parents on benefit (Graham 1993). Many of those who did receive material assistance explained the ways in which it helped them. One was a 37 year old divorcee with two children, who acquired a wide range of support: "Mum and dad help with the bills. They help with paying my insurance once a year. My mother brings food, buys things, furnishings, clothes and shoes for the children." A separated respondent in her thirties spoke of how her family cared for her three young daughters: "They phone and send letters and clothes from India. My in-laws give the children five pounds each on their birthdays." More substantial material support for the children was received by a Hindu divorcee with four dependants, who said that her "brother sends two tickets for the children to go to Canada" to visit him and his family on a regular basis.

According to Table 7.4, the separated mothers were the most probable group to acquire help from either relatives or friends but not from both, which may be because of their more uncertain and unsympathetic status. An illustration of a lack of family support was given by a 40 year old respondent, who, three years following separation, still found herself isolated: "I have only one blood cousin here in Britain, but she and her husband have not been supportive by visiting. If we do meet up and talk, it's always a 'we told you so' attitude."

Two of the 90 mothers said that they received no assistance from anyone. One was a separated respondent who said she had "always coped alone," whilst the other was a divorcee with four dependent sons who had lost contact with her relations in Britain and that she had "very little time to make many friends."

Whether the attitudes of family and friends towards the mothers worsened following marriage breakdown

According to Ahuja, following marriage breakdown "one's relationships to other persons both with those who are aware of his changed status and those who are not, becomes subtly altered by the introduction of this new element into his life" (1994:192). The changes in attitudes of family and friends, however, may have a greater long term impact for Asian lone parents, particularly in the light of their culture disowning marriage breakdown. Studies on divorce in India, however, have shown that, in general, family and friends carry on to be supportive after marriage dissolution. Pothen's survey revealed that in the vast majority of cases (64.5 per cent) there was no substantial change in the attitudes of friends towards the divorcees, with criticism made in about a quarter of cases and avoidance in just 5.5 per cent of cases (1987:195). Bharat's research, although comprising mainly of widows, found that a high percentage (85 per cent) of lone parents reported that they had cordial relationships with both their relatives and neighbours before and after their marriages had ended (1988:233).

Table 7.5 explores whether the attitudes of the family and friends in this sample had worsened following marital disruption, and shows the exclusion of three separated mothers since they had not made anyone aware of their status. The findings indicate that over one-half of the women reported no change in the attitudes of either family or friends, and over a third said they had a mixed reaction.

Table 7.5
Whether attitudes of family and friends towards the mothers had worsened following marriage breakdown by lone parent status

	Div.	Sep.	Wid.	Unm.	Total
All family and friends - no change	22	21	7	1	51
Family & friends - mixed attitude	15	9	8	1	33
Unsure of either's attitudes	2	1	—	—	3
Total	**39**	**31**	**15**	**2**	**87**

The separated followed by the divorced mothers had the greatest tendency to claim that the attitudes of their family and friends towards them had remained the same since lone parenthood, which is somewhat surprising, given that one may have expected the widows to fall into this category. Having been married to a violent and unfaithful former husband was perhaps the reason for family and friends' support towards a separated mother with four dependent children. She spoke of their sensitivity: "My family don't like to talk to me about it as it upsets me. They try to keep things normal. My friends feel for me and help me." A Jain divorcee of ten years explained that "many friends are in the same boat as me," whilst a second divorced mother, whose former partner had both been violent and a heavy drinker said that she had received valuable advice from her family and friends even before marriage breakdown: "Nobody's changed. They all tell me, 'we used to tell you before, leave him, leave him. Now at last it's finished. Don't go back to him now.'"

About a third of the 90 mothers said that they had received a mixed reaction in attitudes towards them since their marriages had ended. Significantly perhaps, of the 33 women who gave this response, 23 reported that whilst their friends had not changed their attitudes in a negative way, all or some of their families had. One of these was a separated Muslim respondent of two years who said of her relatives:

"They do look down on me as I'm separated. My children have suffered, but my parents have never called me. They say that people don't like divorced or separated women." Four more of these repondents reported that a mixture of all or some of both relations and friends had changed their attitudes for the worse, whilst the remaining six mothers said whilst all or some of their friends had changed, their families had remained the same.

Table 7.5 suggests that the widows followed by the divorcees were the most likely groups to have received a mixed reaction. The results pertaining to the widows are somewhat unexpected, given that they did not choose to become lone parents. However, on closer examination of their responses it was revealed that for the majority of them, it was their in-laws' attitudes that had adversely changed rather than those of their own families. One of these mothers, whose husband had died six years previously through kidney failure following a fifteen year marriage, explained that her in-laws actually believed she was the indirect cause of his death:

> It's mainly my in-laws who have changed - my husband's brothers and sisters. They don't like me. They blame me for killing my husband as they think I didn't look after him. They gossip to others that they'll help me, but they don't.

A second widow, aged 41, who had lost her partner four years earlier, said that although her friends still cared for her, some of her husband's relatives no longer did, resulting in her ostracism from the family:

> Only my in-laws have completely disowned me. They are so well off but they don't help me when I'm ill, and the children need help. They don't really see me, only socially sometimes at parties. But they're not pleased to see me at a party looking nice and all dressed up. They talk spitefully about me behind my back.

One mother, aged 36 and who had been married for 20 years, recalled how her own immediate family had abandoned her following her divorce a year ago:

> Nearly all my relatives have changed. They don't talk. Before, my family used to come for a chat and for dinner. No one knows me now. My uncles and aunts are all very traditional and said it's no good.

A small number of separated and divorced women complained that whilst their families had not changed, the attitudes of some or all of their friends had worsened. A 42 year old Bangladeshi mother who took the initiative to end her marriage two years ago spoke of the double standards kept by some of her friends:

> Some of my friends blamed me. They said it's horrid for a woman to divorce a man, but it's not an issue if the man does it though. I've now stopped mixing with them.

Religious affiliation seemed to be a factor in determining the reactions of family and friends, with the Christian, followed by the Sikh and Hindu mothers being more inclined than the other groups to point out that nobody's opinions had adversely changed following lone parenthood. The attitudes of the Christian women's families, in particular, would probably have been more westernised in outlook, and this was echoed by the words of a separated respondent in her forties, whose husband had been both violent and an alcoholic: "No one ever liked my husband anyway. My dad literally hates the man now and thinks I'm better off without him. If I told my dad that he'd phoned, he'd say 'not again!'"

A similar percentage of Sikh and Hindu women said that neither family nor friends had changed their attitudes towards them. One was a Hindu divorcee with an eleven year son who observed of her relations: "On the contrary they care more now than they did before," whilst a Sikh respondent of two years explained that her divorce came as no surprise to her family: "They don't treat me differently as the marriage problems had been going on for ten years, so they expected it and came to terms with it."

Analysis of the data may signify that the Muslim mothers were the least likely group to report no change from their friends and relatives, perhaps because of their more conservative Islamic beliefs regarding the family. One Muslim divorcee in her thirties said she was bewildered by her relations' negative attitudes: "They think it's a disease I have, although I don't know why," whilst another respondent who had been separated for a year, explained that her friends had maintained an incorrect impression of her: "Some of my friends did change. They thought I was a bad girl and kept boyfriends. You know how some of the Indian girls are."

The mothers' contacts with social organisations

Lone motherhood does not necessarily lead to greater social isolation than that of married women, at least in the short term (Crow and Hardey 1992). An alternative for lone mothers to reliance on families and friends as informal networks of support, is greater participation in more formal networks, also often women-based. Chandler stresses the importance of social organisations because:

> relationships in these friendship networks are less intense, more fleeting, reciprocal and ad hoc in contrast to the more complete and obligatory notion of family support (1991:83).

The exchanges are often less gendered with a greater range for services being supplied by other women.

This section will examine the mothers' social contacts by firstly looking at whether they were members of any clubs or organisations, before going on to explore the ways in which the women were helped through membership.

According to Table 7.6, almost two-thirds of the sample were members of clubs and/or organisations. Forty-three of the mothers belonged to Asian women's groups or centres, six were members of other day centres and seven women had joined educational and leisure classes, or were mèmbers of religious groups. A number of the 49 respondents who attended Asian women's or day centres also explained that they participated in other activities. The widows followed by the divorcees were the most likely mothers to belong to a club or organisation, probably because they had much older children than the separated group, and therefore had more time to attend.

Table 7.6
Whether mother was a member of a club or organisation by type and age of lone mother in years

	Divorced	Separated	Widowed	Unmarried	Total
Member of club					**56**
20's	1	3	—	1	5
30's	13	9	3	—	25
40's/50's +	10	7	9	—	26
Not a member					**34**
20's	1	3	1	1	6
30's	8	9	1	—	18
40's/50's +	6	3	1	—	10
Total	**39**	**34**	**15**	**2**	**90**

Age of the respondent also appeared to determine whether she was a member. According to Green et al (1990), women's clubs and organisations tend to be composed of older females, and this was confirmed by the results of this study, which found that the mothers in their forties and fifties were the most likely groups to belong. They were also almost twice as likely as the women in their twenties to have joined, the latter mothers being the least likely participants. The findings indicate a correlation between both type and age of lone parent and club membership. The separated mothers, having the youngest age profile in the sample, were the least likely respondents to have belonged to an organisation, whereas the divorcees and widows, being older, were most probable members.

Further analysis of the data in relation to the religion of the mother has suggested that the Muslim, followed by the Sikh women were the most likely groups to be members. Although Muslim women, generally, are believed to be home-based and non-assimilating, the club members in this sample were found to predominantly belong to Asian women's groups, where they would be interacting with other Asian lone mothers on a social and emotional level. Additionally, as earlier results have suggested, the Muslim mothers faced greater changes in the attitudes of their family and friends towards their lone parent status than did the other respondents, which may have forced them to seek external support from clubs or organisations.

Club and organisation members were also more inclined to have only experienced lone parenthood for under a year, rather than for longer. This could perhaps be attributed to their requiring more support at a time when they were still coming to terms with their new single status. The women who had experienced lone motherhood for a longer time were less likely to have joined a club, probably because they were now more settled and used to their situation, as explained by a Muslim widow of nine years:

> I keep myself busy looking after the house and the affairs of the children. When I'm alone in the house I like neighbours to come for a chat. I don't like to be alone and think of my husband and the children, as I don't want to be depressed. So I go to see other friends.

Women who furthered their education after the sixth form stage were also less likely to belong to a club than those educated up to the age of nineteen, implying that the more highly educated mothers may not have felt the need for external assistance from an organisation.

This was pointed out by a divorcee who attended university: "I don't believe in clubs. There's too much gossip."

There appears to be a connection between the extent of club membership and the number of dependent children of the mother. Women who had joined an organisation tended to have only one or two dependent children, whereas non-members were more likely to have three or four. This would suggest that respondents with more dependants to care for would have less time for outside contacts, as explained by a divorcee with three children aged ten and under who was "too busy looking after the children." The mothers in their thirties had a greater likelihood than the other groups of having three or more dependent children and were less inclined to be club members, thus strengthening the link between participation levels and numbers of dependent children.

The data implies a clear correlation between employment and organisation membership, since the unemployed mothers were twice as likely as the working women to have belonged to a club. Only 11 of the 24 employed women said they had joined an organisation, indicating that the working group may have been too occupied to attend. This point was illustrated by a divorced catering assistant with a thirteen year old son: "There's no time for a club. I work full time. Me and my son are happy and don't need a club." A second employed respondent and a full time assistant manager at a day centre explained that her life revolved around her job: "I've got involved in my work. The centre is open seven days a week and I'm here for seven days with my children. My soul is in this place."

Types of support and benefits received by the club members

The importance of centres as a support for lone parents is shown in Hawthorne and Kirk's study of 85 Scottish households, one-third of which were lone parent households (1995). The latter family type were also headed by women in all but two cases. The survey looked at the use of day centres for families with under fives and showed that the lone mothers tended to use the client-focused centres rather than the neighbourhood family centres or the education nurseries. These client-focused centres tended to depend more on staff and other professionals, probably reflecting the fragile nature of informal support from the mothers' relatives. The lone women were more likely to be poor, to feel stressed, suffer from poor health and be without a car. As members of the centre, these mothers were given advice and information, emotional and practical support, help with child care, someone in whom they could confide, and opportunities to meet others. It was concluded in the research that the centres did provide the kinds of formal assistance that were essential to the lone mothers.

The 56 women in this survey who belonged to a club or organisation were asked about the types of support and benefits they received through membership. Eighteen of the 56 mothers said they had joined a club for social purposes only, 23 women said they received social, financial, legal, housing and general help only, and a further 11 mothers replied that they belonged to an organisation not only for social reasons, but also for attending classes and for practical help. The remaining four respondents said that they acted as volunteers at the centre. Thus, in line with the findings of Hawthorne and Kirk's investigation, the clubs in this study appeared to play a very important role in helping the Asian lone mothers in a wide variety of ways.

The findings suggest that an overwhelming number of the 56 respondents said they were club members for social reasons, reinforcing their need to combat loneliness. According to Chandler, "although membership of women's or single parent groups may be transitory, it appears to supply vital socialisation into the circumstance, plus role models and confidence" (1991:83). One of the mothers in this project who attended an Asian women's centre for social interaction, not only echoed the words of Chandler but also of many of the other women in this research, by saying:

> Before, I cried a lot, but I got together with other women and had to face it and be brave. It has helped a lot at the centre. When you see others in the same situation, your problem doesn't seem that bad as when you're on the outside. My new friends at the centre are all encouraged by talking about their problems, and have become stronger by talking and exchanging ideas.

Of all the lone mothers, the widows were the most inclined to have joined an organisation for social reasons alone, and were less likely than either the divorcees or separated women to ask for practical help with their everyday problems. This could reflect their more "secure" status, in that as widows, being better provided for materially, they would only need clubs to socialise. This was illustrated by a 52 year old widow of eight years, who was an owner occupier and had no debts to pay: "I don't have any financial problems. I like to do things for myself. I come here just to pass time."

The divorcees were less likely than either the widows or separated mothers to belong to organisations for purely social reasons. Instead they also joined classes, and asked for practical help. Seven of the eleven respondents who had attended classes were divorced, and because of their more "finalised" lone parent status, they may have been able to devote more time to their own interests, one of whom was aged 42 and unemployed: "I felt depressed so I decided to do something about it. At college I'm doing a jewellery making course and doing a course in astrology. I've also recently joined a women's group." Another divorcee in her thirties explained that she needed more practical help: "I joined classes to help me get a job - a confidence class. I also want to learn more. I get constant advice with letters and other help."

Club members who received everyday help with housing, legal and financial matters were more likely to have been separated rather than widowed or divorced. These mothers were less inclined to attend classes, which would not be a priority, given their more pressing problems at this uncertain time. For instance, a separated respondent of only a month who was forced into staying in temporary lodging, spoke gratefully of how the Asian women's centre she joined was assisting her: "They're helping me with my court case. They also helped with bed and breakfast accommodation and claiming Income Support." A second separated mother, who also belonged to the same centre mentioned some of the other services provided that she benefited from: "I get counselling help, and help from the DSS, as the women who help me can talk to me in my language."

The one unmarried mother who regularly attended an Asian women's centre only to socialise explained how she tried to keep a low profile: "People here don't know my real situation. They think I'm just a single parent with two children." This may partly reflect the more hidden incidence of single motherhood within the Asian community as compared to the increasing numbers of separated and divorced women now willing to open up and talk about their problems.

The children's contact and attachment with the father

This final section of Chapter Seven will primarily concentrate on the children's contact and attachment with the father. It will firstly look at the effects of marriage breakdown on the children's general well-being as well as on their schooling, before going on to focus on the areas outlined above.

The effects of marriage breakdown on the children

An accumulated body of evidence suggests that children whose birth parents separate run increased risks of adverse health, educational and behavioural outcomes, when compared with those from similar social backgrounds whose parents stay together (Inglis 1982, Maclean and Eekelaar 1983, Walczak 1984, Howard and Shepherd 1987, Parkinson 1987, Burghes 1994)). Where studies once implied that the ill effects were mostly confined to the years immediately after breakdown, it may now be apparent that a few consequences for some children continue into adult life (Utting 1995:45). Wallerstein and Kelly (1980) found that a significant number of children suffered serious damage to their psychological health, not only in the short term, but also in adolescence.

The 90 mothers in this investigation were asked about the reactions of their own children to marital dissolution, with the findings confirming those of the literature. Forty of this sample claimed that all or some of their children had been adversely affected by the breakdown, 16 replied that this was the case for some of their children, and 33 either said that none of their dependants were affected, or else they were too young to understand. Only one of the women was unaware of her children's reactions to her very recent and sudden separation, since they were currently with the father.

As anticipated, the children who had lost their fathers through death were the most likely group to have been negatively affected, with one 41 year old widow observing that her children were "very sad and mentally depressed" after her husband's sudden demise. Divorce also appeared to have a much bigger impact on the children than did separation, partly reflecting the finality of the event in confirming the mother's new lone parent status. Some of the conditions mentioned by the women included insomnia, depression, aggressive behaviour and eating difficulties.

Having a violent father was also a crucial factor in influencing the children's reactions, since all or some children in a family were more likely to be adversely affected by marriage breakdown if their fathers were aggressive than those whose fathers were not. About two-thirds of the women who were victims of violence stated that all or some of their children reacted negatively compared with just over a third of those women whose marriages were free from violence. One respondent whose children were affected by the violent nature of the father was a 34 year old Muslim divorcee, who spoke of the scars that had been left: "They hated their dad because when he left home he hit me very badly and the children saw it. It still affects them. They don't want their dad to ever come home and now hate him." Another divorced mother of eight years spoke of how her then four year old daughter had been even more seriously affected by witnessing domestic violence:

> She was very angry for two years and had to go to the West Middlesex Hospital for psychiatric treatment. She's fine now but didn't want to know men at all. She told me she'll never get married, and used to say that when she grew up she'd kill her dad with a knife. Now she's okay. I've told her that God will look after the bad guys and personal revenge is wrong.

Although children do suffer emotionally and psychologically from having lived in a violent situation, it is worth noting the curious invisibility in the literature on the effects of divorce (Hooper 1994). The best known studies are North American and undertaken by psychologists, and have shown, among other factors, children's problems with eating, sleeping and aggression (Kelly 1994), from which many of the dependants in this research also suffered.

The effects of marriage breakdown on the children's schooling

According to Wells (1994), two-thirds of all children from divorced homes show marked changes in their school behaviour, whereby work suffers from a lack of concentration and through day-dreaming, with behaviour often becoming aggressive or rudely anti-social. Additionally the children can face social criticism when they are condemned or teased and taunted by their school friends, and in this way also encounter personal disorganisation accompanying the rupture of the conjugal family (Ahuja 1994).

Despite this, 46 of the 90 mothers in this survey noted that all their children were always getting on well at school, 29 said that all or some of their children had initially been affected, and only a further 10 replied that all or some of their children were still under-achieving. Three women stated that none of their children were attending school yet, whilst the final respondent said she was unaware of her children's educational progress.

The divorcees followed by the separated women were the two most probable groups to say that none of their children had any schooling difficulties. This is perhaps because the more settled divorced status causes less disruption than does the uncertainty of separation. For example, one divorcee commented on the good progress her five year old son had made: "He's doing well. He's intelligent, mature, takes the lead and mixes well with other children. There have never been any noticeable signs of him being affected." Another divorced respondent spoke proudly of her daughter's achievements in gaining a university place: "People said she wouldn't do well as she was from a broken family. As the daughter of a single parent she passed four A Levels and proved them wrong."

None of the ten mothers who claimed that some or all of their children's education was still being affected were widows. According to Burghes (1994), this may be because children in lone parent widowed families are frequently seen to fare not much differently from their peers in intact families. In this study being divorced or separated did not appear to make any difference to whether their children continued to have educational problems. One Sikh divorcee remarked that her younger daughter still needed extra coaching:

> She tends to seek attention and becomes aggressive in her manner. She's moved on to high school now, but has fallen behind. She gets special tuition within school to catch up, but the damage has been done earlier.

A prolonged illness due to marriage breakdown was the reason given by a separated mother in her thirties for her daughter's educational difficulties: "She was initially with her father. She fell ill and was kept behind at home. She clings to me even now in fear. She's academically behind and can't read very well."

Morrison and Cherlin (1995) argue that any effects of divorce on children reflect not only the stress of the breakup and its aftermath, but also dysfunctional family processes or children's problems that occurred before the dissolution. In a recent review of the literature, Burghes (1994) has also put forward the claim that there is no single or straightforward relationship between family disruption and the consequences for the children. Poorer outcomes can occur separately or in association with other factors such as low income, unemployment, reduced parental supervision, mental and physical illness and inadequate schooling. She also rightly emphasises that there is no inevitable path down which the children who experience their parents' separation can be expected to travel.

This hypothesis may equally be applied to the children of the mothers in this research, in that many of them already came from low income households prior to marriage breakdown. Additionally, the present unemployment situation of the majority of the women, as well as their on-going health problems may also have contributed to some of the negative experiences of the children involved. Moreover, the data has also revealed that only 10 of the 90 respondents said that all or some of their children were still not progressing at school.

The fathers' contact with the children

Despite the introduction of the Children Act (1989), the situation regarding contact between father and child does not appear to have improved. Research on access to children is scarce but suggests that at least 25-30 per cent of fathers lose touch with their offspring not long after separation (Parkinson in Lewis and O'Brien 1990). Marriage breakdown means that most children still lose regular contact, with possibly even a half relinquishing all contact with their fathers (Gibson 1994:158). Bradshaw and Millar (1991:17) found in their survey, that four in ten absent parents no longer had any communication with their children after two years, whilst a more recent study by Hester et al of 70 British and 30 Danish lone mothers, a fifth of whom were of Black and Asian origin (1994:102), revealed that agreed contact began to break down immediately or within a period of six months. Likewise, Leeming et al (1994) discovered a reduction in the ex-partners' relationships with their children, which if did continue, were only on an irregular basis. The loss of the father-child relationship appears to be a wider phenomenon, since most American research has also found that the majority of the fathers disengage from their roles over time (Ihinger-Tallman et al 1995:60). In his Indian study, Pothen (1987:207) also observed that about one-half of divorced fathers did not continue a relationship with their offspring following breakdown.

Echoing the existing literature, the majority of the 70 mothers in this investigation for whom contact was possible - 49 in all - said that the father currently did not see their children. Of the nineteen women whose ex-husbands did have contact, twelve explained that the father saw all his children regularly whilst seven said it was on an irregular basis. Three of these nineteen mothers also pointed out that all their children were presently living with the father, with another two stating that the father saw only some of the children.

Some of the respondents whose children no longer saw the father mentioned that their former partners had either remarried or gone back to live in their countries of origin. One divorcee with three dependent children whose ex-husband was now residing overseas remarked that she would not mind some contact: "If he wanted to see them I'd let him. I still respect him as he's the father of the children even though he didn't do anything for them." A number of other mothers explained that the father was not allowed access to the children, and this was reflected in the words of a divorcee with an eleven year old son: "He's not allowed to see his son by court order. He was given access in the first place, but as he didn't use it, the court took it away."

Not uncommonly, the children's not wanting to see their fathers was mentioned by some of the 49 women and corresponds with other surveys undertaken (Walczak 1984, Parkinson 1987). One divorcee in her forties said that on learning that their father could have access to them, her two children vehemently stated that they never wanted to see him again. Another explanation given by a divorcee as to the father's non-contact with his two teenage children was of a much more serious nature: "He's not allowed to see his daughter after sexually abusing her, and my son doesn't care for his father as he hurt me." Contact being too painful an experience was the reason disclosed by a Hindu divorcee as to why the father no longer wished to see his thirteen year old son:

> He does have access, but never comes. He never said in court that he wanted to see his son. His lady friend told him not to come. They think it's beneficial to my son not to see his father, as it would upset him more to think that other children have a normal relationship with their fathers. She now thinks it'll be easy for me and my son to get over the father as there'll be no contact.

As predicted, the fathers who currently conversed with the mother were also more likely to see their children. For instance, a 31 year old separated respondent who saw her former partner regularly at weekends, said the meetings only took place for the sake of her three sons: "I don't really want him to come but the children have got a right to see their father too." A second mother stated that her young daughters saw their father "now and then, but not regularly though. It's when he feels like it. Sometimes he takes the children to school."

Table 7.7 reviews whether the choice of partner deciding to terminate the marriage and the incidence of domestic violence were factors determining if the father saw his children. The fifteen widows, five mothers whose former partners have since died and one unmarried mother have been excluded from the table.

Table 7.7
Whether father currently sees the children by which partner's decision to terminate marriage and whether violence in marriage

	Her Decision		His Decision		Joint		Total
	V	N/V	V	N/V	V	N/V	
Does not see any children	15	6	6	12	7	2	48
Sees all children regular.	7	2	1	—	—	2	12
Sees all children irregul.	3	4	—	—	—	—	7
Sees only some children	1	—	—	—	1	—	2
Total	**26**	**12**	**7**	**12**	**8**	**4**	**69**

Whilst the findings may indicate that a mutual decision to end the marriage did not make any difference to whether the father saw his children, if the mother initiated family breakdown, she appeared more willing for her former spouse to see his children, either on a regular or an irregular basis. Likewise, if the father dissolved the relationship he was less likely to have contact with his dependants. An association with another woman may have been the motive for some of the fathers ending their marriages, leading to a further loss of interest in their children. This was illustrated by a newly separated mother in her forties with three daughters:

> He has access when he wants, but he doesn't bother or give a damn. When one of my daughters had a car accident and had to go into hospital, he hardly came in for more than five to ten minutes to see how she was doing. When she had to go in again, he didn't bother. At first I wanted him to keep some contact with the children, but he didn't want to. He's far too occupied with his girlfriend.

Evidence from Table 7.7 suggests that there was no correlation between the incidence of violence within the marriage and the father having contact with his children. This can be seen by the similar proportion of violent and non-violent men who currently saw their children. Hester et al's research (in Mullender and Morley 1994) also showed that violence did not make any difference to the father's wanting contact with his children, with the professionals interviewed reporting a rise in applications for access from violent men. Most of these resulted either in informal arrangements or in a failure to take the application through to court, and rather than resisting contact with the violent fathers, the mothers in the study actively encouraged it.

The children's present attachment to the father

Research by Walczak (1984) found that the father remained important to the children only if they were reassured that they still had a place in their absent parent's affections. Despite the distance between them, letters and phone calls by the non-resident parent were often enough to build a positive attachment. In Pothen's Indian study (1987:210), when the children were asked who they felt most attached to, 65 per cent replied it was their mother, whilst only 11.5 per cent said their father. Thus, unless a determined effort is made, the child's ability to sustain a relationship with the absent father is often difficult (Chandler 1991).

The Asian lone mothers were asked whether their children were still attached to the father and as Table 7.8 shows, over two-thirds of them answered that none of their children had retained any positive feelings. An equal number said that all or some of their children had an attachment, with just under a quarter of the respondents stating that they were unaware of their children's feelings or else they were too young to understand.

Table 7.8
Children's attachment to father by lone parent status of mother

	Divorced	Separated	Widowed	Unm.	Total
All children attached	6	10	10	1	27
Some children attached	5	3	—	—	8
All child. not attached	21	13	2	—	36
Don't know/too young	7	8	3	1	19
Total	**39**	**34**	**15**	**2**	**90**

As anticipated, the widows were the most likely group to reply that all their children continued to be attached to the father, one of whom said her four children "still think of him naturally." Another mother who had only lost her husband six months previously said her two dependent children "miss him a lot. They cry a lot at home and at school." These feelings are not unnatural, since unlike divorce and separation, "with the loss of a father through death, a child can idealise the absent parent and won't have his image shattered" (Inglis 1982:57). In comparison, Table 7.8 may signify that the divorcees followed by the separated respondents were the two most likely lone mother types to reply that none of their children were now attached to the father, and may be due to the bigger impact of divorce as opposed to separation in finally terminating the marriage.

Weiss (1975), amongst others, has spoken of the children's anger at the parent they believe to be responsible for the separation. Adolescents, in particular, may suddenly undergo a "precipitous de-idealisation of the parent." Where they had once rested their own self-esteem on identification with that parent, they now not only feel angry for having been disappointed, but also set adrift without internal guidance. One way of this dis-attachment is shown through the child's refusal to see the father when he comes to visit, or to accept his invitations, and an instance of this was illustrated by a Sikh divorcee with three daughters aged ten and under:

> No, they don't want to see their father. My youngest daughter dropped her birthday card he had sent for her on the floor. They all behaved so badly when he had access before because they didn't want to see him. I have tried to persuade them to see their father, but they don't want to. They're old enough to understand.

According to Pothen (1987), children of divorcees are able to maintain permanent relationships with adults who will perform the role of the missing parent, which led a second divorcee in this study to say that her five year old son was "not close at all. His grandfather and uncles have taken over the father figure role." This may not be surprising since "young children have little awareness of family relationships and tend to seek relationships in the immediate family situation" (Robinson 1991:162).

Walczak (1984) argues that apparent indifference to the absent parent can also be related to the non-existence of a bond before the breakdown and this was the reason given by a 39 year old Sikh mother for her two children's dis-attachment:

I do talk about him, but they're not really bothered about him now. They never really ask why their father's away and are used to the fact that he is. He never really cared all that much for them before the separation, so the children never really got the love of a father. It doesn't affect them and now lots of parents have now split up anyway.

Perhaps because of their younger age profile, Table 7.8 goes on to suggest that the separated mothers were the most likely women to either state that they were unaware of their children's feelings, or else that their dependants were still too young. One such respondent whose three year old son had no memories of his father went on to speak about how she would handle this sensitive situation: "I'll tell him when he's older. It'll be up to him to decide what he wants to do."

Additional analysis of the data indicates a strong attachment by all or some of the children to the father if they presently saw him. It would appear difficult for a child to love or feel loved by a father with whom contact is non-existent. Contact, on the other hand, makes it more possible for a parent and child to know each other, to give support and tangible proof of love (Walczak 1984). An example of this was illustrated by a 38 year old divorcee who spoke of her son's fondness for his father: "My son loves his father a lot. He looks forward to his father picking him up on Thursdays when I go on a diploma course. My son and his father are very close."

Conclusion

Chapter Seven has primarily explored the sample's relationships with the father, family and friends and with social organisations. Like many other British and Indian studies, the results of this survey have shown that the mothers' relationship with the father was minimal, with the majority of the women no longer in contact or wanting to see their former partners. Excepting the widows, less than a third of the respondents said they still saw the father. Additionally, more than one-half of the mothers replied that their ex-husbands no longer had any contact with the children, which also appears to be a common finding in other research.

This study found that the women had a stronger relationship with their family and friends, with more than two-thirds replying that both groups knew of their lone parent status. The majority of the respondents also gained a sympathetic reaction from their friends and family when they were told of the marriage breakdown. A great number of the mothers in this project received support from relatives and friends, although this was more likely to be social and emotional, rather than of a material nature. However, whilst just over one-half of the sample said that neither family nor friends had changed their attitudes towards them since lone parenthood, just under a half did face hostility from either family and/or friends.

Almost two-thirds of the respondents sought support from outside contacts through clubs and/or organisations and these women were more inclined to be older, unemployed and with only one or two dependent children. Almost all those mothers who had joined an organisation said they had done so for social reasons, with more than a half also receiving practical help with their everyday problems.

8 Types of Adjustment: Cultural and Psychological

The findings of Chapters Five and Six suggest that the Asian lone mothers feel there are cultural differences between British and Asian values concerning marriage, the family, the position of women, marriage breakdown and lone parenthood, with Asian culture placing far greater emphasis on traditional attitudes and practices within these areas. These prominent differences may therefore imply a possibility of the 90 mothers experiencing a conflict of cultures in their daily lives. Chapter Eight will primarily examine if such a conflict existed, or whether the sample felt they had culturally adjusted to their immigrant status. The latter part of this chapter will go on to explore the psychological adjustment of the women through their emotional and mental states of mind and their general outlook for the future as lone mothers as they perceived them.

The mothers' cultural adjustment

According to Oscar Lewis (1966), culture in an anthropological sense is a "way of life handed on from generation to generation," providing human beings with "a design for living" (quoted in Allen 1982:131). Cultures live and grow, change and sometimes fade away. They amalgamate with other cultures, or they adapt themselves to geographical or demographic necessity (Waldron 1995). Kymlicka (1995:7) argues that cultural membership has a high social profile, as it affects how others perceive and respond to us, which in turn shapes our self-identity. Cultural identity is also especially suited to serving as the "primary foci of identification," since it is based on belonging, and not accomplishment.

Chapter One has shown that various models of race relations have been developed over the years to conceptualise the conflict in the relationship between ethnic groups and the host society. Whilst Park and Stonequist's model in the 1920's and 1930's emphasised the association of marginal personality traits with the immigrant, Dickie-Clark concentrated more on the importance of the marginal situation rather than the marginal personality in the 1960's. The cultural deficit model which also emerged during the 1960's assumed that the majority culture was superior to the ethnic culture, with the immigrant expected to adapt to the life-style and customs of the host nation. Whilst other more contemporary models of race relations have also been developed, such as liberal pluralism, Marxist, Black and feminist perspectives, recent writers in this country such as Hiro and Anthias have put forward the theory of ethnic minorities facing a conflict between two equal but different cultures. Despite the differing perceptions of all the models it is true to say, however, that a conflict of cultures is an inevitability for an immigrant population living in a majority culture today.

Table 8.1 focuses on the cultural adjustment of the sample and looks to see how the replies of the 90 mothers correspond with the numerous models mentioned in Chapter One. The findings of the table clearly show four different types of responses, which appear to match the four stages an immigrant may experience on the way to achieve complete absorption into the host culture. Stopes-Roe and Cochrane give explanations for each of them as follows. The immigrant "may misconceive the reality and lose his given identity in pursuance of contacts in a society which will not accept him, a course that leads to alienation" (1990:126). This would imply that the immigrant experiences a conflict of cultures, whereby he or she is trapped or torn between their original culture and that of the majority culture. Secondly, the immigrant may be accommodated, to a varying degree, into the host and the minority cultures, maintaining attributes of and contacts with both. Thirdly the immigrant may identify clearly with his or her ancestral ethnicity and resist any change towards accommodation; fourthly the immigrant may reject his or her culture of origin and achieve a new identity by assimilating into the new society, changing his or her habits, ways of life and personal attitudes and identifications in response to the patterns encountered in the host society.

According to Table 8.1, just under one-half of the 90 respondents said that they felt caught between the British and Asian cultures, indicating that they were experiencing an identity crisis. About one-quarter of the sample replied that they chose positive aspects of the British and Asian cultures and were thus comfortably accommodated into both. Just under a quarter of the women said that they adhered to their Asian culture and were therefore not undergoing a conflict. A much smaller number of the mothers claimed that they mainly identified with the British culture and were also thus not facing any adjustment problems.

Table 8.1
The mothers' cultural adjustment by country of origin and length of stay in Britain in years

	India	Pak.	E.Afr.	Bang.	Other	**Total**
Caught between two cultures						**40**
Up to 9	1	2	1	—	1	
10-19	4	6	3	—	1	
20 +	7	3	7	2	2	
Chooses positively between both						**23**
Up to 9	2	—	1	—	—	
10-19	5	1	5	1	—	
20 +	2	1	3	1	1	
Feels mainly Asian						**21**
Up to 9	3	1	2	—	—	
10-19	8	1	1	1	—	
20 +	3	1	—	—	—	
Feels mainly British						**6**
Up to 9	—	—	—	—	—	
10-19	—	—	—	1	—	
20 +	2	1	1	—	1	
Total	**37**	**17**	**24**	**6**	**6**	**90**

These groupings, however, are not absolutely distinct from one another. Rather, they overlap at the margins, sometimes considerably. Thus the differences between the first and the fourth group are substantial, but the differences between any two adjacent groups are only minor. Discussion will now turn to each of the four responses in more detail with their implications for the lone mothers in this study.

The largest group of women responded that they were pressed between both the Asian and British culture, since:

living in both socio-cultural systems involves synthesising patterns of identification and developing social skills which enable sudden shifts in time and space from one set of cultural resources to another (Saifullah-Khan 1982:212).

However, through their narratives it became clear that there were varying degrees to which the mothers felt a conflict.

For some of these women the cultural conflict was very pronounced and this was illustrated by an unmarried Christian respondent aged 29, whose mixed ancestry had created a problem for her:

> I'm Anglo-Indian, but I dress in western clothes like my parents do. I'm not more English. I prefer Indian ways, they're more respectable. I eat Indian food all the time. English is our language. I do feel confused about my identity. There's some Indian in us, but no one digs into our background. Most of my friends are Indian and most of my friends go out with Indian blokes.

A 42 year old divorcee from India spoke of how she was finding it difficult to know how to bring up her children because of her own uncertain cultural status:

> Culture gives me a problem regarding the parenting of my two children, as although I'm living in Britain I do have some Asian values and I want the children to respect that. Lots of negotiating goes on, and I often feel caught as to what is best for the children.

Nevertheless, some of the mothers who said they were caught between two cultures explained it in ways which suggested that the culture conflict they experienced was not so pronounced. For instance, an employed Hindu widow in her forties made it clear that she had to adapt her identity according to circumstances:

> I'm caught between two lifestyles. I go to work and mix with English people. Then I come home and change into a Hindu. I change roles and have two lives in one day.

Many of the other respondents also spoke of having to take on both the British and Asian ways of life, one being a 32 year old separated mother from India: "I like and wear English clothes, but I'm also Indian and eat Indian food, and wear saris."

The culture conflict experienced by these 40 women was not of such a severe nature that their personality was impaired. Thus the evidence of this study does not support Park and Stonequist's notion of a marginal personality. To a small degree, however, the findings lend support to Dickie-Clark's claim of a marginal situation.

Table 8.1 goes on to show that 23 of the 90 respondents said they chose positive aspects from both British and Asian cultures. The main difference between this group and some of the mothers in the previous group is one of emphasis, with women in this group being more emphatic about their ability to choose between the values of the two cultures.

As above, there were also degrees to which these respondents felt accommodated into both cultures. In one case, a 37 year old divorcee spoke of how she adjusted on a minimal level: "I accept both cultures. When I'm with English people I'm like them, and when I'm with Indian people I'm like them. I'm satisfied with both cultures and make the most of them both." By comparison, for a separated Hindu mother of ten years, accommodation into both cultures covered a greater sphere of her life:

> Living here, one has to take on much of the English culture. I don't really have an identity problem. I feel both Asian and British. I meet all types of people when I go out. I don't consciously bother about keeping my own culture. I live a lifestyle that suits me and my family, and that means living in a more westernised way. At first it was difficult to be an Asian single parent, but I live as a 'normal' person now. I don't live like a single parent.

The data from the table shows that 21 respondents replied that they had mainly kept their Asian cultures. This is not to suggest that they rejected all aspects of the British way of life. Rather on balance, they relied more on their original than on the British culture. From the responses of these women, it was clear that although they preferred their Asian culture, there were degrees to which they had retained them. For example, a 47 year old separated Sikh respondent from India said she wanted to pass on her culture to her children:

> I can't really speak the English language and I wear Indian clothes. I may be a British citizen but nothing else. I want to maintain my culture totally, as well as teaching my daughter the same. A lot of western ideas are not good. It's best to keep to your own values.

On the other hand, a Muslim divorcee of a year held a preference for her culture because she "liked" her religion, whilst another divorcee, aged 32, explained her feelings in a different way: "Although I am a British citizen, it doesn't matter where I live. I am still Indian inside."

Only six of the mothers said that they felt they had assimilated into the British culture. From what they said, however, it was apparent that these women had not totally relinquished their original culture and identity. For example, an unmarried respondent aged 24 from Kenya commented:

> I was part of the Indian community when I was a teenager, so I was part of both cultures. Now as I have a low profile I can't enter the Indian community again and am living a way of life in England that people come to expect.

A Muslim mother from Pakistan, aged 44, said she felt British but had still retained some of her Asian culture: "I wear salwar kameez and eat Pakistani food, but I relate more to the English way of thinking. I respect it more, and understand it more."

From the results, therefore, it would appear that the model of "cultural pluralism," as advocated by Hiro (1991) and Anthias (1992) in Chapter One, was supported by most of the women in this study. The overwhelming majority of the sample had retained at least some of their Asian culture, regardless of whether or not they were positive about their cultural identities. Within each of the four categories there were also varying extents to which the mothers felt they belonged, implying that they were not really all that far apart in terms of their cultural identifications. Clearly assimilation, as it is understood in the literature, was not supported by any of the mothers. This is not unsurprising in view of the strong physical and cultural differences between Asian and British people as well as because most of the mothers were first generation immigrants.

Looking more closely at the figures from Table 8.1, the data indicates that the respondents from Pakistan were more likely than the other groups to feel that they were caught between both the immigrant and the host cultures. A separated mother in her thirties spoke of her dilemma as follows:

> I still have both Asian and western views. I'm not totally either and am not sure of what my true identity is. I feel Muslim, but my attitudes are both English and Asian. I don't feel fully accepted into either culture. I'm not British because I'm not the right colour, but I'm not Asian because if I was back home, my attitudes would be different from theirs. Even in Britain, some Asians would think my attitudes are different.

The above findings relating to the Pakistani women would seem to be in line with other researchers (Jeffrey 1976, Stopes-Roe and Cochrane 1990,

Shaw 1994), who have all found their Muslim samples to be non-assimilating. This may be because the nature of Islam, which makes a Muslim identity an all-embracing one, is concerned with all aspects of everyday living, and is bound to strengthen further some of the established patterns (Joly 1995).

In comparison, Table 8.1 suggests that the mothers from East Africa had a higher likelihood than the other respondents of saying they were accommodated into both the British and Asian cultures and echoes the findings of previous studies (Bhachu 1985, Robinson 1986, Stopes-Roe and Cochrane 1990), which similarly show the East African group to be more favourably disposed towards being assimilated. This is perhaps because East African Asians are not primary migrants in the sense that they have moved directly from their ancestral homelands to Britain. They have thus aspired to a more westernised lifestyle than migrants from India and Pakistan, and are more concerned with finding and exploiting vacant economic niches in Britain as they had done in Africa (Robinson 1986). According to Bhachu (1985), the emphasis for East African Asians is not on total assimilation. Rather, they stress their own ethnic identity, not by maintaining a distance from the British, but by being more emphatic about their own separate identity.

Some of the women from East Africa who participated in this study spoke of their comfortable accommodation into both the host and immigrant cultures, the first being a 37 year old divorcee who explained that she "switched" cultures to her advantage accordingly:

> I accept both cultures. When I'm with English people I'm like them, when I'm with Indian people I'm like them. I'm satisfied with both cultures, and make the most of them both.

The second respondent, a widow aged 47 and working as a receptionist, explained that she had changed some of her attitudes and values to fit into life in a western society:

> The ideas of my culture have changed. I think differently now than before. I still love my Indian culture but have now evolved. I have taken the good points from both the Asian and the British cultures, so I've got the best of both. I know my colour will never change. I still eat Indian food, live amongst Indians and wear Indian clothes. But on the other hand, some of my attitudes are now western. I will never push my children into having arranged marriages. I know divorces come through unhappy marriages.

According to Table 8.1, the mothers from India were the most inclined group to feel that they had largely retained their Asian culture, implying that they had been less influenced by the British way of life. This finding corresponds with an earlier survey carried out by Robinson (1986) who also revealed that mothers from South Asia, including those from India, were more likely than those from East Africa to hold on to their original cultures.

One 40 year old Indian divorcee of six years in this project spoke of how she had slowly discovered her true cultural identity:

> Today I know my identity...I know who I am and where I belong. When I was first married I was torn between two cultures. I didn't want to be part and parcel of the traditional Asian culture and was more westernised and outgoing. At some stage, however, I realised that things were not going to change and I couldn't be what I wasn't. I'm Indian and I'm proud.

The table may signify that the women who were caught between two cultures were the most probable group to have been residing in Britain for twenty years and over. Although one may have expected these mothers to have been accommodated into both the cultures, on closer examination it was disclosed that thirteen of these nineteen respondents were also in their forties and fifties and had spent much of their upbringing in their countries of origin. This would imply that they had found it much harder to relinquish their traditional culture, despite their extended length of stay in this country.

Mothers who chose positive aspects of both Asian and British cultures were the most likely respondents to have been living in Britain for between ten and nineteen years, perhaps because they had been living here for long enough to have become comfortably accommodated. Much more crucially, perhaps, eight of these eleven women were in their twenties and thirties and were thus more receptive to taking on some of the British culture to create their own identity. For instance, a separated Sikh mother aged 39 and residing here for seventeen years remarked how one should adopt some of the British culture and practices whilst living in this country:

> I don't really have an identity problem. I take the best of both cultures. You can keep your Indian identity, but must accept you're in a foreign country as well. For example, if your marriage isn't working and you have problems, it's better to separate and not stick together. The Indian community has to learn to accept that not all marriages will work.

Respondents who felt mainly Asian in identity had the highest likelihood of having only been residing in Britain for up to nine years. Three of these six women were also in their twenties and three were in their forties, but age did not appear to make any real difference to their responses. Rather, these mothers were still in a position to have kept much of their original cultures intact due to their shorter time in this country, the average length of stay just being three years. One such mother was a 44 year old separated respondent who had migrated to Britain from Tanzania three years previously, which probably accounted for her Asian identity: "I've just arrived here and I'm not that westernised in my thinking. I'm proud of my culture and language. I want to bring up my daughter in an Indian way like that."

Five of the six women who felt that they mainly had a British identity had been resident in this country for twenty years or more and had arrived when they were young. One of these mothers came to Britain aged one year, another when she was aged six, two more when they were fourteen, one at seventeen and the last aged twenty. Thus the average age of this group when they arrived in this country was twelve years, meaning that they would have spent an important part of their socialisation in the UK. In addition to this, whilst only two of these women were educated solely in their countries of origin, another two had received a totally British education, whilst the remaining two respondents were taught both in their countries of origin and in this country. The British education of these mothers may, therefore, have also influenced their feelings of being assimilated into the majority culture and way of life.

Further analysis indicates that the Muslim women were the most likely in the sample to say they were caught between two cultures, and this may be anticipated since Muslims are "fairly successful in insulating those spheres of life in which they particularly dislike British ways and so it is unlikely that they would want to become anglicised" (Jeffrey 1976:107). Likewise, other recent studies (Stopes-Roe and Cochrane 1990, Joly 1995) have found that their Muslim migrants were the most likely group to isolate themselves in their own culture.

Mothers in this study who were accommodated into both the host and immigrant cultures tended to have been of Hindu religion. This was also noted by Stopes-Roe and Cochrane (1990:207) who found that their Hindu sample appeared to be more liberal in their attitudes towards adopting some of the British culture. The researchers went on to qualify this by stating that although "the precepts of Hinduism govern daily life, they are less universally applicable in precisely the same form" as those of Islam, and are thus, in some ways "less rigid. In essence, Hinduism is far more tolerant."

Women in this research who were principally of Asian identity had a greater likelihood of being of Sikh origin. Stopes-Roe and Cochrane (1990) revealed that although their Sikh respondents were between the Muslim and Hindu sample when it came to assimilation, they also appeared to have more stable experiences, and unlike other groups, whose backgrounds varied, the Sikhs came from rural backgrounds and were more likely to have more contact with their own ethnic groups. Because there was less change in the backgrounds between the first and second generation Sikh sample, this may have meant less disruption of their roots on which traditions depend to flourish. Similarly one separated Sikh respondent who took part in this survey explained that she wanted to pass on her Asian culture to her children: "I know I've been in Britain for a while now, but I'm definitely Asian in culture, and I want my children to be too. After all, their colour will never change."

Those who identified with the British way of life were most inclined to be affiliated to the Jain and Christian religions. In the case of the Christian group, this may have been anticipated since they would have a greater affinity with western culture.

Table 8.2
The mothers' cultural adjustment by age of lone mother in years

	20's	30's	40's/50's +	Total
Caught between two cultures	4	19	17	40
Chooses positively between both	2	13	8	23
Feels mainly Asian	4	8	9	21
Feels mainly British	1	3	2	6
Total	11	43	36	90

Table 8.2 explores whether the age of the mothers was a determining factor in deciding the perceptions of their cultural identities, and suggests that the women in their twenties were marginally more likely to feel that they were Asian rather than British. Although one may have expected the youngest respondents to be more westernised as other literature on British Asians has indicated (Shaw 1994, Ballard 1994), a more detailed analysis of these mothers in this

project revealed that, not only were any of them born in Britain, but they had only been living in this country for an average of five-and-a-half years. Therefore, their Asian identities may be attributed to their upbringing in their countries of origin and to their short stay in Britain rather than to their age.

According to one 27 year old separated respondent in this study, strong family ties had helped her to retain her Asian culture: "I've still kept my culture intact. My mother is in Britain as well, so I speak an Asian language. I'm no good at English." Residing in Britain for only two years may have been the reason why a separated mother aged 25 felt she had an Asian identity: "I'm only Indian because I've got all Indian habits. My heart is Indian. I have no identity problem." Stopes-Roe and Cochrane (1990) also found that 57 per cent of their young sample said they perceived themselves to be Asian rather than British, which may imply that the second generation are still willing, to a degree, to keep their original cultures intact.

Respondents in their thirties interviewed for this research were the most probable grouping to say they chose positive aspects from both the host and immigrant cultures. Compared to the older mothers these respondents may have had more open-minded attitudes, as illustrated by a 30 year old Hindu divorcee: "I've picked up the best of both, and I enjoy both cultures. I don't feel an identity problem. I am accepted by both communities."

Those who felt caught between two cultures were most likely to be in their forties and older and least likely to be in their twenties. This may be somewhat surprising, since one may have expected the oldest group to have either felt Asian in identity or else have become more accommodated into both cultures. One 43 year old Jain divorcee, although resident in Britain for 22 years, explained how being an Asian lone parent had partly contributed to her uncertainty regarding her cultural identity:

> I'm neither British nor Asian. I am caught, but being a single parent doesn't help. For example, if an Indian husband and wife are alone in the house I don't want to get too close to them because if anything goes wrong in their marriage, they'll think as I'm a single parent I'm to blame. Sometimes Indian women may think I'm after their husbands. This sort of problem makes me wonder where I stand culturally. Being an Asian lone parent doesn't help because you can't be totally part of that community anymore and you're neither a total part of the English community.

Moving on to employment status, the results of Table 8.3 denote a relationship between this and the mothers' cultural identities, in the sense that the working women were more likely than the non-working group to say they chose positive aspects from both cultures, or else feel they were British in identity. This could be because the women with jobs had greater opportunities to interact, and perhaps were also expected to do so with British people at work. Thus, they were in a better position to "take on" some of the British culture, or else allow it to influence them to a much greater extent. For example, a part time administrator who was accommodated into eastern and western cultures, said she felt privileged to be part of both:

> When I go out to work it's different there, as I'm working with two cultures. At home I'm with my parents and I speak Punjabi, but I don't feel I have an identity problem. I'm lucky in that I can enjoy the English and the Asian cultures.

Table 8.3
The mothers' cultural adjustment by whether or not employed and whether or not a member of a club or social organisation

	Employed	Unemployed	Total
Caught between two cultures			**40**
Member of club/organisation	8	22	
Not a member	2	8	
Chooses positively between both			**23**
Member of club/organisation	2	9	
Not a member	6	6	
Feels mainly Asian			**21**
Member of club/organisation	1	10	
Not a member	3	7	
Feels mainly British			**6**
Member of club/organisation	—	4	
Not a member	2	—	
Total	**24**	**66**	**90**

In contrast, the unemployed respondents had a greater likelihood of either saying that they had an Asian identity or else they felt torn between two cultures. This may be due to their having fewer occasions than the working group in which to mix with the British on a more regular and daily basis. An illustration of this was given by a 60 year old separated mother who said she had retained much of her Muslim culture through being based at home:

> I feel totally Pakistani. I have kept all my culture and am very religious. My English is also very minimal. I mainly stay at home and hardly go out, so I don't mix much with people, especially English people.

The evidence from Table 8.3 implies that women who belonged to a club or social organisation were more inclined than the non-members to perceive themselves as being caught between the British and Asian cultures. Because of this, these respondents may have felt the need for external support, most of whom had joined Asian women's centres, where they received practical help with their day-to-day problems.

Respondents who had not joined a club or organisation were more likely than those who were members to say that they chose positively between both cultures, suggesting that as they were more able to accommodate into society, did not require any specific assistance. For example, a Muslim widow in her forties and with two teenage sons explained how she managed to cope alone:

> I am not caught, but I like both cultures and don't have an identity problem. I like the Pakistani approach to life and my religion which plays a large part. I also take on some of the British culture by mixing with the English when I can.

The findings of this research pertaining to the relationship between ethnic minorities and the host nation corresponds with many others undertaken over the last twenty years. A large and growing academic literature on the lifestyles and habits of British Asian communities (Jeffrey 1976, Anwar 1979, Bhachu 1985, Shaw 1988, Joly 1995), have also all shown how the migrants have retained many of their traditional customs such as diet, dress, language, religious and marriage practices from their countries of origin.

In line with this investigation, Robinson's study of Asian migrants in Blackburn (1986:202) similarly discovered that none of the groups was even near to absorbing into the British culture, never mind achieving total assimilation, whilst, more recently, Stopes-Roe and Cochrane (1990:198) found that almost all the parents and almost two-thirds of the young people in their project identified themselves as Asian. They also went on to reveal that language use was the point of greatest difference in changing customs for the sample. More than half of the younger women interviewed dressed in traditional clothing by choice, at home at least, whilst the majority of the ethnic group kept traditional diet regulations. Significantly, perhaps, the young Asian respondents did not indicate a general tendency to break away from parents and family and adopt British ways of selecting future partners in marriage.

All these patterns in the above research, as well as in this study, tend to imply that Asian migrants "seek to create an environment which will strengthen, rather than challenge" their traditional values (Robinson 1986:79). Although the surrounding environment may have had much more influence on migrants' lifestyles than they themselves are aware of, the notion of cultural pluralism practised today has meant that "the boundaries around their own domestic worlds are still sharply drawn" (Ballard 1994:34). This would imply that the immigrants continue to identify with and evaluate the norms of their original cultures in a positive way, whilst rejecting any aspects of the majority culture which they do not find agreeable.

The mothers' psychological adjustment

According to Spanier and Casto (1979), divorced and separated mothers must adjust to feelings such as loneliness, fear, frustration or inadequacy, as well as to possible feelings of happiness, heightened self-esteem and freedom if their adjustment is to be successful. This section of Chapter Eight will firstly explore whether the 90 women in this survey had adjusted to their status as lone mothers mentally and emotionally, and secondly if they now felt more confident and independent in the light of their marriages dissolving.

Types of emotional and mental conditions suffered by the mothers

There is a very substantial body of empirical evidence to show that marriage breakdown both in India and Great Britain leads to mental and emotional difficulties. Some of the findings of these studies shall be compared with those of this research.

Table 8.4 examines the types of mental and emotional conditions suffered by the respondents, and shows an overwhelming majority of the sample admitting to being affected by at least one of the listed conditions. On closer examination of the data, it became apparent that six of the seven mothers who did not suffer from any of the problems also said they were in physically good health and did not complain of any physical illnesses. Two of these seven respondents explained further that they always had good friends around them, whilst a widow in her thirties said she was now "happy with life." A core of 53 women claimed to be suffering from three or more of the emotional and mental conditions listed, echoing Bharat's study (1988:234) which similarly found that sixty per cent of the sample manifested combinations of three to four symptoms.

Table 8.4
Types of emotional and mental conditions suffered at present

I *Suffers from no emotional and mental illnesses*	**7 mothers**
II *Suffers from the following emotional and* *mental complaints*	**83 mothers**
Loneliness	66 mothers
Stress	63 mothers
Depression	59 mothers
Unable to cope	47 mothers
Guilt	19 mothers
Suicidal	7 mothers

In this project, the widows were the most likely group to suffer from three or more complaints, which may be anticipated since, according to Chandler:

> bereavement is seen as amongst the most traumatic of human experiences which stirs a gamut of emotions and feelings that border on those of the physically ill and mentally disturbed (1991:61).

In one case a widow in her forties complained of feeling stressed, lonely and depressed: "I'm always crying all the time. There's no one to talk to anymore. I'm all alone without my husband. It's all still too much for me, even after five years."

The findings for the nucleus of 53 mothers also denotes that perceptions of physical health (discussed in Chapter Four) was an additional factor in determining the extent of the mental and emotional symptoms suffered, since twelve of the fifteen respondents who felt they were in poor health, were afflicted by three or more of the listed ailments.

According to Table 8.4, the most common single complaint given by the 83 women was that of being lonely. Similarly, Wallerstein and Kelly (1980:155) found that eighteen months following the separation, two-fifths of the divorced men described themselves as lonely as did two-thirds of the females, about half of them painfully so. Bradshaw and Millar (1991:14) also revealed that for their sample, loneliness was the worst thing about being a lone parent (48 per cent).

Loneliness is not simply a desire for any company. Rather it refers to very specific forms of relationship. In their study, Wallerstein and Kelly (1980:193) observed that more women than men "quietly, longingly wished for someone with whom they could talk, share and be affectionate on a daily basis." Likewise, a widow in her forties with three daughters in this research spoke of how loneliness was attributed to her no longer having a husband: "Even though everyone is there, you're still on your own really. The children understand but it's not the same thing as having a partner."

Through the responses of other mothers it became clear that there were different kinds of loneliness, as well as differing degrees to which the women suffered from it. According to Chandler (1991), women without husbands may also be lonely because they are socially isolated and marginalised in a society built around couples and the conventionally married. This type of solitude was portrayed by a divorcee in this project: "Everyone is married. No one wants to know me." In contrast, a Sikh divorcee in her thirties claimed that being lonely was only an occasional problem for her: "I can get lonely at times. Well, now and then. But on the whole I'm okay on my own."

An almost comparable percentage of the respondents interviewed said they suffered from stress. As with loneliness, there were various extents to which the stress was endured. For a 34 year old separated mother, strain was the result of looking after three children as well as holding down a full time job: "I feel stressed because of work and being a mum and dad at the same time. The children require a lot of attention." The pressures of being a lone parent took on a more acute form for another separated mother in her thirties: "I'm suffering mainly from stress. That's why I couldn't carry on working as I was too poorly."

Just under two-thirds of the sample explained that they felt depressed, and this may have been foreseen since whilst the presently married are the most free of depression, those whose marriages have ended are the most burdened with it (Pearlin and Johnson 1981). Bharat (1988) and Siganporia (1993) also noted that the majority of their Indian lone mothers claimed to have suffered from depression, whilst Wallerstein and Kelly (1980:155) similarly observed that eighteen months after marriage breakdown close to one-half of their female divorcees were depressed to some considerable degree, and significantly more so than the men.

The respondents in this study who were disconsolate expressed this in various forms, and again in differing gradients. For some women being depressed merely meant having "good days and bad days" as a Muslim divorcee put it, or else the despondency was "not that bad" as expressed by a 47 year old widow. However, for other mothers, grimmer forms of depression were caused by specific worries. A Sikh divorcee of ten years with a thirteen year old son had this to say: "I worry too much about the mortgage, and I need clothes, dinner money, books and clothes for my son." A widow whose husband had passed away four years ago had suffered from a more acute form of depression which had affected her whole way of living: "I've been in and out of hospital because of my depression. It all started after my husband died."

Just under a fifth of the respondents admitted to feeling guilty about their present situation. This is likely to be manifested in "the individual's self-condemnation for having failed to maintain a home for the children, or simply for having failed at marriage" (Weiss 1975:76), and was illustrated by a Sikh divorcee with two children, who said:

> I feel guilty all the time as I was the one who wanted the divorce, and I can't do everything for my children. I can't give them a father's love, but the children don't want to see their father. I now want to be the best mother for them.

Despite being a widow, a second mother in her forties and with two children, explained why she blamed herself: "I feel guilty now that I'm not a good mother. I keep asking myself if I've done enough for my children."

A very small number of the women alleged that they currently felt suicidal. This is in line with Siganporia's survey (1993) which also revealed that although many of the respondents suffered from depression, loneliness, anxiety and fear about their futures, most of them did not admit to having suicidal feelings. For the majority of the seven respondents in this project who felt suicidal, the children's need for them as mothers provided them with a sense of being valuable to some degree. One of these was a Hindu widow who said she only lived for her two dependants: "Even now when I feel very down, I would rather die than suffer, but I know I have to be strong for the children. I have to live for them. If I died, what would happen to them?" Seeing her grandchildren on a regular basis was the reason given by a Hindu divorcee in her forties for stopping her suicidal thoughts: "Yes, I do feel suicidal sometimes, but I always think of the girls and am happy when they come with my grandchildren."

Although not directly asked, 23 of the 90 mothers made it known that they had felt suicidal in the past. Some of them gave accounts of their previous experiences, one being a divorcee in her thirties who explained that she needed therapy:

> I used to have feelings of suicide at least three times. I was very depressed. I had one nervous breakdown and had to have homeopathic treatment. I'm okay now as I've got good friends around me.

Another of these respondents, a young widow, said it was only having two children to care for that prevented her from committing suicide: "When my husband died, at first I thought of suicide, but as I had children I knew I had to live for them. If I'd had no children I would have killed myself." A third mother, separated and in her forties, gave a brief description of how she had actually made an attempt to take her own life: "I tried once in the past to kill myself. I drank domestos. It was a stupid thing to do."

When questioned, 78 of the 83 women under study who endured at least one mental or emotional condition also claimed that their present state of mind was attributed to their lone parent status. In one case, a separated Muslim mother said she suffered from guilt following the breakdown of her love marriage because she did not heed the advice of her family: "I feel guilty now about not listening to my parents about marrying someone of their choice. I don't feel as if I can cope anymore being on my own."

Only 5 of the 83 respondents said that their emotional or mental symptoms were not connected to their single status. According to Chandler (1991), this may be because although conditions such as loneliness are commonly reported by lone mothers, to regard these simply as emotional problems implies that they exist primarily in the minds and attitudes of the women. To depict this, Bharat's study (1988) significantly found that the symptoms of emotional disturbance suffered by the lone mothers were ascribed not merely to the absence of the spouse, but mainly to the resultant conditions of economic hardship, poverty and problems regarding the children. Similarly, in this investigation, the five mothers gave various external explanations for their complaints. One of these was a Sikh respondent who associated her stress with her cramped housing conditions; another, an unmarried mother, said she was depressed because of her over-dependence on her parents, with whom she still lived; two more of the women explained that they felt guilty because they had not been in contact with their families for a long while, whilst suffering from a hereditary illness was the reason given by one mother for her feelings of depression.

The mothers' personal outlook

It has been argued by many that recovery from marriage breakdown is gradual and goes through different stages. Weiss (1975) has put forward the view that there are two distinctive phases in the movement towards recovery. The first is a period of transition in which the pre-existent of life has been disrupted, a new pattern not yet integrated, and is for many a time of disorganisation, restlessness and chaos, with a frantic search for escape from distress. The second stage which begins is a period of recovering, "in which the individual has established a coherent pattern of life but has not yet integrated it firmly enough so that it can withstand new stress" (1975:236). This phase would usually end from between two to four years following the separation, as a stable and resilient new identity and way of life is established. Thus, although overwhelming upset may disappear before the first year after the marriage has broken down, the achievement of full recovery requires more time than one may expect.

Table 8.5, later in this chapter, examines whether the 90 women in this survey believed they had recovered from marriage breakdown, with the data clearly showing that the vast majority of the sample were presently more optimistic about their lives. This has also been confirmed by other research on lone parenthood.

Kohen, Brown and Feldberg's American study of divorced and separated mothers (1979:233) found that twelve of the mothers expressed relief or happiness at the the ending of their marriages, another six felt similarly but had some reservations and twelve were unhappy. One year after breakdown, 17 of the 30 mothers reported that things were easier now than with their husbands, 3 said things were harder and 10 explained that things were different with both good and bad aspects. Whilst the drawbacks were primarily a lack of income and too many responsibilities, the benefits were seen as control and emotional growth. Wallerstein and Kelly (1980) also noted that despite on-going problems of loneliness and financial difficulties, five years post-separation the majority of adults felt that their divorces had been successful. As well as this, the researchers observed that the divorce had proved more beneficial to the women than to the men involved. Whereas only half of the male divorcees replied that their self-esteem had risen notably in addition to their contentment with life, this response was expressed by two-thirds of their female counterparts. The women especially felt they were now more competent, readily articulated and more capable of handling themselves as adults and parents. Whilst fewer men seemed to have utilised the divorce experience to bring about a positive transformation in their lives, this was more so for over half the women in their investigation. It was found that one-half of this latter group had undergone striking and decisive changes that appeared to have lifelong implications.

More recent surveys have also produced similar results. Bradshaw and Millar (1991:14) found that by far the most common response to the benefits of lone parenthood given by the parents was independence (60 per cent). This was followed by the freedom it gave them to do as they wished (31 per cent) and to make unilateral decisions about the children (21 per cent). Fifteen per cent of the respondents said that they now had peace of mind, with the divorced and separated placing more emphasis on this than did the unmarried mothers. Corresponding to this, Siganporia's Indian study (1993:361) discovered that despite the problems encountered, a large number (88 per cent) of the respondents interviewed felt happy following their divorces and envisaged a positive future for themselves through education and training for work.

The responses of many of the women in this sample reflected those of the mothers in the above mentioned studies. The general impression given was that the optimistic outlook was due to the fact that they had "disentangled themselves from a marital relation that had been mutually destructive, debilitating, or completely ungratifying" (Wallerstein and Kelly 1980:158). In her book "Single Women" (1994:165), Gordon uses phrases such as "challenge, strength, women's capacities, being in control, defining oneself, having one's own lifestyle, not being dependent on a man, being complete and being a human being" to describe the experiences of women alone. Many of these sentiments were also expressed by the Asian respondents in this project.

Table 8.5
The mothers' outlook following lone parenthood by lone parent type and age in years

	Divorced	Separated	Widowed	Unmarried	Total
Positive Outlook					73
20's/30's	23	21	2	2	
40's/50's +	14	7	4	—	
Negative Outlook					17
20's/30's	—	3	3	—	
40's/50's +	2	3	6	—	
Total	**39**	**34**	**15**	**2**	**90**

Table 8.5 suggests that the divorced followed by the separated mothers were the two most inclined groups to have positive outlooks regarding their situation. There were a number of reasons for this. Firstly, further analysis shows that 28 of these women had also been victims of domestic violence, which may have been a contributing factor to their feelings of relief and independence following marriage breakdown. This was the impression given by a divorcee of six years from Kenya with two sons, whose former husband had been both violent and an alcoholic:

There's no more 'yes sir, no sir, please sir, thank you sir, your food's ready, your ironing's ready.' The children are happier now there's no arguing. I've been to discos but realised it was a cattle market, and didn't like it, so stopped going. But at least I could go if I wanted. No one stopped me. It's a learning process. In my time I was like a pussy cat. I didn't know how to buy a stamp at the post office or go to the DSS or do the shopping. I've had to learn every single thing from scratch. I have to be strong on the outside, but it took me five years to get stronger after being beaten up like an animal. What I've been through is a therapy. When I look back even two years to see how I was then and how I am now, I realise it was all worth it.

For other divorced and separated respondents the heightened feelings of optimism were attributed to their having brought up their children successfully on their own, as put by a divorcee of seven years with a twelve year old son:

> I can do lots of things for myself I thought I couldn't do before, but it's a great responsibility bringing up a child on your own. It sort of makes me feel proud that I have achieved this alone and have watched my son grow up without a father.

As expected, Table 8.5 indicates that the widows were the most inclined of the mothers to say they did not feel confident or independent since their marriages had ended. This is "especially so when the man has been the manifestly dominant partner in a marriage which encased the woman in her dependence, and diminished her capacity to function on her own" (Chandler 1991:61) and an instance of this was illustrated by a widow of four years with two children: "I was very dependent on my husband. I had no worries then. I'm not feeling good at all. It's depression really. Why do I have to suffer all this?"

Examining whether age was a determinant in the sample's levels of psychological adjustment, the figures from Table 8.5 imply that there was a correlation between the two. This can be seen by the greater tendency of the respondents in their twenties and thirties to express a positive attitude towards their situation. Several explanations for this are as follows. Due to their younger age as compared with the older, more traditional women, these mothers may have held more liberal views regarding the acceptability of a lone parent status. Secondly, because of their youth, they could have also felt that they had more options open to them, such as gaining employment or remarriage, which could change their lives for the better. For example, a respondent in her mid-twenties and separated for only seven months spoke of how taking up education again may prove beneficial to her becoming more assertive and confident:

> I go to college to learn English and meet other people. Before I came to Britain I never knew anything. I lived with my husband for two years and knew nothing. I want my rights now, and to stand on my own two feet.

By comparison, those in their forties and older were almost three times more likely than the younger age groups to say that they had a pessimistic outlook on their lives, perhaps because, being more orthodox, they had been more dependent on their spouses during marriage. As well as this, they may have had more traditional values regarding the approval of lone parenthood, particularly within the Asian culture, and this was the reason given by a 44 year old separated Sikh respondent:

It's not a matter of being confident and relieved really. I keep to my own tradition and culture as much as I can. It's not really something to be happy about being a single parent. You shouldn't feel proud of it.

Further analysis of the data in relation to length of lone parenthood suggests that the women who had experienced marriage breakdown for under a year had a higher likelihood than the other mothers of having negative feelings about their situation. This was probably because they were still trying to come to terms with their loss, as explained by a 60 year old separated mother of only eight months: "I feel less confident and am always crying. I feel totally helpless without my husband."

Respondents whose relationships had been terminated for over a year were more likely than the other groups to say they had adjusted more positively to their lone parent status, and may indicate that, having got over the initial shock, these mothers had now begun to rebuild their lives. A 30 year old Muslim respondent and separated for a year said she was now beginning to integrate more into society: "I feel really good. I can go out with friends. I feel confident meeting people. I used to get really scared if someone saw me, but now I don't care, and talk to everyone with a smile."

Not surprisingly, perhaps, those respondents who were in paid work had a greater tendency than the unemployed mothers to feel more confident about their predicament, amounting to 22 of the 24 employees. One of these was a 32 year old divorcee and full time secretary and administrative assistant, who spoke confidently about managing alone:

I certainly feel more confident knowing I can cope both financially and socially on my own. I think it is expected that once an Indian woman becomes a lone parent, for whatever reason, she should somehow be satisfied with perhaps just bringing up the children.

A second employed respondent, a 38 year old divorcee and full time receptionist, claimed that having a job had made her more self-reliant in other aspects of her life:

I've had to come out into the open and use my hidden skills in that I've had to sort out financial and housing problems. Before I never used to sort out these things with my husband, but now I do them all on my own.

Those with depressed prospects were almost three times more likely to be unemployed than working, indicating that the lack of financial security may have contributed to their present worries. For example, a Muslim respondent in her thirties and with two children aged thirteen and twelve explained that she had been forced to give up her previous job due to an illness brought about by her separation. Because of her current financial difficulties she admitted she would rather be part of a couple again:

> I was confident until I lost my job. I now feel more dependent on other people as I've found it quite hard to cope alone. My husband's slightly changed for the better and I want to get back with him in the near future.

It also appeared that the women who did not belong to a social organisation were more inclined than the members to have a positive attitude towards their single status. This may suggest that 30 of the 34 non-members who gave this response did not need to rely on outside contacts to adjust to their situation, one being a 47 year old divorcee and university degree holder from India who commented on how she had rebuilt her life with no external support:

> Circumstances have made me a stronger person. There are lots of ladies who won't divorce because of what could happen, and put up with their husbands just for the sake of it, and because they've got two or three children. I don't think of culture. Lots of ladies do at my age. It's better to make a break than be at each other. It's not good for the child, but it's better than being in an unhappy environment. When my husband threw me out of the house, I had no time to think about what other people would say. I've just got on with my life.

Likewise, mothers who had despondent feelings about their lives were almost three times more likely to belong to a club or organisation than not to be a member. This could perhaps be because these women depended on more specific forms of assistance, as did a 52 year old widow who attended an Asian women's centre for social reasons and financial help:

> I feel more depressed now. I mainly like to sit alone at home and think. I don't like to go out much. I like to chat on a one-to-one basis with someone to listen to me, and with a friend to listen to, like at the centre.

The findings of this study have also revealed that whilst 53 of the 90 respondents said that they were happy on their own and had no plans to remarry, another 28 women expressed a wish to marry again. These tended to be younger women and divorcees, one being a 34 year old divorcee from Pakistan: "Yes I would like to, if I can find a good person, who is better than my ex-husband." Another Muslim divorcee in her mid-thirties gave a slightly more detailed response: "There'll be no more arranged marriages. I'd want to know the person first. It'll be the second time so I have to be very careful." For a 36 year old divorcee from Kenya, remarriage was already a distinct possibility: "I've got a boyfriend at present, and am planning to marry. He's an Indian man living here, and he gets on with the children." The last nine women in the sample said they were unsure of their future marital status. The overall data may, therefore, indicate that remaining as a lone parent was a reality for over half of the Asian lone mothers in this research and as Table 8.5 has indicated, the vast majority of the sample had begun to come to terms with their single status in a positive way.

These results can be compared to those found by Bradshaw and Millar (1991:13), who observed that a smaller proportion of their sample (47 per cent) said that they preferred to stay as a lone parent in the near future, 23 per cent would rather remarry, whilst a further 13 per cent would prefer to live with another partner.

Conclusion

Chapter Eight has concentrated on the two types of adjustment the 90 respondents in this project have had to make as immigrants living in London and as lone mothers. The results have shown that just under one-half of the sample said they were experiencing a conflict between the British and Asian cultures. The remaining 50 mothers, nevertheless, did appear to be culturally adjusted, in that 23 of them were accommodated positively into both cultures, 21 had retained their original Asian culture and 6 had assimilated into the British way of life.

Detailed responses of the sample, however, made it clear that the differences between the mothers in adjacent groups were not as great as the categorisations of the table implied. Moreover, Park and Stonequist's notion of marginal personality received no support, in that none of the sample suffered, for example, from irrational or unstable personalities. Even Dickie-Clark's claim of a marginal situation received minority support. Finally, none of the mothers felt totally assimilated into the British culture.

The second part of the chapter has explored the psychological adjustment the women have had to make as lone mothers. It was found that all but seven of the respondents said they suffered from at least one mental or emotional condition, although there were varying degrees to which these were experienced. Despite this, the overall outlook for the sample appeared to be a positive one, with the majority of women now valuing confidence and independence to a greater extent than when they were married. Not surprisingly, the widows were the most likely group to have not yet come to terms with their loss.

9 Conclusions

The principal aim of this study was to explore the two situational difficulties faced by Asian lone mothers from the Indian and African sub-continent residing in London: the first being their lone parent status, and the second their being of ethnic background. A subsequent objective of the research was to compare the living and material conditions of this sample with those of lone parents nationally. Finally, the implications for social policy were also to be addressed from the appropriate results of the project.

Since only 90 respondents from London participated in this investigation, any conclusions and comparisons made are only tentative and far from conclusive. With this in mind, Chapter Nine presents a summary of the major findings of this project.

The research process

The methodology procedures carried out in this study were discussed in Chapter Three. Of the 90 women interviewed, 39 were divorced, 34 separated, 15 widowed and 2 were unmarried. All had at least one dependent child aged sixteen and under or aged up to nineteen and in full time education. Due to Asian lone mothers in London being such an exclusive group, the quota sampling procedure proved both unavoidable and practical, with most of the respondents being located through Asian women's centres and general practitioners' lists. After undertaking two pilot studies, the final questionnaire was drawn up, consisting of 95 open-ended and closed questions. Each interview lasted from between 45 minutes to an hour and following completion of the 90 questionnaires, the data was then sorted into categories, coded and presented as required for analysis. Because much of the research was based on the respondents' personal sentiments, opinions and experiences, this project was mainly of a qualitative nature.

The mothers' living standards

Chapter Four examined the material and living conditions of the 90 mothers, with the early hypothesis in Chapter Three which assumed that the women would experience a low standard of living being confirmed by the results of the study. Although any comparisons made can only be provisional, many of the findings have generally suggested that there were similarities between the circumstances of this sample and the general lone parent population in this country.

Reflecting both the national trend and those of other studies, over two-thirds of the mothers were not working, with only 24 women in paid employment. Those with jobs tended to be divorcees and widows in their forties and over and working full time rather than part time. Most of the employed were found in low paid, skilled non-manual and unskilled jobs such as secretarial, reception, catering and factory work. Only seven mothers were engaged in highly salaried professional and managerial posts, and these included a doctor and a psychiatrist. Echoing other research findings, the majority of the unemployed Asian respondents also expressed a wish to work in the near future. Whilst 21 of these 66 women said they were currently available and looking for a job, another 18 explained that they would do so once their children were older, indicating that a lack of affordable child care may have prevented them from taking up employment.

In this survey, two-thirds of the mothers were living entirely on state benefits, with only nine respondents not in receipt of any at all. This over-dependence of lone parent families on state support was similar to the overall picture revealed by other investigations. However, only 11 of the 68 Asian women eligible for maintenance payments actually acquired this source of income, a ratio that was lower than that of other studies. Predictably, three-quarters of the mothers complained that their incomes were insufficient, with all but twelve of them having to cut back on commodities such as food, clothing and presents. Because of this, only a small minority of the respondents said they could afford to take a family holiday. Just over one-half of the women had incurred heavy debts at some stage and this was more likely to occur if the mother was unemployed or had more than one dependent child. Payments of bills was a constant worry for 71 of the sample and a lack of income was also highlighted by the fact that only 39 of the women had access to a car.

Likewise, the housing situation of this sample also seemed to correspond with that of the lone parent population at large. Over a half of the mothers were living in council properties and these were mainly younger separated and divorced women who were unemployed or living on low wages. The third of those who were owner occupiers tended to be older widows and divorcees, and working in better paid jobs.

The three-quarters of the respondents who expressed satisfaction with the physical condition of their accommodation were more likely to be home owners. The dissatisfied mothers, who tended to be residing in council properties, were mainly aggrieved about damp, overcrowding and a lack of hygiene, with centrally heated homes also the domain of owner occupiers rather than of local authority tenants. Seventy-three of the women had a telephone, television and a washing-machine, and were more likely to possess these if a home owner and employed. Only two of the sample were without any of these commodities. The mothers were divided about their future housing plans. Whilst those who owned their homes were happy where they were living, council house tenants wanted to move to bigger and better properties.

One-third of the mothers perceived themselves to be in good physical health, one-half in average health, and only a sixth in poor health, with widows and older women more inclined to make up the latter group. Fifty-three of the respondents said they suffered from at least one physical illness, the most common maladies being arthritis, asthma and back problems, and for 36 of these women, the ailments were also connected to their lone parent status. Compared to other research findings, the respondents in this sample also appeared to endure more physical illnesses, perhaps because of their older age profile.

The mothers' cultural attitudes

The discussion presented in Chapter Two showed that Hindu, Muslim and Sikh cultures are profoundly different from the British culture with regard to marriage, the family, the position of women, marriage breakdown and lone parenthood, with far greater emphasis placed on conservative ideologies and practices within all these areas. Since these inner cores of cultures are very deep-seated and thus very difficult to change, this may have had important implications for the lone mothers in this study. Chapter Five focused on the sample's attitudes towards marriage, the family and the position of women, with their responses confirming the literature in Chapter Two. Sixty-nine of the mothers believed that Asian and British values towards marriage differed, 67 said that marital disruption meant a loss of family honour and this was a greater problem for Asian than for British lone mothers and 72 respondents claimed that Asian women were less independent than their British counterparts. Some of the differences highlighted by the mothers included the arranged marriage system, dowry payments and over-dominance and control by Asian men over women.

Chapter Six examined the respondents' attitudes towards marriage breakdown and lone parenthood, with the findings again largely corresponding with the discussion in Chapter Two. Although two-thirds of the sample held no views about this prior to family breakdown, 84 of the 90 women were sympathetic following their own marriages failing. However, 72 of the mothers did feel that people generally disapproved of lone parent as compared to traditional families, 30 of whom also stressed that the Asian culture, in particular, was more condemning.

When questioned more specifically about the Asian community in London, not unexpectedly, over three-quarters of the sample replied that they were less sympathetic towards lone parenthood than were the British, and this was mainly attributed to cultural differences between the two groups. Despite this, studies by Bharat (1988) and Siganporia (1993) have both revealed a slow but growing acceptance of lone parent families in India. Although 64 of the mothers in this investigation went on to say that a loss of marital status caused greater dilemmas for Asian women than for their British counterparts, they also evaluated their self-perceptions positively. Somewhat surprisingly, only 26 mothers felt they were betraying their Asian culture through marriage breakdown and these tended to have only been lone parents for six years and under and residing in Britain for a relatively short period of time. The 52 respondents who explained that they had never felt ashamed of their single status were more inclined to have been lone parents for seven years and over. A further 20 mothers initially felt ashamed, with only 16 currently feeling so.

The mothers' relationships

The results of Chapters Five and Six suggested that the mothers were facing hostility from their communities, which would support the assumption made in Chapter Three. Chapter Seven primarily explored the women's relationships with the father, family and friends and found that, despite the on-going difficulties, not all their experiences were negative. This largely disproved the assumptions made prior to the research being carried out. Only 19 of the 70 women who could see the father, actually did, and these were mainly separated rather than divorced. This result differs somewhat from other studies (Pothen 1987, Bradshaw and Millar 1991), which found that their samples retained more contact with their former partners. Some of the explanations given by mothers in this survey for not seeing their ex-husbands included the latter having left the country or else their having remarried. Not unpredictably, due to loss of communication, 57 of the respondents in this investigation were no longer emotionally attached to their former partners, and this resembled the findings of other studies. Of the 30 Asian mothers who were still attached, 14 were widows and married for a longer length of time.

The women appeared to have stronger and more continuous relationships with their family and friends. Only three of them had not told any relatives of their lone parent status, with 69 women claiming that all their family were sympathetic on hearing of their lone parent status. Nine mothers had received a mixed reaction and another nine had unsympathetic kin. Whereas a slightly higher proportion of the sample said all their friends had reacted favourably, more of the women, nine in all, had not made their friends aware of their new status. None of the mothers, however, faced negative reactions from all of their friends.

Just two of the respondents received no support from family and/or friends, with the main kinds of help given to the majority being writing, telephoning and social visits. Over a third of the women received social and emotional help from family and friends, 23 received this in addition to material support, whilst only 13 of the mothers were not helped by their relatives. For over half of the sample, attitudes of family and friends towards them had not worsened following the onset of lone parenthood, with just over a third of them saying they had received a mixed reaction. Interestingly, for 23 of this latter group, it was family rather than friends who had changed their opinions.

Almost two-thirds of the mothers also belonged to clubs and social organisations, which were largely Asian women's centres. This refuted the earlier theory that the sample would be isolated from their local communities. These respondents were more disposed to being older, unemployed and lone parents for only under a year. For practically every member, social interaction was the main reason why they had joined, but for 34 of these women, practical help with everyday problems and attending classes were also benefits received.

The final section of Chapter Seven was devoted to the outcomes of lone parenthood on the sample's children, and corresponding with other research, found that a large majority of them were adversely affected by the marriage breakdown of their parents, through suffering from such problems as depression, aggressive behaviour, eating and sleeping difficulties. However, the children in this study appeared to be performing well educationally, with only ten mothers claiming that their offspring were still under-achieving at school. In line with other recent surveys which found that contact weakened over time, more than one-half of the children no longer saw their fathers. Only about a third of them were still attached to the father, and these tended to be children of widows.

The mothers' adjustments

Chapter One discussed various models of race relations theorising the conflict of relationships between an ethnic population and the host society. Whilst Park and Stonequist associated negative personality traits with the immigrant in the 1920's and 1930's, Dickie-Clark concentrated largely on the inferior marginal situation of the settler in the 1960's. The cultural deficit model which also emerged during the 1960's similarly presumed that the culture of ethnic groups was inferior to that of the majority nation and condoned an assimilationist position. Whilst the chapter also went on to examine other models such as liberal pluralism, Marxist, Black and feminist perspectives, more recently, the notion of cultural pluralism has gained more support, maintaining that any conflict faced by ethnic minorities is between two equal but different cultures.

The first half of Chapter Eight concentrated on the sample's cultural adjustment as immigrants and indicated that 40 mothers said they were experiencing a conflict of cultures, 23 felt comfortably accommodated into both the British and Asian cultures, 21 claimed to be mainly of Asian identity, with only 6 women perceiving themselves to be British. Through their replies, however, it became apparent that not only were there varying degrees to which each respondent identified with each category, but also that the differences between the mothers in bordering groups were not as large as the divisions implied. None of the 90 women experienced a marginal personality as argued by Park and Stonequist, and only a minority of the respondents felt they were in a marginal situation as suggested by Dickie-Clark. Confirming other literature on Asians living in Britain (Jeffrey 1976, Robinson 1986, Shaw 1988, Stopes-Roe and Cochrane 1990, Joly 1995), none of the women were totally assimilated into the British way of life, with the majority of the sample having retained many aspects of their original cultures, which they appraised positively. This would imply that far from experiencing major cultural dilemmas as suggested they would in the third chapter, the respondents were largely able to adjust to life as Asian lone mothers from the Indian and African sub-continent living in London.

The concluding section of Chapter Eight explored the sample's psychological adjustment, and echoing both the literature and the assumption made in Chapter Three, found that almost all the mothers currently suffered from at least one mental or emotional condition in varying degrees. The most frequent conditions mentioned were loneliness, stress and depression. Despite this, 73 of the 90 respondents presently felt more independent and self-confident about their lives as lone mothers. These were more likely to be divorcees and separated women, many of whom had been victims of domestic violence within their marriages, in the younger age bracket and employed.

Policy implications

Research of this kind inevitably has policy implications. From the replies given by the women interviewed, the following appeared to be the main policy issues.

The results of Chapter Four have shown that two-thirds of the sample were totally dependent on government benefits for their revenue, with only 9 of the 90 mothers not in receipt of this form of support. Not surprisingly, the data also corresponded with 67 of the respondents expressing dissatisfaction with their present levels of income. This would imply that state benefits are too low to sustain a reasonable standard of living, with the result that most of the women interviewed were living in or on the margins of poverty. This would mean that their level of wages have to be improved in some way in order not to create strong work disincentives.

Lone parents should be encouraged, but not coerced to work if they so wish. Prevailing social policies, however, as it will be shown, fail to support lone mothers to become financially independent. This enforced dependency on social security benefits is linked not only to the present social security system, but also to the dynamics of the labour market. Although only 24 of the 90 women in this research were employed, 55 of the remaining 66 respondents not working said that they were currently looking for a job or else would be doing so in the near future. For many ethnic minority mothers, such as those in this sample, their search for employment may be further compounded by the fact that they do not speak English as their first language. Policy makers should, therefore, link welfare benefits with incentives to work such as intensive training and retraining schemes, with the Race Relations Act (1976) also being properly enforced to ensure that jobs are fairly allocated to immigrant groups.

The types of jobs available to lone mothers may also discourage them from entering into the labour market. As both this and other investigations have revealed, employment offered to these women tends to be underpaid and of a menial status, such as cleaning, catering and factory work. For many lone mothers, working part time and receiving its equivalent deficient part time wages within such sectors are, in reality, no better than living on government benefits. In many cases, this may actually produce a disincentive to work, trapping the mother in a state of enforced dependency on welfare for her income. If the government wants to discourage lone mothers from refusing to take such jobs, the rates of Family Credit should be increased yearly in accordance with rising inflation in order to supplement the women's low wages.

Similarly, many lone mothers engaged in full time, low paid jobs and who are eligible to claim some benefits, find that part of their Family Credit is deducted from their already meagre wages. In order to prevent the mothers from losing valuable income in this way, the government need to also take into account child care and travelling expenses involved in taking up employment before making deductions from their benefits. In this investigation, only those very few respondents working in full time, highly paid professional posts such as medicine and teaching were not forced onto welfare, suggesting that for a very large group of employed lone mothers, additional income from Family Credit is vital in helping them to raise their standards of living.

The Labour government are now attempting to raise standards of living for the poorest working sections of society, such as lone parent families, in two ways. Firstly, plans have been unveiled for the introduction of a national minimum wage which will be enforced from April 1999. Those aged over 21 and in employment will be paid a minimum of £3.60 an hour, with the wage rate for those aged 18-21 being phased in starting at £3 hourly. It is hoped that the initiative will ensure that those currently working in very low paid jobs – three-quarters of whom are women – will see a rise in their wages. Secondly in order to reward poor income households for working, the Labour government have introduced a new working families tax credit, whereby families with someone working full time are guaranteed £180 per week and no income tax on earnings below £220 per week. This would mean an increase in actual take-home pay for many of those on lower incomes.

There are also other factors preventing lone mothers' access to an independent wage. The constraints on labour market participation may not stem solely from low wage rates but also from having child care responsibilities. As confirmed by the data in Chapter Four, this was found to be a major obstacle for the unemployed sample to enter into paid employment and is another issue to be addressed. It is already well documented that Britain provides one of the lowest publicly funded day care provision of nearly all the European countries, with demand for places far outstripping supply (Monk 1993). None of the three employed lone mothers in this study with some or all pre-school children who had to make child care provision for their dependants used local authority nurseries, and had to turn to informal networks such as family and friends instead. Because of this lack of state provision, 18 of the 66 mothers who were not currently working expressed a wish to do so once their children were older and could look after themselves. These women would also then not have to pay the high cost of child care, which was not presently possible whilst living entirely on benefit payments for their incomes.

In order to give lone mothers the option of taking up jobs if they have children under school age, the number of local authority child care places must not only be increased but also be made more affordable to those who use them, since, as it has been shown, these women may already be on low wages. The current situation means that a significant group of lone mothers who want to work are being forced into receiving welfare for a considerable length of time through no choice of their own.

The Labour government is now actively trying to increase the number of pre-school places available. In their Early Years Development Plan they have guaranteed a nursery place for every child of four for up to three terms, depending on when each child has their birthday. This can be at a private day nursery, a playgroup or an early years/nursery class within a primary school.

Each local education authority now has the duty to agree plans with the private and voluntary nursery providers in its area, and means that 650,000 places will have become available from September 1998. Twenty per cent of the places are to be provided by the private and voluntary sectors and the rest by the local authorities. The free places will be available for five half-days a week in some areas and full days in others. However, parents choosing from the private day care nurseries would only be entitled to a government limit of £1,100 for three terms' schooling, which it believes covers the cost of education for four year olds. Parents who wish to place their children in private nurseries which charge above this will, therefore, have to meet the additional fees themselves.

Although the new scheme is supposed to allow parents to choose the nursery education that suits their children from the places available, the poorer parents will inevitably be unable to afford the extra income necessary for the better quality forms of child care in the private sector. However, it is deemed that low income households, such as lone parent families who would otherwise not have had the chance to send their children to nursery school, will gain in some way from the initiative.

Another area of concern which has come to light through the findings of Chapter Four is the very poor take up rate of maintenance payments for the divorced and separated sample, amounting to only 11 of the 73 mothers who were eligible to claim, and lower than the average for the white lone parent population and in other recent studies (Bradshaw and Millar 1991, McKay and Marsh 1994).

There are several reasons for this. Firstly, given their heavy workload, the Child Support Agency may not have yet started to deal with the mother's case, especially if she is relatively new to her status. Secondly, the former partner may be unemployed and because he is living on benefits himself, would not be able to contribute to the child's upkeep. Thirdly, the mother may know the father's current address, but because she does not want to have any further involvement with him, can make it difficult for the Child Support Agency to trace him. Fourthly, if the mother is receiving cash in hand from the father, she may not want to declare this to the Child Support Agency, and therefore pretends she is unaware of his place of residence.

The Child Support Agency was initially set up by the Conservative government in order to trace absent parents to make them more responsible for their own children's welfare, and thereby reducing public expenditure on state benefits at the same time. However, since its introduction, it has been widely recognised that the system has been over-complicated and ineffective, with staff currently spending 90 per cent of their time on assessments and just 10 per cent enforcing payments. Moreover, the maintenance system has not been financially beneficial to lone mothers on Income Support, since this form of payment is deducted pound for pound from their benefits. Therefore, only the minority of employed lone mothers in highly paid posts and not in receipt of Income Support have gained economically in this way.

In order to recify the failings of the Child Support Agency, the Secretary of State for Social Security, has announced plans for a radical upheaval of the maintenance system, simplifying awards and introducing a fixed formula of payments. A higher rate will be paid for a first child, with lower percentages of earnings awarded for a second and third child. Another key element of the package is a plan for a "disregard" - a mechanism which would allow lone parents to keep more of their benefit payments, probably amounting to about £10 per week, enabling them to feel they are better off if they co-operate with the system.

The fourth chapter highlights the inadequate housing situation of a large proportion of the 64 mothers living in local authority accommodation. Many of them said they were housed in high-rise estates or flats with no play areas or gardens for their children, whilst others attributed their poor physical health to the inferior physical state of their homes, with damp and lack of hygiene being some of the main complaints. Overcrowded conditions were also mentioned by some of the respondents, a problem perhaps more greatly experienced by Asian lone parents, given the larger size of many of their families in contrast to the smaller nature of their white counterparts. With all these difficulties in mind, local authorities must be more sensitive to the needs of lone mother families when rehousing them following relationship breakdown. As a high proportion of these women do not command a decent income, and therefore cannot afford to pay for existing repairs or make improvements to their dwellings, they should be accommodated in more appropriate forms of housing from the outset. Unfortunately, housing policy is currently moving in the opposite direction, whereby under the Homeless Persons Act (1977), lone parents are no longer regarded as a priority group for housing.

Chapter Seven has shown that far from being isolated at home, the majority of the lone mothers in this study - 56 in all - had joined at least one club or organisation, with 43 of them belonging to Asian women's centres. Since none of the respondents were affiliated to any national organisations for lone parents such as the "National Council for One Parent Families" or "Gingerbread," this stresses the importance of the Asian women's centres in helping to restructure the mothers' lives following marriage breakdown, especially those new to their single status. Here, within their own local communities, these women could communicate in their own languages and in confidence with their group leaders. More importantly, they could receive invaluable practical day-to-day help and socialise with other mothers in a similar situation to themselves.

In the present climate of scarce resources, however, the threat of cut backs and closures are very much a harsh reality for such valuable small local organisations which rely so much on state assistance to remain open. To prevent many such existing centres from shutting down, the government must, therefore, be prepared to grant them more financial aid to ensure that they maintain the high standards of support given to the lone mother population. In order to keep in line with the ever-growing numbers of lone mothers from the Indian and African sub-continent living in this country, the government should also invest more capital into the establishment of further similar organisations so that more women have easier access to such services at a local level.

Finally, in this research as in others on lone parenthood, domestic violence appeared to be a major factor in the mothers initiating relationship breakdown, with 44 of the 90 women interviewed experiencing this form of abuse at the hands of their former partners. As the literature in Chapter Two has illustrated, Asian culture tends to look upon violence within a marriage as an acceptable form of control by the man, and because of this, the issue still remains more hidden and less well addressed than within the population at large. However, the figures from this study would suggest that fewer Asian wives are now willing to tolerate such unreasonable behaviour from their spouses, with the result that more of them are escaping from unhappy marriages. This trend can only point to the increasing significance of women's refuges in safely sheltering the victims of domestic violence and their children whilst the former decide their marital futures away from their partners. However, as with the women's centres, many of these refuges are also in danger of losing their grants and closing due to a lack of funding. The government clearly must not underestimate the vital role played by women's refuges by lending more financial support not only towards sustaining existing refuges, but also towards the construction of additional shelters throughout the country.

Through the findings of this study, the above discussion has suggested that in order to improve the situation of both the Asian and the lone mother population at large in Britain, many of the social policies implemented by the present government must be amended or changed accordingly. Current policies would only ensure that the general standard of living remains at subsistence levels for a great many of these women and their children.

A small study cannot provide definitive answers to the issues faced by lone mothers from the Indian and African sub-continent living in this country. Clearly, more research, both qualitative and quantitative is needed to provide a fuller and more comprehensive picture of this particular situation of this group of lone mothers in the UK. Of notable interest, further examination into these women's everyday living conditions as well as their cultural predicaments, would prove of great value.

Nevertheless, this investigation has shown that in addition to experiencing low standards of living, the women also encountered more specific dilemmas as a result of the many differences in attitudes and practices between British and Asian cultures. Hence, adjustments had to be made, not only because of their lone parent status, but also because of their differing ethnic and cultural backgrounds. Hopefully, this study has gone some way to bring to light a problem, which until now, has not been tackled in any great depth.

Appendix

The Questionnaire

Date of interview:

Place of interview:

Section one:

Personal

1.1   Were you born in this country?
1.2   If not, which country are you originally from?
1.3   How long have you been living in Britain?
1.4   What is your age?
1.5   What is your religion?
1.6   What kind of education did you receive?
1.7   In which country/countries did you receive your education?

Section two:

The process of lone parenthood

2.1   What category of lone parent do you fall into?
2.2   For how long have you been a lone parent?

FOR DIVORCED AND SEPARATED MOTHERS ONLY
2.3   Did you become a lone parent gradually over some time or was it suddenly?
2.4   Did you marry a man of the same ethnic group as yourself?
2.5   How long did your marriage last?
2.6   What were the problems in your marriage that led to the separation/divorce?

2.7 Whose decision was it to separate/divorce - yours, your husband's or was it a mutual decision?
2.8 Did you part on good terms or were you bitter?
2.9 Did you have many difficult decisions to make or was the divorce/separation an easy choice to make?

FOR UNMARRIED MOTHERS ONLY
2.10 Was the father of your child/ren of the same ethnic group as yourself?
2.11 Was the relationship a serious or a casual one?

FOR WIDOWS ONLY
2.12 Was your husband of the same ethnic group as yourself?
2.13 Did your husband die suddenly or had he been ill for a time?

Section three:

The children

3.1 How many children do you have?
3.2 What are their ages?
3.3 Where do your children live - all with you, some with you or none with you?
3.4 Has the separation/divorce/death affected the children, and if so, how?
3.5 How are the children getting on at school with their lessons?
3.6 Has the separation/divorce/death had any effect on their schooling? If so, please expand.

Section four:

Material and living conditions

HOUSING
4.1 Are you an owner occupier, do you rent from the local authority (council housing, housing association), rent from a private landlord, stay with family or friends, other?
4.2 For how long have you been living at your present address?
4.3 Is the accommodation in good physical condition?
4.4 Is it centrally heated?
4.5 On the whole, are you satisfied with your housing condition?

EMPLOYMENT

4.6   Do you have a paid job?

4.7   What is its description?

4.8   Is it part time, full time or occasional?

4.9   How long have you been employed there?

4.10   What kind of child care arrangements do you make while you are at work?

4.11   If you do make arrangements, how much does it cost, even if you use family help?

ASK ALL WOMEN

4.12   Did you work before marriage, and if so what was your job?

INCOME

4.13   What are your wages/salary?

4.14   Do you receive any benefits?

4.15   If so, what are they? (Income Support, One Parent Benefit, Child Benefit, Housing Benefit, Widows Pension)

4.16   Do you find that your wages/benefits are sufficient to manage on?

4.17   If not, what kind of things do you have to go short of/go without?

4.18   Have you ever run into heavy debts?

4.19   Do you worry about paying the bills?

4.20   Do you have enough money to go on holiday with your children?

COMMODITIES

4.21   Do you have access to a car?

4.22   Do you have a telephone?

4.23   Do you own a television set?

4.24   Do you have a washing-machine?

HEALTH

4.25   How would you rate your physical health - good, average or poor?

4.26   Do you suffer from any physical illnesses, and if so, what are they?

4.27   Are any of these illnesses connected with your lone parent status?

4.28   In addition to these illness do you suffer from any of the following - stress, depression, loneliness, guilt, being unable to cope, feelings of suicide?

4.29   Have any of the above anything to do with your present situation?

Section five:

The father

5.1   Do you ever see your former partner?
5.2   If so, is it on a regular basis, an irregular basis, or very infrequently?
5.3   If you only see him irregularly, how do you feel about not seeing him on a regular basis?
5.4   How emotionally attached are you to the father now?
5.5   Does the father see the children regularly, now and then or never?
5.6   How does he feel about the children now?
5.7   If he still sees them, do you think he is still attached to the children, or is he now more distant?
5.8   Are the children still emotionally attached to the father, or are they now more distant?
5.9   What was your former partner's last job when you were married?
5.10 Did he earn good wages/salary?
5.11 What is his job now?
5.12 Does he earn good wages/salary?
5.13 Does he pay maintenance for the children's upkeep regularly, now and then or never?
5.14 If he pays maintenance, how much is this?

Section six:

Family and social contacts

6.1   Do your immediate relatives know about your lone parent status?
6.2   Do your friends know about your lone parent status?
6.3   What do your family think of your situation - have they accepted it, or are they unsympathetic?
6.4   What do your friends think of your situation - have they accepted it, or are they unsympathetic?
6.5   What kind of support, if any, do you receive from your relatives?
6.6   What kind of support, if any, do you receive from your friends?
6.7   Now that you are a lone parent have any of your family/ friends changed their attitudes towards you - have they deserted you, are they unsympathetic, or understanding?
6.8   Do you belong to any clubs or social organisations?
6.9   In what ways does the club/organisation help you - socially, practically, educationally?

Section seven:

Cultural issues

7.1   Before you became a lone parent, what kind of ideas did you have about lone parent families?

7.2   Now that you are a lone parent yourself, have your ideas on this changed? If so, how?

7.3   Do you find that people in general think less well of lone parent families compared to two parent families? Please expand.

7.4   As you know, Asian lone parent families are not so common here in Britain. Do you feel that the Asian community in London accepts lone parenthood less, the same or to a greater extent than British society does? Please tell me more about this.

7.5   Being of Asian origin yourself, do you feel that being in your situation, you are betraying your culture, ethics and values? Please expand.

7.6   Has it ever worried you or made you ashamed in any way that being a lone parent is contrary to the Asian culture? Please expand.

7.7   Living in London do you feel mainly British or Asian, or caught between the two cultures? Please expand.

7.8   Do you feel that there are any differences between British and Asian values regarding marriage; birth control and abortion; the independence of women? Please explain.

7.9   Do you think these differences can cause any difficulties for Asian women living in London? Please expand.

7.10   Do you think that being an Asian lone parent makes any difference to the way you are treated by the local authorities? Please expand with examples of discrimination, even if you have heard of your other lone parent friends being discriminated against.

7.11   Do you think there are any problems of lone parenthood that apply more to Asian lone mothers than to white lone mothers regarding financial problems; losing the family honour; loss of marital status in the community; bringing up daughters? Please explain.

7.12   Are you able to practise your religion?

7.13   Do you think your religion has influenced/had anything to do with your views on marriage, the family and marriage breakdown? Please expand.

7.14 Despite all the problems that you may have encountered, has anything positive come out of the ending of your relationship - becoming more independent, confident, having feelings of relief? Please give examples.

Section eight:

Future plans

8.1 Do you have any plans to marry in the future?
8.2 Do you have any plans regarding employment?
8.3 Do you have any plans regarding your housing situation?

Bibliography

Abd Al 'Ati, H. (1977), *The Family Structure in Islam*, USA: Trust Publications.

Abdullah, T. and Zeidenstein, S. (1982), *Village Women of Bangladesh -prospects for change*, Oxford: Pergamon Press.

Abul A'la Maududi, S. (1986), *Purdah and the Status of Woman in Islam*, Lahore: Islamic Publications.

Ahuja, R. (1994), *Indian Social System*, Jaipur: Rawat Publications.

Allen, S. (1982), 'Perhaps a seventh person?' in C. Husband (ed.) *Race in Britain: continuity and change*, London: Hutchinson and Company.

Anthias, F. (1992), 'The problem of ethnic and race categories and the anti-racist struggle' in N. Manning and R. Page (eds.) *Social Policy Review 4*, London: Social Policy Association.

Anthias, F. (1995), 'Rex' in V. George and R. Page (eds.) *Modern Thinkers on Welfare*, Prentice Hall/Hemel Hempstead: Harvester Wheatsheaf.

Anwar, M. (1979), *The Myth of Return - Pakistanis in Britain*, London: John Murray.

Austerberry, H. and Watson, S. (1986), 'A woman's place: a feminist approach to housing in Britain' in C. Ungerson (ed.) *Women and Social Policy - a reader*, Hampshire: Macmillan Education Limited.

Balchin, P. (1985), *Housing Policy - an introduction*, London: Routledge.

Ballard, R. (1994), 'The emergence of Desh Pardesh' in R. Ballard (ed.) *Desh Pardesh - the South Asian presence in Britain*, London: Hurst and Company.

Banton, M. (1967), *Race Relations*, London: Tavistock.

Bechhofer, F. (1992), 'The research process' in P. Worsley (ed.) *The New Introducing Sociology*, London: Penguin Books.

Berry, B. (1965), *Race and Ethnic Relations*, Boston: Houghton Mifflin.

Bhachu, P. (1985), *Twice Migrants -East African Sikh settlers in Britain*, London: Tavistock Publications.

Bharat, S. (1986), 'Single parent family in India - issues and implications' in *The Indian Journal of Social Work*, Vol XLVII No 1, April.

Bharat, S. (1988), 'Single parent families - consequences for single parents' in *The Indian Journal of Social Work*, Vol XLIX No 3, July.

Bourne, J. with Sivanandan, S. (1980), 'Cheerleaders and ombudsmen: the sociology of race relations in Britain' in *Race and Class - the sociology of race relations in Britain - a journal for Black and third world liberation*, Vol XXI No 4, Spring.

Bourque, L. and Clark, V. (1992), *Processing Data - the survey example*, California: Sage Publications.

Boyden, J. (1993), *Families - celebration and hope in a world of change*, London: Gaia Books Limited.

Bradshaw, J. and Millar, J. (1991), *Lone Parent Families in the UK*, Dept. of Social Security, Research Report No 6, London: HMSO.

Brewer, J. and Hunter, A. (1990), *Multimethod Research - a synthesis of styles*, California: Sage Publications.

Brijbhushan, J. (1980), *Muslim Women in Purdah and Out of it*, New Delhi: Vikas Publishing House.

Brown, M. (1986), *Introduction to Social Administration in Britain*, London: Hutchinson and Company.

Burghes, L. (1994), *Lone Parenthood and Family Disruption - the outcomes for children*, London: Family Policy Studies Centre.

Calvert, S. and Calvert, P. (1992), *Sociology Today*, Hemel Hempstead: Harvester Wheatsheaf.

Caplan, P. (1985), *Class and Gender in India - women and their organisations in a South Indian city*, London: Tavistock Publications.

Cashmore, E. and Troyna, B. (1983), *Introduction to Race Relations*, London: Routledge and Kegan Paul.

Central Statistical Office (1995), *Family Spending - a report on the 1994-95 Family Expenditure survey*, London: HMSO.

Chandler, J. (1991), *Women Without Husbands - an exploration of the margins of marriage*, Hampshire: Macmillan Education Limited.

Chowdhury, P. (1994), *The Veiled Woman - shifting gender equations in Haryana 1880-1990*, New Delhi: Sage Publications.

Cochrane, A. (1993), 'The problem of poverty' in R. Dallos and E. McLaughlin (eds.) *Social Problems and the Family*, London: Sage Publications.

Cole, W. and Sambhi, P. (1978), *The Sikhs - their religious beliefs and practices*, London: Routledge and Kegan Paul.

Collins, R. (1992), 'Upholding the nuclear family: a study of unmarried parents and domestic courts' in C. Marsh and S. Arber (eds.) *Families and Households, Division and Change*, Hampshire: Macmillan Education Limited.

Crow, G. and Hardey, M. (1992), 'Diversity and ambiguity among lone parent households in modern Britain' in C. Marsh and S. Arber (eds.) *Families and Households, Divisions and Change*, Hampshire: Macmillan Education Limited.

Dale, J. and Foster, P. (1986), *Feminists and State Welfare*, London: Routledge and Kegan Paul.

Denney, D. (1983), 'Some dominant perspectives in the literature relating to multi-racial social work' in *The British Journal of Social Work*, Vol 13.

Denney, D. (1995), 'Hall' in V. George and R. Page (eds.) *Modern Thinkers on Welfare*, Hemel Hempstead: Prentice Hall/Harvester Wheatsheaf.

Department of Environment (1993), *English House Condition Survey 1991*, London: HMSO.

Desai, D. (1989), 'Women in Indian society' in P. Dandvate, R. Kumari and J. Verghese (eds.) *Widows, Abandoned and Destitute Women in India*, London: Sangam Books Limited.

Desai, N. and Krishnaraj, M. (1987), *Women and Society in India*, New Delhi: Ajanta Publications.

Devandra, K. (1985), *Status and Position of Women in India - with special reference to women in contemporary India*, New Delhi: Shakti Books.

Dhagamwar, V. (1987), *Women and Divorce in Bombay*, Bombay: Somaiya Publications Limited.

Dickie-Clark, H. (1966), *The Marginal Situation - a sociological study of a coloured group*, London: Routledge and Kegan Paul.

Dixon, B., Bouma, G. and Atkinson, G. (1991), *A Handbook of Social Science Research - a comprehensive guide for students*, Oxford: Oxford University Press.

Donnellan, C. (ed. 1993), *One Parent Families*, Cambridge: Independence.

Donnellan, C. (ed. 1995), *Lone Parents*, Cambridge: Independence.

Duskin, E. (1990), 'Overview' in *Lone Parent Families - the economic challenge*, France: OECD.

El Saadawi, N. (1982), *The Hidden Face of Eve - women in the Arab world*, Boston: Beacon Press.

Esposito, J. (1992), *Islam - the straight path*, New York: Oxford University Press.

Fadhlalla Haeri, S. (1993), *The Elements of Islam*, Dorset: Element Books Limited.

Fruzzetti, L. (1990), *The Gift of a Virgin - women, marriage and ritual in a Bengali society*, Oxford: Oxford University Press.

Gardner, K. and Shukur, A. (1994), 'I'm Bengali, I'm Asian and I'm living here - the changing identity of British Bengalis' in R. Ballard (ed.) *Desh Pardesh - the South Asian presence in Britain*, London: Hurst and Company.

Gaur, A. (1980), *Women in India*, London: The British Library.

Ghadially, R. and Pramod, K. (1988), 'Bride burning, the psycho social dynamics of dowry deaths' in R. Ghadially (ed.) *Women in Indian Society - a reader*, New Delhi: Sage Publications.

Gibson, C. (1994), *Dissolving Wedlock*, London: Routledge.

Giddens, A. (1992), *Sociology*, Oxford: Polity Press.

Gilroy, P. (1993), *There Ain't no Black in the Union Jack - the cultural politics of race and nation*, London: Routledge.

Glendinning, C. and Millar, J. (1992), 'It all really starts in the family: gender divisions and poverty' in C. Glendinning and J. Millar (eds.) *Women and Poverty in Britain*, Hemel Hempstead: Harvester Wheatsheaf.

Gordon, M. (1978), *Human Nature, Class and Ethnicity*, New York: Oxford University Press.

Gordon, T. (1994), *Single Women*, Hampshire: Macmillan Education Limited.

Goulbourne, H. (1991), 'Varieties of pluralism: the notion of a pluralist post-imperial Britain' in *New Community*, Vol 17 No 2, Winter.

Graham, H. (1992), 'Budgeting for health: mothers in low income households' in C. Glendinning and J. Millar (eds.) *Women and Poverty in Britain*, Hemel Hempstead: Harvester Wheatsheaf.

Graham, H. (1993), *Hardship and Health in Women's Lives*, Hemel Hempstead: Harvester Wheatsheaf.

Green, E., Hebron, S. and Woodward, D. (1990), *Women's Leisure, What Leisure?*, Hampshire: Macmillan Education Limited.

Gregory, J. and Foster, K. (1990), *The Consequences of Divorce - the report of the 1984 OPCS Consequences of Divorce survey*, London: HMSO.

Guillaume, A. (1990), *Islam*, London: Penguin Books.

Haralambos, M. with Heald, R. (1985), *Sociology - themes and perspectives, second edition*, London: Bell and Hyman.

Haralambos, M. and Holborn, M. (1991), *Sociology - themes and perspectives, third edition*, London: Collins Educational.

Haskey, J. (1993), 'Trends in the numbers of one-parent families in Britain' in *Population Trends*, No 71, London: HMSO.

Hawthorne Kirk, R. (1995), 'Social support and early years centres' in M. Hill, R. Hawthorne Kirk and D. Part (eds.) *Supporting Families*, Edinburgh: HMSO.

Helweg, A. (1979), *Sikhs in England - the development of a migrant community*, New Delhi: Oxford University Press.

Hester, M., Humphries, J., Pearson, C., Qaiser, K., Radford, L. and Woodfield, K. (1994), 'Domestic violence and child contact' in A. Mullender and R. Morley (eds.) *Children Living With Domestic Violence - putting men's abuse of women on the child care agenda*, London: Whiting and Birch Limited.

Hiro, D. (1991), *Black British, White British - a history of race relations in Britain*, London: Grafton Books.

HMSO (1974), *Finer Report - report of the Committee on One Parent Families*, London: HMSO.

HMSO (1996), *Social Trends*, No 26, London: HMSO.

Holtermann, S. (1993), *Becoming a Breadwinner - policies to assist lone parents with child care*, London: Daycare Trust.

Hooper, C. (1994), 'Do families need fathers? The impact of divorce on children' in A. Mullender and R. Morley (eds.) *Children Living With Domestic Violence - putting men's abuse of women on the child care agenda*, London: Whiting and Birch Limited.

Horrie, C. and Chippindale, P. (1991), *What is Islam?*, London: Virgin Books.

Howard, J. and Shepherd, G. (1987), *Conciliation, Children and Divorce - a family systems approach*, London: B.T. Batsford Limited.

Hughes, E. (1968), 'Social change and status protest: an essay on the marginal man' in R. Mack (ed.) *Race, Class and Power*, New York: Litton Educational Publishing.

Hyatt, J. and Parry-Crooke, G. (1990), *Barriers to Work: a study of lone parents' training and employment needs*, London: National Council for One Parent Families.

Ihinger-Tallman, M., Pasley, K. and Buehler, C. (1995), 'Developing a middle-range theory of father involvement post divorce' in W. Marsiglio (ed.) *Fatherhood - contemporary theory, research and social policy*, USA: Sage Publications Limited.

Inglis, R. (1982), *Must Divorce Hurt the Children?*, London: Maurice Temple Smith Limited.

Innes, S. (1995), *Making it Work - women, change and challenge in the 90's*, London: Chatto and Windus Limited.

Jacobs, B. (1988), *Racism in Britain*, Bromley: Christopher Helm Publishers.

Jameelah, M. (1993), *Islam in Theory and Practice*, Lahore: Mohammed Yusuf Khan and sons.

James, A. (1974), *Sikh Children in Britain*, London: Oxford University Press.

James, A. and Wilson, K. (1986), *Couples, Conflict and Change - social work with marital relationships*, London: Tavistock Publications.

Jeffrey, P. (1976), *Migrants and Refugees - Muslim and Christian Pakistani families in Bristol*, Cambridge: Cambridge University Press.

Jewson, N. and Mason, D. (1992), 'The theory and practice of equal opportunities policies: liberal and radical approaches' in P. Braham, A. Rattansi and R. Skellington (eds.) *Racism and Antiracism - inequalities, opportunities and policies*, London: Sage Publications in association with the Open University.

Joly, D. (1995), *Britannia's Crescent - making a place for Muslims in British society*, Aldershot: Avebury.

Jomier, J. (1989), *How to Understand Islam*, London: SCM Press Limited.

Judd, C., Smith, E. and Kidder, L. (1991), *Research Methods in Social Relations - international edition*, USA: The Drysden Press.

Kakar, S. (1988), 'Feminine identity in India' in R. Ghadially (ed.) *Women in Indian Society - a reader*, New Delhi: Sage Publications.

Kalra, S. (1980), *Daughters of Tradition - adolescent Sikh girls and their accommodation to life in British society*, Birmingham: Diana Balbir Publications.

Kapur, P. (1979), 'Women in modern India' in M. Singh Das and P. Bardis (eds.) *The Family in Asia*, London: George Allen and Unwin Limited.

Kelly, L. (1994), 'The interconnectedness of domestic violence and child abuse: challenges for research policy and practice' in A. Mullender and R. Morley (eds.) *Children Living With Domestic Violence - putting men's abuse of women on the child care agenda*, London: Whiting and Birch Limited.

Khanna, G. and Varghese, M. (1978), *Indian Women Today*, New Delhi: Vikas Publishing House.

Kiernan, K. and Wicks, M. (1990), *Family Change and Future Policy*, York: Joseph Rowntree Foundation.

Kiernan, K. (1992-93), 'Men and women at work and at home' in R. Jowell, L. Brook, G. Prior and B. Taylor (eds.) *British Social Attitudes*, Aldershot: Dartmouth Publishing Company.

Kohen, J., Brown, C. and Feldberg, R. (1979), 'Divorced mothers: the costs and benefits of female family control' in G. Levinger and O. Moles (eds.) *Divorce and Separation - context, causes and consequences*, New York: Basic Books Publishers.

Korson, J. (1979), 'Modernisation and social change - the family in Pakistan' in M. Singh Das and P. Bardis (eds.) *The Family in Asia*, London: George Allen and Unwin Limited.

Kumari, R. (1989), 'Dowry victims: harassment and torture' in P. Dandvate, R. Kumari and J. Varghese (eds.) *Widows, Abandoned and Destitute Women in India*, London: Sangam Books Limited.

Kymlicka, W. (ed. 1995), *The Rights of Minority Cultures*, Oxford: Oxford University Press.

Labour Market Trends (1996), *Women in the Labour Market: results from the spring 1995 Labour Force survey.*

Lazerwitz, B. (1971), 'Sampling theory and procedures' in H. Blalock and A. Blalock (eds.) *Methodology in Social Research*, London: McGraw-Hill.

Leeming, A., Unell, J. and Walker, R. (1994), *Lone Mothers*, Dept. of Social Security Research Report No 30, London: HMSO.

Lemu, A. and Heeren, F. (1978), *Woman in Islam*, Leicester: The Islamic Foundation.

Liddle, J. and Rama, J. (1986), *Daughters of Independence: gender, caste and class in India*, London: Zed Books Limited.

Lund, M. (1990), 'The non-custodial father: common challenges in parenting after divorce' in C. Lewis and M. O'Brien (eds.) *Reassessing Fatherhood - new observations on fathers and the modern family*, London: Sage Publications.

MacLean, M. and Eekelaar, J. (1983), *Children and Divorce - economic factors*, Oxford: SSRC Centre for Socio-Legal Studies.

MacLean, M. (1991), *Surviving Divorce - women's resources after separation*, Hampshire: Macmillan Education Limited.

Madge, J. (1971), *The Tools of Social Science*, London: Longman Group Limited.

Mama, A. (1992), 'Black women and the British state - race, class and gender analysis for the 1990's' in P. Braham, A. Rattansi and R. Skellington (eds.) *Racism and Antiracism - inequalities, opportunities and policies*, London: Sage Publications in association with the Open University.

Mann, J. (1973), 'Status: the marginal reaction - mixed bloods and Jews' in P. Watson (ed.) *Psychology and Race*, Middlesex: Penguin.

Marsh, I., Keating, M., Eyre, A., Campbell, R. and McKenzie, J. (eds.1996), *Making Sense of Society - an introduction to sociology*, London: Longman.

Mason, D. (1995), *Race and Ethnicity in Modern Britain*, Oxford: Oxford University Press.

May, D. (1980), 'Women in Islam: yesterday and today' in C. Pullapilly (ed.) *Islam in the Contemporary World*, Indiana: Cross Roads Books.

McKay, S. and Marsh, A. (1994), *Lone Parents and Work*, Dept. of Social Security Research Report No 25, London: HMSO.

McNeill, P. (1992), *Research Methods*, London: Routledge.

Mernissi, F. (1985), *Beyond the Veil - male-female dynamics in Muslim society*, London: Al Saqi Books.

Millar, J. (1989), *Poverty and the Lone Parent Family: the challenge to policy*, Aldershot: Gower.

Millar, J. (1992), 'Lone mothers and poverty' in C. Glendinning and J. Millar (eds.) *Women and Poverty in Britain*, Hemel Hempstead: Harvester Wheatsheaf.

Miller, W. (1983), *The Survey Methods in the Social and Political Science: achievements, failures, prospects*, London: Frances Pinter.

Minai, N. (1981), *Women in Islam - tradition and transition in the Middle East*, London: John Murray.

Minces, J. (1982), *The House of Obedience*, London: Zed Press.

Modood, T. (1990), 'Catching up with Jesse Jackson: being oppressed and being somebody' in *New Community*, Vol 17 No 1, Autumn.

Modood, T. (1992), 'British Asian Muslims and the Rushdie affair' in J. Donald and A, Rattansi (eds.) *Race, Culture and Difference*, London: Sage Publications.

Monk, S. (ed. 1993), *From the Margins to the Mainstream - an employment strategy for lone parents*, London: National Council for One Parent Families.

Morgan, P. (1995), *Farewell to the Family? Public Policy and Family Breakdown in Britain and the USA*, London: Health and Welfare Unit.

Morris, J. and Winn, M. (1993), *Housing and Social Inequality*, London: Hilary Shipman.

Morrison, D. and Cherlin, A. (1995), 'The divorce process and young people's well-being: a prospective analysis' in *Journal of Marriage and the Family*, Vol 57 No 3, August.

National Council for One Parent Families (1995), *Key Facts*.

Newman, W. (1976), 'Multiple realities: the effects of social pluralism on identity' in A. Dashefsky (ed.) *Ethnic Identity in Society*, Chicago: College Publishing Company.

Oakley, A. (1981), 'Interviewing women: a contradiction in terms' in H. Roberts (ed.) *Doing Feminist Research*, London: Routledge and Kegan Paul.

O'Brien, M. (1990), 'Patterns of kinship and friendship among lone fathers' in C. Lewis and M. O'Brien (eds.) *Reassessing Fatherhood - new observations on fathers and the modern family*, London: Sage Publications Limited.

Office of Population Censuses and Surveys (1993), *General Household Survey*, No 24, London: HMSO.

Oppenheim, C. (1993), *Poverty: the facts*, London: Child Action Poverty Group.

Pahl, J. (ed. 1985), *Private Violence and Public Policy - the needs of battered women and the response of the public services*, London: Routledge and Kegan Paul.

Parikh, I. and Garg, P. (1989), *Indian Women: an inner dialogue*, New Delhi: Sage Publications.

Park, R. (1950), *Race and Culture*, Glencoe: The Free Press.

Parker, G. (1992), 'Making ends meet: women, credit and debt' in C. Glendinning and J. Millar (eds.) *Women and Poverty in Britain*, Hemel Hempstead: Harvester Wheatsheaf.

Parkinson, L. (1987), *Separation, Divorce and Families*, Hampshire: Macmillan Education Limited.

Pascall, G. (1986), *Social Policy: a feminist analysis*, London: Tavistock.

Patterson, S. (1965), *Dark Strangers*, Harmondsworth: Penguin Books.

Payne, S. (1991), *Women, Health and Poverty: an introduction*, Hemel Hempstead.

Pearlin, L. and Johnson, J. (1981), 'Marital status, life strains and depression' in P. Stein (ed.) *Single Life - unmarried adults in social context*, New York: St Martin's Press.

Peil, M. with Mitchell, P. and Rimmer, D. (1982), *Social Science Research Methods - an African handbook*, London: Hodder and Stoughton.

Phoenix, A. (1991), *Young Mothers?*, Cambridge: Polity Press.

Popay, J. and Jones, G. (1990), 'Patterns of health and illness amongst lone parents' in *Journal of Social Policy*, Vol 19 No. 4.

Pothen, S. (1987), *Divorce, its Causes and Consequences in Hindu Society*, New Delhi: Vikas Publishing House.

Raza, M. (1993), *Islam in Britain - past, present and future*, Leicester: Volcano Press Limited.

Rex, J. (1986), *Race and Ethnicity*, Milton Keynes: Oxford University Press.

Reynolds, V. and Tanner, R. (1995), *The Social Ecology of Religion*, Oxford: Oxford University Press.

Richards, M. (1995), 'Changing families' in M. Hill, R. Hawthorne Kirk and D. Part (eds.) *Supporting Families*, Edinburgh: HMSO.

Richardson, J. and Lambert, J. (1985), 'The sociology of race' in M. Haralambos (ed.) *Sociology: new directions*, Lancashire: Causeway Press.

Richmond, A. (1965), 'Coloured colonials in the United Kingdom' in A. Rose and C. Rose (eds.) *Minority Problems: a textbook of readings in intergroup relations*, New York: Harper and Row.

Rimmer, P. and Rossiter, C. (1983), *One Parent Families: parents, children and public policy*, London: Study Commission on the Family.

Robinson, M. (1991), *Family Transformation Through Divorce and Remarriage - a systemic approach*, London: Tavistock/Routledge.

Robinson, V. (1986), *Transients, Settlers and Refugees - Asians in Britain*, Oxford: Clarendon Press.

Rose, E. et al (1969), *Colour and Citizenship: a report on British race relations*, Oxford: Oxford University Press.

Rozario, S. (1992), *Purity and Communal Boundaries - women and social change in a Bangladeshi village*, London: Allen and Unwin.

Rudestam, K. and Newton, R. (1992), *Surviving Your Dissertation - a comprehensive guide to context and process*, California: Sage Publications.

Saggar, S. (1992), *Race and Politics in Britain*, Hemel Hempstead: Harvester Wheatsheaf.

Saifullah-Khan, V. (1982), 'The role of the culture of dominance in structuring the experience of ethnic minorities' in C. Husband (ed.) *Race in Britain - continuity and change*, London: Hutchinson and Company.

Sambhi, P. (1989), *Sikhism*, Cheltenham: Stanley Thorne Publishers.

Sharma, U. (1980), *Women, Work and Property in North West India*, London: Tavistock Publications.

Shaw, A. (1988), *A Pakistani Community in Britain*, Oxford: Basil Blackwell Limited.

Shaw, A. (1994), 'The Pakistani community in Oxford' in R. Ballard (ed.) *Desh Pardesh - the South Asian presence in Britain*, London: Hurst and Company.

Shipman, M. (1982), *The Limitations of Social Research*, Harlow: Longman Group Limited.

Siganporia, M. (1993), 'Indian Muslim Women: post divorce problems and social support' in *The Indian Journal of Social Work*, Vol LIV No 3, July.

Sinha, R. (1992), 'Trends and correlates of widowhood in India' in *The Indian Journal of Social Work*, Vol LIII No 1, January.

Sivanandan, A. (1983), *A Different Hunger - writings on Black resistance*, London: Pluto Press.

Spanier, G. and Casto, R. (1979), 'Adjustment to separation and divorce: a qualitative analysis' in G. Levinger and O. Moles (eds.) *Divorce and Separation - context, causes and consequences*, New York: Basic Books Publishers.

Stacey, M. (1969), *Methods of Social Research*, Oxford: Pergamon Press.

Stonequist, E. (1961), *The Marginal Man - a study in personality and culture conflict*, New York: Russell and Russell.

Stopes-Roe, M. and Cochrane, R. (1990), *Citizens of This Country*, Clevendon: Multilingual Matters Limited.

Tajfel, H. (1965), 'Some psychological aspects of the colour problem' in R. Hooper (ed.) *Colour in Britain*, London: British Broadcasting Corporation.

Tajfel, H. (1982), 'The social psychology of minorities' in C. Husband (ed.) *Race in Britain: continuity and change*, London: Hutchinson and Company.

Thompson, J. and Priestley, J. (1996), *Sociology - 2nd edition*, Oxford: Made Simple Books.

Tomlinson, S. (1991), 'Education and training' in *New Community*, Vol 17 No 3, Spring.

United Nations (1991), *The World's Women 1970-1990 - trends and statistics*, New York.

Utting, D. (1995), *Family and Parenthood - supporting families, preventing breakdown*, York: Joseph Rowntree Foundation.

Wadley, S. (1988), 'Women and the Hindu tradition' in R. Ghadially (ed.) *Women in Indian Society - a reader*, New Delhi: Sage Publications.

Walczak, Y, with Burns, S. (1984), *Divorce: the child's point of view*, London: Harper and Row.

Waldron, J. (1995), 'Minority cultures and the cosmopolitan alternative' in W. Kymlicka (ed.) *The Rights of Minority Cultures*, Oxford: Oxford University Press.

Wallerstein, J. and Kelly, J. (1980), *Surviving the Breakup - how children and adults cope with divorce*, London: Grant McIntyre Limited.

Wasoff, F. (1995), 'Families, the Child Support Act and the welfare state' in S. Asquith and A. Stafford (ed.) *Families and the Future*, Edinburgh: HMSO.

Weiss, R. (1975), *Marital Separation*, New York: Basic Books Publishers.

Wells, R. (1994), *Helping Children Cope With Divorce*, London: Sheldon Press.

White, S. (1992), *Arguing With the Crocodile - gender and class in Bangladesh*, London: Zed Books Limited.

Whyte, R. and Whyte, P. (1982), *The Women of Rural Asia*, Colerado: Westview Press.

Williams, F. (1994), *Social Policy - a critical introduction - issues of race, gender and class*, Cambridge: Polity Press.

Wilson, A. (1978), *Finding a Voice - Asian women in Britain*, London: Virago Press.

Youssef, N. (1979), 'The status and fertility patterns of Muslim women' in L. Beck and N. Keddie (eds.) *Women in the Muslim World*, Massachusetts: Harvard University Press.